CHANDLER STUDIES IN
INTERNATIONAL AND INTERCULTURAL RELATIONS

Nationalism and International Progress: Revised and Enlarged Edition
Compiled and Edited by Urban G. Whitaker, Jr.

Nuclear Weapons, Missiles, and Future War: Problem for the Sixties
Compiled and Edited by Charles A. McClelland

Propaganda and International Relations: Revised and Enlarged Edition
Compiled and Edited by Urban G. Whitaker, Jr.

The Underdeveloped Lands: A Dilemma of the International Economy
Compiled and Edited by DeVere E. Pentony

United States Foreign Aid: Readings in the Problem Area of Wealth
Compiled and Edited by DeVere E. Pentony

The United Nations: The Continuing Debate
Compiled and Edited by Charles A. McClelland

Democracies and International Relations: Can Ours Survive?
Compiled and Edited by Urban G. Whitaker, Jr.

Soviet Behavior in World Affairs: Communist Foreign Policies
Compiled and Edited by DeVere E. Pentony

China, the Emerging Red Giant: Communist Foreign Policies
Compiled and Edited by DeVere E. Pentony

Red World in Tumult: Communist Foreign Policies
Compiled and Edited by DeVere E. Pentony

PROPAGANDA AND INTERNATIONAL RELATIONS

Compiled and Edited by

URBAN G. WHITAKER, Jr.

San Francisco State College

Revised and Enlarged Edition

CHANDLER PUBLISHING COMPANY

San Francisco

Acknowledgments

This book was made possible by funds granted by the Carnegie Corporation of New York. That Corporation is not, however, the author, owner, publisher or proprietor of this publication, and is not to be understood as approving by virtue of its grant any of the statements made or views expressed herein.

The editor gratefully acknowledges permission to reprint materials for which the following hold copyrights: The *American Scholar*, Leslie B. Bain, Devin-Adair Company, Johns Hopkins Press, The Macmillan Company, *The Nation, New York Times, New York Times Magazine*, Prentice-Hall Company, *Reader's Digest, Saturday Review of Literature, The Reporter*, and the University of Chicago Press.

The preparation of this book would not have been possible without the assistance of Miss Merrit Cross of the San Francisco International Studies Project. Robert V. Edington assisted with the original selection of readings. Frank Keenan Sloan not only worked on the selection of readings and made valuable suggestions on the entire project but also prepared the commentary for Chapter I. Miss Jean Ternoir, assisted by Arlyn Webster, supervised the assembling of materials for the revised and enlarged second edition.

Preface to the Revised and Enlarged Edition

The first version of this reader was prepared in 1958 as part of an experimental program in the teaching of international relations at San Francisco State College. Published in mimeographed form, it was used along with nine other booklets as a text for lower-division undergraduates enrolled in a required course, "International and Intercultural Relations."

This general education course was created in 1948 to meet the citizenship needs of students as determined by an intensive faculty study. It is a one-semester course taught by eight to ten instructors who handle sections of thirty to fifty students as individual classes. There are no common lectures or common examinations. Course outlines vary from section to section and the instructors do not always use the same text materials.

The 1958-60 experimental program from which this book of readings emerged was supported by a grant from the Carnegie Corporation. The International Relations faculty at San Francisco State College organized the San Francisco International Studies Project and were given released time to develop: (1) new approaches to the teaching of international relations at the undergraduate level; (2) appropriate text materials for each new approach developed; and (3) pre- and post-tests to evaluate the new approaches and materials.

Two approaches were developed, the "transformation" course and the "area" course. The former concentrates on the problems of change in international politics, economics and communications. The latter studies the principles of international relations and the processes of intercultural communication through the case study of a major geocultural area.

The evaluations program did not reveal significant differences between the two approaches in terms of their success with students. Indeed, the evidence strongly suggests that the proper choice of an approach or of text materials will vary with the instructor and the composition of the class.

This book of readings on *Propaganda and International Relations* was originally prepared as part of the international communications section of the "transformation" course. It was soon found, however, that it served a variety of purposes in a variety of courses depending on the instructor's choice of approach to his subject. It is with this flexible use in mind that this second edition, revised and enlarged, has been prepared.

New readings have been added to the section which describes the information agencies of the United States and to the section which describes the information activities of both the United States and the Communist powers. The treatment of the Communist states has been extended to include more Chinese materials. The case study on nuclear testing has been reorganized to emphasize the fact that this is an issue which gives rise primarily to propaganda of the *word* rather than of the *deed*. Although some new materials have been added, no attempt has been made to cover the nuclear-testing question *per se*. The new materials are primarily for the purpose of illustrating that the unilateral cessation of testing by the Soviet Union in 1958 was not, as it appeared then, a marriage of propaganda *deed* and *word* but primarily the clever use of circumstance to get maximum mileage from propaganda pronouncements. The 1961-62 exchanges between the great powers underline the fact that each seeks through the propaganda of the *word* to minimize the psychological impact of its contrary *deeds*.

A new concluding section has been added to illustrate the propaganda of the *deed* through a case study of the United States Peace Corps.

Urban G. Whitaker, Jr.

San Francisco
April 3, 1962

Contents

Acknowledgments iv
Preface to the Revised and Enlarged Edition . . . v
Introduction 1

I. THE NATURE AND ROLE OF PROPAGANDA IN
INTERNATIONAL RELATIONS

History and Definition of Propaganda 3
STRATEGIC PSYCHOLOGICAL OPERATIONS, by Robert T.
Holt and Robert van de Velde 6
Propaganda and the Cold War 8
THE STRUGGLES FOR THE MINDS AND LOYALTIES OF MAN-
KIND, by William S. Benton 10
PRESTIGE AND FOREIGN POLICY, by Paul H. Nitze . . 20
AMBASSADOR STEVENSON STATES U.S. VIEWS ON UNITED
NATIONS, by Adlai E. Stevenson 23

II. PROPAGANDA AGENCIES OF THE
SUPERPOWERS

Information Activities of the United States . . . 26
PSYCHOLOGICAL WARFARE, by William E. Daugherty . 28
SPRAGUE COMMITTEE REPORTS TO THE PRESIDENT ON U.S.
INFORMATION ACTIVITIES ABROAD 38
THE USA GOES TO THE FAIR, by J. D. Ratcliff . . 62
INDUSTRY COMMUNICATIONS PROGRAMS IN SUPPORT OF
U.S. FOREIGN POLICY, by Roger W. Tubby . . 66
Information Agencies of the U.S.S.R. and Communist
China 72
COMMUNICATION MEDIA AS CHANNELS FOR THE COM-
MUNIST MESSAGE, by Evron M. Kirkpatrick . . 72

III. PROPAGANDA ACTIVITIES OF THE
SUPERPOWERS

Publications 96
AMERIKA ILLUSTRATED, *New York Times* . . . 98
SOVIET NEWSPAPERS, by Mark Arkadyev . . . 99
PEOPLE'S COMMUNES TAME THE WATER DRAGONS, by
Chu Chi-min 106
OVERSEAS CHINESE 107
FOREIGN GUESTS 109
MARK TWAIN: EXPOSER OF U.S. IMPERIALISM, by Lao
Sheh 110

Radio Propaganda 112
TEXT OF VOICE OF AMERICA BROADCAST TO THE USSR 113
REMARKS BROADCAST ON RADIO MOSCOW, by E. M. Baza-
rina 114
HUNGARY: THE FIRST SIX DAYS, by Leslie B. Bain . 117

IV. PROPOSALS FOR GOVERNMENT ACTION ON
THE PSYCHOLOGICAL FRONT

Evaluations of Present Agencies and Activities . . 122
WHY WE ARE LOSING THE PSYCHOLOGICAL WAR, by
Arthur Krock 123
BALANCE SHEET IN THE WAR OF IDEAS, by Andrew H.
Berding 132
PSYCHOLOGICAL WARFARE AND FOREIGN POLICY, by Saul
K. Padover 140
CAN PROPAGANDA MAKE FRIENDS?, by Victor Lasky . 143

Suggestions for Changes in Government Programs . . 153
OPPOSITION TO THE UNITED STATES INFORMATION PRO-
GRAM, by Eugene W. Castle 154
PROPAGANDA VS. DIPLOMACY, by Theodore Sands . . 158
FIGHT FALSE PROPAGANDA WITH TRUTH, by Harry S.
Truman 163
A COOPERATIVE PEACE FOR ALL MANKIND, by Dwight D.
Eisenhower 170

V. CESSATION OF NUCLEAR TESTING: A CASE
STUDY IN PROPAGANDA OF THE *WORD*

Official Announcements 179
    Text of Soviet Announcement 180
    United States Views on Soviet Announcement of
        Cessation of Bomb Tests 182
    Secretary Dulles' News Conference of April 1, 1958 184
    Letter from Khrushchev to Eisenhower . . 192
    Eisenhower's Reply to Khrushchev . . . 195
Press Reactions in the United States and Japan . . 197
    It's Our Move Now 198
    Japanese Reaction to Soviet A-Test Halt Statement 199
Epilogue 203
    U.S. and U.K. Propose Banning Nuclear Tests in
        Atmosphere 204
    U.S. Resumes Nuclear Testing in Laboratory and
        Underground 208
    Declaration of Premier Khrushchev . . . 208
    Japan Protests Resumption of Nuclear Tests . . 213

VI. THE PEACE CORPS: A CASE STUDY IN
PROPAGANDA OF THE *DEED*

    The Crisis and America's Image, by Roger W. Tubby 220
    Statement by President Kennedy, by John F. Kennedy 227
    Message to Congress, by John F. Kennedy . . 229
    The Peace Corps Act, Section 2 234
    The Peace Corps, by R. Sargent Shriver . . . 234
    The First Peace Corpsmen Report for Work: Ghana 236
    The Peace Corps: A New Dimension of Public Service, by Lawrence E. Dennis 237

Conclusion 243
Selected Readings 245

Introduction

It is easy to become accustomed to looking at international relations within an innovating-conserving frame of reference. It is also quite helpful in developing an understanding of current international problems to get the habit of asking what are the institutions, processes and arrangements currently in use and whether they are still adequately serving the function for which they were established.

Most people have quite a bit of experience in applying this innovating-conserving approach to familiar problems of economics and politics. In the former field we have discussed and debated for years many questions about whether tariffs and other trade activities are serving legitimate functions and should be continued or whether they are the practices of a former day and have no place in current international life. In the political field we have, as a society, begun to seriously question whether the nation-state as a primary institution in international affairs has outlived its day and should be succeeded by new supranational institutions.

Similar questions are bound to arise in the area of human communications. Contacts of all kinds between people have increased in frequency and intensity so rapidly that institutions and processes of communication among them have hardly had time to take on recognizable form in one situation before a new situation develops. In a sense there has been continuous innovation in the field of international and intercultural communication in recent years and the question has not been *whether* to develop new methods and techniques but *how*.

In the field of international communications "propaganda" has become a key word. It is used in many different senses. Sometimes it is synonymous with "information." More often it has negative

1

connotations of distortion or of untruth. We hear the terms "propaganda war," "psychological war" and the "propaganda of the *word*" as distinguished from the "propaganda of the *deed*." We are sometimes advised to become better at *using* propaganda. But, we are sometimes told *never* to be *guilty* of it. We are often told to be properly afraid of it or to at least be aware of its potential effects on us and on others' feelings about us.

In this book we will concentrate primarily on problems of verbal conflict between the United States and the Soviet Union. Many important and interesting areas of discussion cannot be covered within such a narrow framework but it is hoped that a study of the information and propaganda activities of these two major nations will serve as an introduction to the over-all problem of international and intercultural communications in the present day.

We will discuss, first, the nature and role of propaganda with emphasis on the question of its place in the struggle between the forces of international communism led by the Soviet Union and the forces of the democracies led by the United States. We will then look at the organization of information and propaganda agencies in each of these nation-states and briefly sample some of their actual activities. After getting some idea *what* each is doing we will compare their strengths and weaknesses and consider some of the alternatives from which the United States might now choose in this field.

Finally, we will look at two case studies: (1) the nuclear-testing issue—a case study in the propaganda of the *word;* and (2) the Peace Corps—a case study in the propaganda of the *deed.*

I

The Nature and Role of Propaganda in International Relations

History and Definition of Propaganda

Although the word "propaganda" came into the language relatively recently, activities that we now term propaganda go far back into history.

In the Book of Judges it is recorded that in the thirteenth century B.C., Gideon used a form of propaganda to confuse and panic the Midianites. In The Book of War (a Chinese classic) Sun Tsu advises the use of beacons and drums at night, banners and flags during the day to deceive the enemy regarding the size of the forces facing him. Herodotus described how Themistocles engraved inscriptions on stones in the path of the Ionians, direly threatening them if they continued to advance. In Rome in 45 B.C., Caesar's most recent victory was celebrated with a parade featuring victims to be sacrificed, slaves and loot taken from the conquered and placard signs—veni, vidi, vici. Similarly, in later years, from Tom Paine's Common Sense, the Jacobin Clubs, the Communist Manifesto to Lord Bryce's publication of Germany's atrocities in World

3

War I, the dropping of leaflets in World War II, and Herter's report on the failure of the first part of the 1959 Geneva Conference—all can be broadly classed as propaganda.

Etymologists trace the origin of the word to the Latin propago—*to extend, enlarge, increase, carry forward, advance, spread—and find its first usage in 1622 as a result of the creation of the College for the Propagation of the Faith by Pope Gregory XV. Since that time, the word has lost its neutral meaning of propagating or spreading and has developed connotations of an evil nature. For our purposes, it is necessary to define it in the general sense in which it will be used in the following articles. It is also necessary to define psychological warfare and attempt to distinguish it from propaganda, if such a distinction is possible.*

Three reference-book definitions of propaganda may be examined:

2. . . . any institution or systematic scheme for propagating a doctrine or system . . .

3. Effort directed systematically toward the gaining of support for an opinion or course of action.

> *—Funk and Wagnalls' New Standard*
> *Dictionary of the English Language*

2. . . . Any organized or concerted group, effort, or movement to spread a particular doctrine or system of doctrines or principles;
. . .

3. . . . (a) A doctrine, system, or ideas, spread through propaganda (sense 2); . . . (b) A scheme or plan for the propagation of a doctrine or system of principles; . . .

> *—Webster's New International*
> *Dictionary, Second Edition*

. . . Propaganda is the making of deliberately one-sided statements to a mass audience. It is an act of advocacy in mass communication . . . to reach the mass audience, propagandists rely upon every medium of communication—oral, printed, pictorial, plastic, musical or dramatic. . . .

> *—Encyclopaedia Britannica (1959)*

In order to eliminate the Madison Avenue variety and such others that are nonpolitical in nature, our definition will be:

Propaganda consists of the planned use of any form of public or mass-produced communication designed to affect the minds and emotions of a given group for a specific public purpose, whether military, economic or political.[1]

The definition of psychological warfare is somewhat narrower:

Comprises the use of propaganda against an enemy, together with such other operational measures of a military, economic or political nature as may be required to supplement propaganda.[2]

The second part of this definition may be clarified by an example. During the Quemoy crisis of 1958, the United States sent a squadron of F-104's to Formosa for the purpose of intimidating the Red Chinese by letting them pick up a 1400-m.p.h. blip on their radar screens. Per se *this was a supplemental act of psychological warfare. When this fact was published, at home and abroad, especially throughout the Far East, it was interpreted as more in the nature of a propaganda move.*

It must be added that in a shooting war the use of psychological warfare is narrowed to the use of mass communications in order to destroy the enemy's will to fight.

The first reading reprinted below is selected from the Preface to a recent book entitled Strategic Psychological Operations and American Foreign Policy. *It deals specifically with the problem of selecting appropriate terms to describe the kinds of intercultural communication processes which are the subject of both that book and this one.*

---

[1] Paul M. A. Linebarger, *Psychological Warfare* (Washington, D.C.: Infantry Journal Press, 1948), p. 39.

[2] *Ibid.*, p. 40.

STRATEGIC PSYCHOLOGICAL
OPERATIONS*

ROBERT T. HOLT AND ROBERT VAN DE VELDE

ROBERT T. HOLT *and* ROBERT VAN DE VELDE *are both scholars in the developing field of international communications. Mr. Holt is the author of* Radio Free Europe, *published by the University of Minnesota Press in 1958. This reading is from the Preface to* Strategic Psychological Operations and American Foreign Policy, *which Holt and van de Velde co-authored.*

This book deals with the use of the psychological instrument of statecraft. Had it been written a decade ago, it quite likely would have been entitled *Psychological Warfare*. The authors would not have been altogether happy about that term. They undoubtedly would have suggested several alternatives—international political communication, international information, battle for men's minds, and others—but finally would have accepted with reluctance *Psychological Warfare*.

We have decided to use a new term. There will certainly be those among our readers who will be unhappy with our selection of *Strategic Psychological Operations*. It is reasonable that they should expect some sound arguments, if not sincere apologies, for the introduction of a new term in an area already suffering from an overabundance of half-accepted labels. The reasoning behind our choice combines both positive and negative considerations.

The principal negative consideration was a compulsion to get rid of the words "warfare" and "information." "Warfare" cannot, or at least should not, be applied to the larger concepts involved here. Furthermore, it is "psychologically unsound—if not definitionally ridiculous—to apply that word to activities conducted in the absence of overt hostilities, or at any time when applied to the activities of a

* Reprinted from *Strategic Psychological Operations and American Foreign Policy* (pp. v-vi) by Robert T. Holt and Robert van de Velde by permission of The University of Chicago Press. Copyright © 1960 (by) The University of Chicago.

government of a democratic and peaceful people toward the government and people of an allied, friendly, or neutral nation. The term "information" so widely used in our government simply fails completely to cover the situation or to convey any idea of the scope of the operations involved. "Operations," then, is our answer to these negative considerations. We believe "operations" implies a large-scale, continuous process in which are included the functions of planning, coordinating, directing, and acting. No other single word seems to us so aptly to include all these elements on the level and in the magnitude herein considered.

We recognize the negative aspects of the word "psychological," but it has been retained *faute de mieux*. It was once said that the efforts of almost all people concerned with psychological warfare to rid themselves of that distasteful term was reminiscent of the Australian bushman who longed for a new boomerang. For years this chap strove to obtain a new and better implement. Finally his wish was fulfilled, but the result was he drove himself mad trying to throw away his old one. The truth of the matter is that, despite the dislike of many government people for the application of a word connoting little-understood theories to their everyday activities, the word "psychological" is not inappropriate here. As will be seen in the text, the operations *are* psychological in a common-sense usage in that they are designed to provoke certain behavioral responses or attitudes, by bringing about changes in *the meaning that men attach* to objects and events in the material world, rather than by changing directly those objects and events. In keeping this word, too, we hope to maintain the interest of the psychologist and social psychologist in developing further their studies on the nature of the instrument with which we are dealing.

On the positive side is the inclusion of the word "strategic." We use it to imply breadth of scope both organizationally and geographically. It also implies continuation over a long period of time. The use of this word is meant to convey something quite different from "campaign" as President Truman used that word in labeling our overseas information program a "Campaign of Truth." To us the word "campaign" implies a specific course of action designed to last a foreseeable length of time and to culminate in "victory." We see no "victory" to be achieved, but rather a constant striving for "success." The use of "strategic" here also means something quite different from the meaning of that word when it is used in such phrases as "the strategy of terror." This usage seems to us false, for it is used to label what is at most really a tactic. "Strategic" as we use it means something national in its origins, international or world-wide in its effect, and decades long in its implementation. . . .

Propaganda and the Cold War

Since there have been nation-states there has been conflict among them. It does not seem likely that this situation will disappear at any time within the foreseeable range of man's history on the planet Earth. But the nature of man's approach to the process of conflict resolution can and does change.

We have seen this change take place in the development of national states. For example, there is conflict between states of the United States. California and Arizona have argued about the Colorado River, Iowa and Nebraska have disagreed about the Mississippi and there has been a court case involving the conflicting claims of New Jersey and Delaware to the river which runs between them. But these disagreements have long since been removed from the arena of physical warfare.

For some of the arguments between some of the nation-states this is also true. The United States has had disagreements over boundaries and other problems with both its northern and southern neighbors, but it has been many years since hot, physical, military war with either Canada or Mexico has been a real possibility. Even in the major international conflicts it has been true for a long time that there has been a psychological element in the resolution of disagreements between nations. Until the end of World War II, however, it was also true that the really serious conflicts had always been settled primarily by physical means. The question which we take up now is whether this is still true.

Probably most of the commentators and scholars in the international field agree that the psychological means of conflict resolution have gained in utility relative to the physical means. But there is considerable disagreement concerning the extent of the nuclear stalemate. If you believe that it is a complete stalemate and that there will be no further opportunity for the major world powers to settle their differences by resort to "hot" war then you may feel that this book is a "Handbook for Winning the Next War." If, on the other hand, you believe that the final resolution of major international conflicts is still likely to be on a military battlefield you may consider the discussions in this book to be somewhat irrelevant.

The speech by Senator Benton, which begins on the following page, reflects the view that the psychological *components of conflict resolution have become at least as important as the purely* physical *components.*

The two short readings by Paul Nitze and Adlai Stevenson which follow Senator Benton's speech were written ten years later. Both of them reflect the deepening awareness among American leaders that the role of propaganda in international relations has changed significantly in recent years. But there are sharp differences between Nitze's view that negotiations between hostile powers may actually be more for propaganda purposes than for purposes of reaching agreement, and Stevenson's plea for a "moratorium on propaganda" and a return to "quiet diplomacy."

Students of the role of propaganda in contemporary international relations may find it profitable to study Ambassador Stevenson's criticism as, itself, a very successful piece of propaganda. In fact, careful study of all the readings in this collection may strongly suggest that the best propaganda of the word *is opposition to its use, and that the most successful propaganda is that of the* deed, *performed as in the example of the U.S. Peace Corps (see Chapter VI), "purely" for the benefit of others.*

THE STRUGGLES FOR THE MINDS AND LOYALTIES OF MANKIND—PROPOSING A MARSHALL PLAN OF IDEAS*

SPEECH BY MR. WILLIAM S. BENTON
Senator from Connecticut

WILLIAM S. BENTON *is an advertising executive and a federal government official from Connecticut. He was Vice President of the University of Chicago (1937–1945), United States Senator from Connecticut (1949–1952) and has been Assistant Secretary of State for Public Affairs and a member of the United States delegation to UNESCO.*

. . . I wish to invite the attention of the Senate to an aspect of our foreign relations which seems to me at once crucially important and relatively neglected. It is an aspect toward which all the events of the past several years, and particularly the events of the past several months and weeks have pointed. Today, I should like to make some proposals concerning this neglected aspect of our foreign relations. . . .

In the field of foreign policy, let us in Congress now devote ourselves to those things which we the people of the United States can really do something about. Let us talk more about the things we can do and much less about the things we cannot do. I do not mean that I necessarily object to speeches about what the Russians should do. I object to them only when they divert us from the things which we ourselves can and should do. Such talk about Russia is of course needed; it is needed to clear the air and to show the American people what we are up against; but I fear it has temporarily so focused our minds on the obdurate men of the Kremlin that we bury our heads in the sands of our own frustration.

There is, of course, one point that is constantly valid. This point is not whether the Russian tyranny is terrible. It is terrible.

* Reprinted from *Congressional Record* (March 22, 1950), pp. 3763-65.

It is not whether the Russian surge of aggression should be halted. It should be halted. The constantly valid point is, "What action is it now legitimate for us to take; what is today within our potential power of achievement?" While it takes two parties to make an agreement, it takes only one to do something intelligent about the lack of agreement.

One obvious area within our own power is our armed forces. Unhappily, we must have these, and to this fact we are trained by tradition and by history. Another area is the hydrogen bomb, and this, too, is an old area, but in a new dress. The hydrogen bomb is the 1950 version of Attila and Genghis Khan. But surely we are beginning to learn that we cannot win the struggle now raging between the allies of freedom and slaves of communism merely by force and threat of force, or even by the threat of extermination.

It has been charged that no great idea has been forthcoming in the field of our foreign policy—no new challenging and constructive idea to which the Nation and the world will rally.

I do not agree with this charge. The United States has backed such vital ideas as UNRRA, of which the Senator from New York (Mr. Lehman) was the head, the Marshall plan, the Atlantic Pact, and now point 4. The ideas themselves are big, even if on occasion perhaps they have been imperfectly projected and little understood.

But history is seldom written in terms of big ideas, and surely never by big ideas unaided by bold projection and courageous leadership. While the critics may bewail our lack of the big idea, I suggest that our democratic ideals are indeed the biggest idea of all. Let us now begin to create a big package through the clarification and projection of these ideals. Let us make a package so big and so strong that it will give new faith to our own people and to struggling peoples everywhere.

Walter Lippmann recently wrote:

> We are losing touch with the peoples of the world—with their fears, their hopes, their needs, their purposes, and their will to survive—and we are talking not to them but to ourselves in a self-induced mood of defeatism and impotence about how much we must distrust one another and our own better instincts and our own capacity to think and believe.

We Americans have been told a hundred times in the five years since the end of the shooting war—I suppose it has been said a hundred times on the floor of this Chamber—that the contest now raging all over the world is, in its essence, a struggle for the minds and loyalties of men. We have been reminded again and again that, in this struggle, bullets and bombs, shell and flame, do not change men's minds or win their loyalty. Yet at the end of five years we are still preoccupied with physical force as though this were the answer to our present problems with the Russians.

Secretary Acheson has stated the new orientation of our foreign policy in five words: "Strength at points of weakness." This leads me to ask my colleagues in the Senate, wherein are we weak? Is it in military power? Is our industry weak? Is our diplomacy a point of weakness? No; our weakness, our Achilles heel, springs from a failure of analysis, a failure to accept the basic proposition that the struggle for the minds and the loyalty of mankind is the heart of the matter. We have failed in analysis and we have failed in action. Here is an area where we can act boldly. Here we can be imaginative. In this area we are not dependent on the Kremlin. We do not need a meeting with Marshal Stalin. I suggest that we quit wringing our hands. Let us give to this area the great faith and the great talent of which we are capable. Indeed, we should be devoting ourselves to it if there were no Politburo and if the Russian power instantly vanished from the earth. But how many Americans are there who recognize—as the Russians so clearly do—that the prime objective of total diplomacy is to win men's minds and loyalties? Total diplomacy, to be total, must include as a major element psychological efforts directed at whole peoples. It must include practical means, direct as well as indirect, for waging psychological diplomacy. Only last Sunday, Bertrand Russell wrote in the *New York Times Magazine* that

> Before very long psychology, and especially mass psychology, will be recognized as the most important of all sciences from the standpoint of human welfare.

He said further:

> Whether civilization can long survive—now—depends upon psychology.

My plea today is not a new one for me and it is familiar to many in the Senate, notably the members of the Foreign Relations and Appropriations Committees before which I have appeared so often. But with each passing day in the three years since those appearances it has become increasingly clear that, as Mr. Acheson has said, agreements with the Russians have had no value other than to record an existing situation and to register power balance. Are we not now ready to admit that what people in various areas of the world know, think, and feel is a key factor in the power balance? In the older diplomacy force, military might, lay in the background of most negotiations, sometimes very close to the surface. In most recent years economic considerations have played an increasing role. Today the diplomacy of public opinion is the emerging factor. Indeed, the diplomacy of public opinion is here for all to see—or perhaps I should say for all who will look.

Mr. President, it was not until the 1930's that the State Department set up a major division for economics, as the Senator from Illinois (Mr. Douglas) will recall, and not until 1945 that it began to organize to deal with international public opinion. Yet it seems to me much of the justification for military and economic measures has always been psychological—the military measures to convince the potential war-maker that he will not get away with it, and the economic measures because hungry and hopeless people have always been easy victims of subversion.

By far the most imaginative step we have taken in our foreign relations since 1945 has been the Marshall plan. Is it an accident that it now seems the most successful step? It has had perhaps the most brilliant leadership of any operating department of our Government, but it was brilliant in concept as well. The Marshall plan has been no mere containment of communism. It has aimed at a positive rollback for communism, an ideological as well as an economic defeat for communism. It was boldly conceived on a scale adequate to the need. It was designed to close the dollar gap until recovery could permit Europe to earn its own way.

With this success before us, is it not time—and past time—for us to create a world-wide Marshall plan in the field of ideas? Let us now aim to close the mental gap between ourselves and the people of the world. The mental gap is far more dangerous than the dollar gap. Unless we close it, our efforts to close the dollar gap may boomerang upon us. The mental gap cannot be easily and quickly cured. It cannot be bought by money alone. It is the gap through which communism is now pouring its deadly poison into the mind, into the conscience, and the emotions of mankind.

Communism began as propaganda. It survived for more than half a century as propaganda. Its greatest heroes have been propagandists. It is Lenin and Marx, the propagandists, who are enshrined in Red Square and in the hearts of their countrymen. Its greatest advances have been scored by a combination of propaganda and political warfare. It is not the Red Army which is fighting for the victories.

Mr. George Kennan, counselor of the State Department, and one of our keenest students of Russia, writes in this month's *Reader's Digest* that

> It is hardly likely that the Russians are now charting an early military onslaught on the Western World.

We all hope he is right.

And indeed, why should they attack us? The very milk of the Marxist doctrine is that a capitalist economy such as ours must collapse because of what the Marxists call our inner contradictions. That belief that we will collapse is as basic to Communist thinking as the belief in life after death is to the Christian faith. The real military danger to Russia, Communists believe, is that capitalism, vainly trying to avert collapse, must engage in ever greater imperialistic ventures and, in its death throes, lash out at the Soviet Union. Fortunately our death throes do not seem very imminent.

However, say the Communists, this final Armageddon can be avoided if the non-Communist countries can be weakened from within, confused, and divided and set against each other. Thus, communism by its very nature must be aggressive. But its characteristic form of aggression is not that of hurling armies across frontiers. Mr. Kennan describes Soviet expansion as sly and cautious.

We of the Western World have, of course, had decribed for us a thousand times the methods of Communist aggression—incessant and skillful propaganda followed up by political infiltration, sabotage, and disruption and then the seizure of power by a minority and the consolidation of power by suppression and terror. In this process the Russian Army is merely a reserve component. The front line is propaganda and political skulduggery.

Even where a shooting war develops, propaganda is the key for the U.S.S.R. China is an example. The State Department white paper tells us that in 1945 the army of Generalissimo Chiang was stronger than the Chinese Communist army. The Russian Army was not involved. But Chiang could not produce—or at least could not project—a program that appealed to the masses of the Chinese people. The Communists, with Moscow guidance, and with incessant, skillful, and usually lying propaganda, could and did project such a program. That is why so many tens of millions of Chinese welcomed the Communists as liberators.

The Communists, employing Moscow-trained Chinese propagandists in the villages, centered their attack on the ancient evils of land tenure, under which landlords could and did lay claim to as much as 75 per cent of a peasant's produce. They promised reforms. There was no one in the villages, with equal vigor and skill, telling the Chinese peasants that the entire theory and history of communism could lead only to the forced collectivization of the land they love. Yet, if that single point had been explained, the outcome of the Chinese war might have been different.

We sent to China billions of dollars' worth of arms and armaments. We might more effectively have sent motion-picture projectors and radio sets.

Day in and day out in two score languages, in every medium of communication from a whispered rumor to a globe-girdling radio, everywhere from a remote Burmese village to the Security Council of the United Nations, Communists play the same propaganda tune, though the words are sometimes changed to fit the time and place; the tune never changes. For two years in the State Department, I read daily reports on communism's propaganda program throughout the world. Make no mistake, it is very skillful and it is very effective. There has never been anything like it, anything so skillful and so effective in its mass impact. As applied to its principal target of abuse, the United States, the tune is always the same. It revolves around five themes which never vary:

First. The United States is headed for a cataclysmic economic crash.

Second. The rulers of the United States are Fascists, warmongers, and monopolists.

Third. Although the rich in the United States are getting richer, everybody else is getting poorer and there is starvation, unrest, and growing sympathy for the Soviet Union among the masses.

Fourth. America's vaunted freedom is a fraud, and our doctrine of equality is belied by racial and religious discrimination.

Fifth. Our character is bad—we are culturally barbarous, money-mad, lawless, crime-ridden, and effete.

If you were a voter in a nation subject to Communist attack and trying to make up its mind, or a legislator, or a foreign minister, and if wherever you turned you heard rumors and forecasts of economic disaster for America, and if you heard nothing in rebuttal would you care to tie your political and economic future to that of the United States? Would you care to emulate America's methods? Let us not forget that the first victims of propaganda are the propagandists themselves; the Kremlin and Communists everywhere survey the American scene through the acute distortion glass of their own dogma. They never hear anything but their own propaganda. This miscalculation of America can be highly dangerous—as Hitler and the Japanese demonstrated to us.

In many countries, the news about the United States gives the impression that we are continuously in the grip of a major crisis. Our production dip last year was compared with the early months of 1929. Our potato surplus is pictured as a typical example of capitalist mishandling.

If the United States refuses loans and favors, it is portrayed as rich and selfish. If it makes foreign loans, or grants favors, or embarks on an historical program, such as the Marshall plan, it is seeking to enslave foreign people. If it takes a firm position on any matter, it is militaristic and imperialistic. If it yields, it is weak-kneed and its action is an indication that the United States is withdrawing again to isolationism.

What do the Communists tell the world about themselves? They say they are the true champions of peace; that they are the protectors of national sovereignty, the hope of subject people who are striving for independence; that their social system is the only one that offers justice and equality for all; that their economic system is the only one that can efficiently convert the resources of the earth to human use; and that only through their system can mankind reach its fullest development in art and in science.

The Communists practiced the technique of the "big lie" long before Hitler discovered it and wrote it in *Mein Kampf.* They learned that, in propaganda, the best defense is an attack. They not only seem to be getting away with it; they are getting away with it.

Mr. President, we must question the truth of the old adage that actions always speak louder than words. Here I must disagree most emphatically with Secretary Acheson in his San Francisco speech. The words may do the job alone for the Communists, but for us the words must at least accompany the actions if the actions are to be understood.

Indeed, if the Communists can fool enough of the people enough of the time—long enough to seize power in these critical areas and suppress all critical voices in their purges—they do not need to worry about whether they can fool all the people all of the time.

We are in the crucial moments, it seems to me, of a struggle for the minds and loyalties of mankind. The United States is in a world political campaign. What the United States stands for must be freely elected by the peoples of the world. Every day must be a campaign day for the United States.

The Russians are conducting a very dirty campaign, and I am sure there are Members of this body who out of their own experience should know what it is like to be up against a dirty political campaign. For our part, we are scarcely campaigning at all. A campaign demands the systematic clarification of issues. It means the projection of a "platform." It means developing and hammering a few positive themes. As the Senator from Connecticut (Mr. McMahon) so eloquently pointed out, it means doing these things in a loud enough voice so it can be heard. Yes, no one campaigns in a whisper.

Specifically in behalf of the United States, let us begin in earnest to dramatize abroad the strength and stability of our economy. Let us make clear that, although we have many problems, under the American business system our whole people, and not just the few, share a high and rising standard of living. Let us dramatize our peaceful record and our peaceful intentions—our devotion to the ideal of political and economic independence for all peoples, our desire to help all friendly peoples. Let us demonstrate that we seek to practice democracy here at home, and that we are making steady progress in the elimination of the undemocratic aspects of our national life. We should not boast about our scientific and cultural achievements, but neither should we let others underrate them. Finally, let us explain that we are a people slow to anger, but united and mighty in a righteous cause.

Any campaign, Mr. President, even a moral crusade, requires organization. I, therefore, propose that the United States now undertake to organize its campaign for men's minds and loyalties on a scale commensurate with the need and commensurate with the stakes. Fortunately, we have on our side a priceless asset: we have no need to lie.

Specifically, I propose six steps:

First. Maintenance, through the United Nations and through our own diplomacy, of a steady and steadily increasing pressure in behalf of world-wide freedom of information. The entire American press, I may say, is deeply interested in that subject.

Second. Acceleration of the work of the United Nations Educational, Scientific, and Cultural Organization to the point where, with effective leadership, it has a chance to make a significant, perhaps decisive, contribution to peace.

Third. Development of the activities of the Office of International Information and Educational Exchange in the Department of State, in the following ways, among many others:

(a) Preparation and execution of a comprehensive world-wide program to exhibit documentary and educational motion pictures designed to explain the democratic principles and ideals which underlie our foreign policy.

(b) Significant and immediate expansion of our program for bringing foreign students to the United States.

(c) Creation of a world broadcasting network capable of broadcasting on long wave, short wave, or medium wave, with an ultimate goal of reaching virtually every radio set in the world.

I may say parenthetically, while our present domestic radio and the publicity it gets in the American press is effective, our international radio does not reach an appreciable number of the world's sets with a satisfactory signal. It is a very weak reed. It is indeed, as I once stated and as the senior Senator from Connecticut (Mr. McMahon) has stated, a whisper, not a voice.

(d) The use of any and all possible means to reach people who are shut off from the free world by censorship and by suppression.

Fourth. Promotion of democratic education abroad, notably in the occupied areas of Germany and Japan.

Fifth. Convening of a conference of non-Communist nations

now conducting international information programs, with a view of reaching a better understanding on common themes and on greatly increasing the effectiveness of the projection of such themes.

Sixth. Encouragement of the establishment of a nongovernmental agency to help inspire and guide the efforts of the millions of private American citizens who might use their talents and resources and contacts overseas in furtherance of the programs and objectives of this resolution.

Mr. President, these six steps have been incorporated into a resolution, which I now submit on behalf of myself and a group of twelve other Senators who have associated themselves with me.

THE PRESIDING OFFICER (MR. WITHERS *in the chair*). The resolution will be received and appropriately referred.

The resolution (S. Res. 243) submitted by MR. BENTON (for himself, MR. DOUGLAS, MR. FLANDERS, MR. FULBRIGHT, MR. GRAHAM, MR. HENDRICKSON, MR. LEHMAN, MR. McMAHON, MR. MORSE, MR. MUNDT, MRS. SMITH of Maine, MR. SPARKMAN, and MR. TOBEY) was received and referred to the Committee on Foreign Relations, as follows:

> *Whereas* the struggle now raging between freedom and communism is a contest for the minds and loyalties of men; and
>
> *Whereas* in such a struggle force and threat of force do not change men's minds or win their loyalties; and
>
> *Whereas* the real methods of Communist aggression—incessant and skillful propaganda designed to prepare the way for political infiltration, for sabotage and for the consolidation of power by suppression and terror—whereas these tactics have poisoned and continue to poison the minds of hundreds of millions throughout the world; and
>
> *Whereas* we have learned that such Communist methods cannot be beaten back by arms and dollars alone but require world-wide offensive in behalf of the ideas which express our democratic principles and aspirations: Therefore be it
>
> *Resolved,* That the United States should initiate and vigorously prosecute a greatly expanded program of information and education among all the peoples of the world to the full extent that they can be reached—with a view of closing the mental gulf that separates the United States from other peoples and that now blockades the universal hope for freedom and peace. . . .

PRESTIGE AND FOREIGN
POLICY*

PAUL H. NITZE

PAUL H. NITZE, *writer, lecturer and foreign-service official, served during World War II in the Office of the Coordinator of Inter-American Affairs and other government agencies. In 1946 he moved to the Department of State and later became Director of its Policy Planning Staff (1950-53).*

Today it would appear that the most important tool of foreign policy is prestige. Prestige is a complex concept. It has a number of elements. Like the economic tool, it is a mixture of immemorial principle and new scope. One component of a nation's prestige is the belief of others that the nation has the will and the capability to bring about whatever it indicates as its serious intentions. From this standpoint the brutal Soviet suppression of the Hungarian uprising contributed to the growth of Soviet prestige. The failure of the British and French to press their intervention in Suez with speed and effectiveness was a blow to England and France in this component of prestige.

A second component of prestige is the respect and agreement which the other nations and peoples hold for what they understand to underlie a nation's policy. In this component of prestige, the United States has had, and in my opinion still has, a decided edge over the Soviet Union. The fact that we have had no territorial ambitions, that we do not seek world hegemony, that we have been understanding of diverse viewpoints, that we have been on the side of self-determination by important national groups, that we have attempted actively to assist others in making the transition to the modern technological, economic, and politcal world have all contributed to the strength of this component of prestige. Whether our assets

* Paul H. Nitze in *The Secretary of State,* by The American Assembly, Columbia University, N.Y. © 1960. By permission of Prentice-Hall, Inc., publisher. This reading is from Mr. Nitze's article, "The Secretary and Foreign Policy," which appeared in Don K. Price (ed.), *The Secretary of State,* pp. 15-17.

here can long outweigh a growing debit in the other component is doubtful.

With respect to both of these components of prestige, the precision with which we indicate our serious purposes and intentions is important. If we give the impression that we intend to support the liberation of the satellites and then do not do so, our prestige suffers. If on one day we say that U-2 flights are vital to our security, and a week later cancel them, we damage our prestige.

The same principle applies to many of the terms which today provide the framework within which peoples judge our purposes. If we permit "peace" and "peaceful coexistence" to become associated in people's minds with a cessation or mitigation of resistance to Soviet intentions and do not ourselves intend any such one-sided abandonment of the struggle, we do ourselves a disservice. If we permit "relaxation of tensions" and "ending of the cold war" to be understood as good things to be obtained, by a modification not of Soviet purposes, but largely of ours, we put ourselves in a box the moment it is found that Soviet purposes have not changed and that we must continue to oppose them and thus continue tensions and the cold war or else give up the struggle.

The point about prestige is that it provides a multiplier to all other elements of national power. If people respect and agree with our purposes, they will wish to do what we wish to do; they will add their strength to ours. If they believe we will be able to do, and will in fact do, what we indicate our intention of doing, they will accommodate themselves to our intention (even if they disagree with it) without forcing us in most instances to prove our point by doing it. Obviously the same holds for Soviet prestige.

This brings us to a consideration of the tool of negotiation. The ancient principles of negotiation still seem to apply, although sometimes apparently forgotten.

It still is true that negotiations between two or more parties having a large measure of common interests, in relationship to which the matter under negotiation is of minor significance, generally place greater value upon agreement than upon victory for their particular viewpoint. Our negotiations with the British, French, and Germans may not have produced dramatic or startling results, but they have produced agreement.

It also seems still to be true that in negotiations between hostile powers, the stronger power may seek victory for its side and be unwilling to agree unless he secures advantages commensurate with what he considers the strength of his position. Success is more important to him than agreement. In such negotiation among hostile powers, the limits of the negotiating possibilities are set by the alternatives available to the two sides in the event of non-agreement.

In today's world of mass communication and mass opinion the public-opinion effect of negotiations may be more important to the participants than the agreements arrived at. The Soviet Communists have always made a clear distinction in their theoretical papers between negotiations primarily for support of their propaganda positions and negotiations entered into to produce agreement. Generally they try to exploit all the possibilities of the first type before they get down to wringing the last possible drop out of the second.

Many on the Western side believe that there is virtue in negotiation as such, that to continue to talk is in some way to avoid action other than talk. Certainly keeping the lines of communication open with the adversary is important; and negotiation is one way of so doing. Furthermore, it is important that we always have a clear view of our negotiating position versus our adversaries on every important point at issue between us. But the proposition suggested by some, that the tool of negotiation provides an escape from the necessity of developing the other tools that support policy, seems dubious in the extreme. . . .

But the hour is too late, the times too dangerous, for name calling and rhetorical violence. I believe that the world would benefit from a moratorium on propaganda and abuse and by a return in this great parliament to the courtesy and dignity of traditional diplomatic usage.

The United Nations is now an organization of 99 member states —double its size when I last served here. We cannot afford to neglect the opportunities which our membership gives us, nor do we intend to do so. We look to the United Nations not as an arena in which to fight the cold war but, rather, as an instrument which can help us to end it and to liberate man from the scourges of war, poverty, disease, ignorance, and oppression. We are not seeking here military alliances; we shall not try to impose our system or philosophy on others. We seek only that they should make good their national independence and advance the well-being of their people.

The United States is the oldest anticolonial power, and we are in favor of freedom and self-determination for all peoples. The United States views with satisfaction the rapid political revolution of independence which has swept the world. Like the former colonial powers—the United Kingdom and France, for example—we are now interested in the orderly, peaceful transition to self-government and a healthy national life, without creating new enmities to plague the world. Hence we deeply regret the disaster that has befallen the Congo in its first months of national independence.

By trial and error we have learned a great deal about economic development. The United States attaches the first importance to improving the well-being of peoples, and the United Nations has proved its ability to administer economic and technical aid without fear of ulterior motives. So we shall support expanded efforts of the United Nations to aid countries whose peoples are determined to aid themselves. Much unrest in the world would be eased if millions of people were sure of at east one square meal a day.

We believe that the United Nations can be used much more than it has been to facilitate quiet diplomacy. I recall that the solution of the Berlin crisis in 1948 had its origin in quiet talks here at United Nations to aid countries whose peoples are determined to aid a great opportunity to anticipate crises as well as to deal with the urgent problems of the moment. To prevent fire is often better than to extinguish fire.

AMBASSADOR STEVENSON STATES U.S. VIEWS ON UNITED NATIONS*

ADLAI E. STEVENSON

ADLAI E. STEVENSON was a member of the first United States Mission to the United Nations. In 1948 he was elected governor of the State of Illinois. In 1952 and 1956 he was Democratic candidate for the presidency of the United States. In 1961 he became Permanent Representative of the United States to the United Nations.

This is my first meeting with the United Nations press corps since I last served with the United States delegation to the General Assembly in 1947. I am happy to be back with you and also to see so many old friends. I look forward to cooperating with you in every possible way so that the people of the United States and of the world may know, through your efforts, about the objectives and ideas and ideals of the United States and our people.

The United States is on every stage in every region of the world, and there is nothing larger or more important or more influential, in our judgment, than the United Nations. I hope that we can play our part actively and consistently to advance the peace and security and to strengthen and expand the influence and authority of the United Nations.

Let me suggest some general policies or attitudes that I expect will govern our actions here.

President Kennedy, in his inaugural address last week, described the United Nations as "our last best hope" and renewed our pledge to support the Organization and "enlarge the area in which its writ may run." I believe that there has been too great a tendency to use the forum of the United Nations for narrow propaganda purposes.

* This statement by Ambassador Stevenson was made at a press conference held at U.N. headquarters on January 27, 1961 (U.S./U.N. press release 3642). Reprinted from *The Department of State Bulletin* (February 20, 1961), pp. 276-277.

The priceless value of the United Nations in all these fields depends on the integrity of the office of the Secretary-General and the adequacy of the Organization's financial resources. Attacks on the Secretary-General are attacks on the institution itself. I should think that the small powers would rise as one in defense of the institution which is their best protection. The United Nations exists in order that no nation need be powerful in order to be independent and secure.

The United States cherishes free institutions and is committed to the growth of law across national and cultural frontiers. We believe our goals and interests are shared with the masses of people throughout the world. We will not shrink from the burdens of our membership in this Organization. The United States will not always have its way, we know, but I hope we will always have a decent respect for the opinions of others and will act reasonably in settling disputes, reducing armaments, achieving normal relations, even with those with whom we disagree.

We believe that the United Nations offers the best possible means to find common ground with the nations of the world and thereby to achieve a peace in which the free and the just can dwell in safety. Upon that common ground we devoutly believe that the nations and the peoples of the world must ultimately stand.

I have made courtesy calls on the Presidents of the Security Council and the General Assembly. I have also called, of course, upon the Secretary-General. I am calling on all the members of the Security Council, and I would like to pay my respects to all of the representatives, all of my colleagues, of other countries. I will not have time to visit them all, but I am sending out invitations for a series of lunches at which I hope to have an opportunity to meet everyone. I hope to have the representatives of our neighbors, the Latin American Republics, dine with me this coming week.

We are just finishing, as you all know, a new building to house the United States mission. I hope it is a good sign for Soviet participation in the United Nations that they too are interested in new quarters. We have offered our help if they need it. . . .

II

Propaganda Agencies of the Superpowers

Information Activities of the United States

The images of the United States which are formed in the minds of other peoples have many sources. Because we are a society of free people we have many contacts with others which are not regulated by our government. Americans travel to foreign areas and entertain foreign guests in the United States with almost no official control over the nature of their international and intercultural contacts. We also write letters, books and musical compositions and in hundreds of other ways do things which help to determine how others view us. There are countless millions of these individual contacts every day as Americans and their words and deeds are introduced into the lives of foreign peoples.

Individual contacts, numerous as they are, do not tell the whole story, however. Business, social and religious groups organize much of our association with other nations and cultures. The impact of the movie industry, for example, is extensive and profound. The great press associations, Associated Press and United Press International, which distribute news throughout the world may be the vehicles of more contact between the United States and other nations than even the government. There are even some private or-

ganizations such as the Asia Foundation and Radio Free Europe which are devoted particularly to the task of making information about the United States available in other parts of the world.

As a result of all these "information" activities it should be clear that the United States is continually broadcasting some image of itself to others whether there is any official government attempt to do so or not. Yet the focal point of most public discussion about the role of propaganda or information in world affairs is the activity of the government. The following article by William E. Daugherty describes the development of American governmental services concerned with these activities.

The excerpts from the Sprague Committee's report analyze the full range of activities, official and private, which carry images of the United States abroad. The Committee's recommendations for strengthening U.S. information programs are also included.

The articles by J. D. Ratcliff and Roger Tubby describe less formal agencies of U.S. information work. Mr. Ratcliff's description of the American program for participating in world fairs is several years old but still serves as an informal history of this phase of government participation in the fair program. Mr. Tubby, writing more recently, reflects the government's interest in private agencies whose activities are directly concerned with exporting information about the United States.

PSYCHOLOGICAL WARFARE: ORGANIZATION AND PERSONNEL IN THE UNITED STATES SINCE WORLD WAR II*

WILLIAM E. DAUGHERTY

WILLIAM E. DAUGHERTY *is with the Operations Research Office at Johns Hopkins University.*

Little more than ten years have elapsed since the end of World War II. In this period many changes have taken place in the organization and personnel of the United States agencies engaged in foreign information and psychological warfare activities. In a few short pages it is impossible to do more than to describe rather crisply some of the more important of these changes, with little discussion of the conflicting political pressures—domestic and foreign—that have led to the alterations in organizational structure and the increased or decreased emphasis on continued propaganda output that has occurred from time to time.

OWI LIQUIDATED—1945

President Truman on 31 August 1945, two days prior to the formal surrender of Japan, by Executive Order 9608, established an Interim International Information Service (IIIS) in the Department of State and transferred to it the overseas information functions of OWI and the information activities of CIAA. The executive order authorized the Secretary of State to continue within the Department of State such foreign information functions as he considered necessary, to abolish any he thought desirable, or to transfer any to other executive agencies.

* Reprinted from *A Psychological Warfare Casebook*, by William E. Daugherty in collaboration with Morris Janowitz (Baltimore: Johns Hopkins Press, 1958), pp. 135-145.

28

The order also provided for the liquidation of OWI and IIIS by 31 December 1945. In the meantime the Secretary of State was to study the problem of continuing a foreign information program and to recommend a solution to the President.

William Benton (later Senator from Connecticut) was appointed Assistant Secretary of State for Public Affairs and as such was made the responsible head of the new IIIS. Benton drew most of the key personnel for the new agency from OWI and CIAA. Among the major tasks facing him in his new office were these: to win congressional understanding and approval for a new peacetime propaganda service including the necessary funds with which to operate; to gain from top-echelon and rank-and-file members of the Department of State a sympathetic understanding of the requirements of the new service; and to establish effective liaison, adapted to peacetime conditions, with responsible intelligence-collecting and policy-making officers both inside and outside the Department of State.

As a result of the study requested by President Truman, the Office of International Information and Cultural Affairs (OIC) was established in the Department of State in early 1946. The activities of this office remained largely unchanged until 1948; however, its name was later changed to the Office of International Information and Educational Exchange.

When funds were being considered for the 1948 fiscal year (FY48) Representative Taber, Chairman of the Appropriations Committee in the 80th Congress, called attention to the fact that Congress was being asked to appropriate money for an agency for which there was no enabling legislation. As a result of congressional action, funds for the overseas information program were drastically curtailed. However, thanks to the efforts of Senator Smith of New Jersey and Congressman (now Senator) Mundt of South Dakota, the United States Information and Educational Exchange Act of 1948 was passed. Funds appropriated for a foreign information service for FY49 were then more than doubled.

UNITED STATES INFORMATION AND
EDUCATIONAL EXCHANGE ACT OF 1948

The Smith-Mundt Act directed the Secretary of State "to provide for the preparation and dissemination abroad of information about the United States, its people, and its policies, through press, publications, radio, motion pictures, and other information media, and through information centers and instructors abroad." The administration of the act was placed under the International Information Administration (IIA) of the Department of State.

With the passage of the 1948 act the major objective of the information service became that of promoting abroad understanding and trust of the United States. This line was undertaken largely as a response to the Soviet campaign of vilification of the United States and distortion of United States international intentions. This objective was interpreted as a gigantic advertising campaign, carried on for the most part by the broadside telling of America's story. However, by 1950 it came to be recognized that the advertising method adopted to tell the "American Story" sometimes overwhelmed and confused people abroad, not infrequently leading to increased resentment rather than better understanding.

In 1950 after the outbreak of the Korean conflict, the emphasis of the program shifted sharply from a "full and fair picture" of this country to one with more definite objectives. Programs were designed specifically to deter further aggression, to help maintain the stability and cohesion of the countries of the non-Communist world, and to inspire in them confidence in their mutual capacity to meet any eventualities. With this change came the development of a system of priorities among countries in programming and a highly specialized approach to each country or area and to the various social or economic groups within them. In short, an attempt was made to adjust the content and the techniques of the program to needs growing out of the widened schism in the world.

The shifts in emphasis through the years have been reflected in changes in the organizational pattern of the agency principally responsible for administering the information program. Major changes occurred in a reorganization in January 1952. From a position subordinate to the Assistant Secretary of State for Public Affairs, IIA was reconstituted as a relatively autonomous unit of the department. The role of Assistant Secretary in the program became essentially that of a channel through which foreign policy and information policy could be coalesced. Authority over operations formerly divided among the general manager of the information program, the Assistant Secretary, and the regional bureaus of the department was concentrated in the Administrator.

FOREIGN INFORMATION ACTIVITIES OF OTHER EXECUTIVE AGENCIES

. . . In the military establishment in Washington, staff planning activities involving psychological warfare ceased with the end of World War II hostilities. Several months after the outbreak of hostilities in Korea, in June 1950, the Department of the Army created the Office of the Chief of Psychological Warfare as a special staff section. The duties of this office are largely planning and advisory in character. The Department of the Air Force later established a Psychological Warfare Division in the Air Force headquarters' Directorate of Plans. This division was a relatively small one and after several months in being was renamed the Subsidiary Plans Division. Planning for the future use of psychological warfare in the United States Navy headquarters involved even fewer individuals, the task being entrusted to a branch of the Strategic Plans Division, Office of the Chief of Naval Operations.

In addition to the three military services and the Department of State's IIA, at various times in the post-World War II era the following United States agencies operating in the international field also possessed their own overt international information service: the Technical Cooperation Administration (TCA) (of the Department of State); the Economic Cooperation Administration (ECA); and Mutual Security Administration (MSA).

COORDINATING THE EFFORTS OF VARIOUS AGENCIES

The seemingly ever-growing tendency for the various agencies interested in international operations to engage directly in propaganda and information activities, as well as the increasing awareness that acts of governments themselves carry great psychological warfare implications, led to the demand for some coordinating machinery on the United States government executive level. Accordingly on 17 August 1950 President Truman announced the establishment of a national Psychological Strategy Board that in time came to be known as PSB. At the time of its establishment it was stated that the mission of PSB would be to coordinate "foreign information and psychological strategy in situations where joint action by more than one agency of the Government is required in this field."

The original PSB was in fact only an interdepartmental committee. It was composed of the following: a representative of the

Secretary of Defense; a representative of JCS; a representative of the Director of CIA; and the Assistant Secretary of State for Public Affairs serving as chairman. Representatives of a few other agencies sat with the board as observers and advisers. In late 1951 a new PSB was established, this one presided over by a specially appointed chairman and with the following members: the Under Secretary of State, the Deputy Secretary of Defense, the Director of the Central Intelligence Agency (CIA) and the Director of MSA. PSB was given a small operating staff. The members of the original board on the establishment of the new one became the Psychological Operations Coordinating Committee. The precise line of demarcation of authority between the new PSB and the coordinating committee was never clearly defined. In general, however, the principal functions of PSB seemed to lie in the planning for long-term objectives, whereas the mission of the interdepartmental committee lay in the direction and determination of current psychological operations and policies.

Former Assistant Secretary of State for Public Affairs, Edward W. Barrett, who headed both the original PSB and the Interdepartmental Committee, has written concerning their achievements:

> Both did some good in coordinating strategy and operations. Both have thus far fallen far short of being cure-alls. In retrospect, it appears that both have attempted too much Washington masterminding of complex tactical problems that could best be solved by first-rate men in the field.

After General Eisenhower became President he appointed a special committee to prepare recommendations for reorganizing the foreign information and psychological warfare effort of the United States government. This committee was headed by William H. Jackson, Chairman, with C. D. Jackson, White House adviser, as one of several members. Following the report of this committee two major changes were accomplished. PSB was abolished and replaced by an Operations Coordinating Board (OCB), with membership comparable to PSB, but with a revised and smaller supporting staff.

UNITED STATES INFORMATION AGENCY ESTABLISHED—1953

A second and equally important step in the reorganization of the United States foreign information program was the creation of the United States Information Agency (USIA) on 1 August 1953. This agency was given independent status, with the director reporting to the President through the National Security Council. The agency was made responsible for all United States information activities overseas, except for those that might fall under the jurisdiction of a military commander in time of armed conflict [chart, p. 24]. Thus information activities formerly carried out by IIA and TCA of the Department of State and by MSA were transferred to USIA. The administration of the Exchange of Persons Program was retained by the Department of State.

The activities of the USIA, although not identical with, nevertheless closely follow, those of the predecessor agency, IIA of the Department of State. The major media of communications employed in reaching overseas targets are shortwave radio (VOA); press material radioed to Public Affairs officers overseas, and placed by them in local newspapers; films; and information center service, including circulation of books and the supplying of reference material. To ensure that the agency speaks with authority on foreign policy matters it receives from the Secretary of State complete, day-by-day guidance on matters involving United States foreign policy.

RECENT DEVELOPMENTS

In the more than three years that have elapsed since the establishment of USIA as an independent agency a number of developments have occurred that are of great significance in the field of international communications, propaganda, and psychological warfare. Many of these developments occurred as the result of efforts to correct deficiencies in the manner in which the United States foreign information effort was being planned and administered. Many of these changes suggest that some of the criticisms of past efforts, implicit in some of the accounts appearing in this casebook, are no longer valid.

Recent Developments with Respect to Administration and Coordination of USIA Efforts. A number of significant steps have been taken to increase the status of the Director of the agency within the Executive branch of the government and to improve the effectiveness of liaison and coordination between USIA and other agencies, either directly or indirectly concerned with the administration of the foreign information program. During the first half of 1955 the Director of USIA was designated a member of OCB and the agency was given representation on OCB's staff. Thus the agency became a full-fledged participant in the deliberations of OCB. Along with this important development, the Director was invited to become an observer at the meetings of the highly important National Security Council.

In addition to the formal recognition of importance accorded to USIA, a number of administrative and procedural arrangements have been undertaken that add greatly to the efficiency and effectiveness of operations. The Director and key members of his staff have met regularly once a month with the President. Close and continuing liaison has been established at various echelons between officers in the agency and appropriate personnel in the Departments of State and Defense and in such *ad hoc* agencies operating in the field of foreign relations as the Foreign Operations Administration (FOA).

Further evidence of the far-reaching changes that signify the new importance attached to effective planning and implementation of a foreign information program is the designation of one top-level presidential assistant to devote his major effort to this field of endeavor. A number of prominent men, well known for past accomplishments in the field, have been assigned this duty by President Eisenhower. These have included: C. D. Jackson, a World War II civilian deputy director of PWD/SHAEF, and a member of the special committee appointed by the President in 1953 to prepare recommendations with respect to future psychological warfare efforts; Nelson Rockefeller, World War II director of CIAA; and, William H. Jackson, a former deputy director of CIA, and chairman of the 1953 Presidential Commission on Foreign Information.

As a result of top-level planning and the recognition accorded the effectiveness of foreign information activities, four individuals from the Office of the Assistant Director for Policy and Programs were assigned as work members of the United States delegation to the conferences held in Geneva in 1955. The idea incorporating the President's "Summit" proposal that the United States and the Soviet Union agree to mutual aerial reconnaissance and open exchange of military blueprints actually originated during preconference deliberations conducted by Presidential assistant Nelson Rockefeller.

Personnel from key overseas areas, as well as from Washington, were in attendance at Geneva during both the Summit conference and subsequent Foreign Ministers Conferences. In addition to their advisory functions, such personnel performed two other important duties: They directed the flow of information from the American delegates to the world's press and provided on-the-spot news coverage to United States posts around the world. This development truly marked a wide departure from the practices followed at prior international conferences.

Another relatively recent development that has led to the improvement of liaison and coordination between separate offices within USIA as well as with outside agencies and departments in Washington was the move of the VOA's studios from New York to Washington, completed in November 1954. This move, directed by the Congress, greatly improved integration of the broadcasting services within the agency and made possible closer liaison with other governmental departments.

Improved Facilities for Intelligence, Research, and Evaluation. During the latter half of 1954 the Office of Research and Intelligence was created in order to provide facts and analyses about foreign conditions and issues to both planners and output personnel. This new office inaugurated a greatly expanded program of internal research on world-wide Communist activities, including analyses of their current propaganda "line." A widened program of public opinion polls was undertaken to provide policy planners more informed estimates of peoples' reactions, anxieties, etc., in foreign areas.

"Country plans" for every key area in the world have been revised on the basis of the agency's restatement of mission and new estimates of the situation abroad. Objectives in each area and country have been stated with greater clarity and simplicity. These are changed as circumstances dictate.

Developments with Respect to Evaluation and Improved Operational Efficiency. In order to assist and advise the Director of USIA on the proper management of the agency's resources, at home and abroad, a small independent inspection staff was established in 1954. A Broadcast Advisory Committee and a Committee on Books Abroad continue to advise relevant sections of the agency on specialized activities that come under their separate jurisdiction.

The United States Advisory Commission on Information is the principal channel for reports of effectiveness to Congress. This commission, consisting of five citizens, is charged by the Congress with the task of making an independent assessment of the foreign information services of the United States government.

Expanded Operations. The expansion of output operations of USIA have kept pace with developments in the field of expanded internal services, the development of better planning facilities, and the establishing of improved liaison with all other government departments. VOA, the radio voice of the agency, has expanded operations to include transmissions in 41 separate languages and to 56 or more foreign countries or autonomous areas. In recent months President Eisenhower's pronouncements on "Atoms for Peace," "Mutual Inspection for Peace," and similar themes, have been highlighted in output in all media operations.

The number of program hours broadcast to the Soviet Union has reached 79 daily. Programs in Cambodian, Hindi, Tamil, and English, addressed to crucial areas in south and southeast Asia and Africa, have been added. Programs suitable for rebroadcast over local facilities are prepared and sent abroad to be aired.

Among the more significant recent developments, however, are these: Films that are especially suitable for release over local television outlets have been prepared and sent to overseas areas where that medium of communication is increasing in importance. Private groups, particularly universities and private industry, have been encouraged to undertake or expand foreign operations in line with information objectives of the agency. Also there has been a greatly expanded utilization of exhibits and participation in trade fairs by the United States government and private interests.*

The increase in the use of films for overseas television outlets was occasioned in part by requests from abroad for coverage of special events in the United States. Material of this type has been in widespread demand so that, by the end of 1955, films were being sent to more than 100 stations overseas. In order to increase the opportunities for information dissemination by this new medium, the USIA has provided, on request, technical assistance and advice to local television stations abroad.

* See "The USA Goes to the Fair," which follows the selection on the Sprague Committee's report, the next reading in this chapter.

The Office of Private Cooperation had been in existence for quite some time prior to the creation of an independent USIA, but it has only been in recent months that its efforts have begun to bear real fruit. All manner of American groups, extending from corporate cities through veteran and civic organizations to private industry, have undertaken projects in furtherance of our international information objectives. Foreign cities have been saluted with appropriate musical programs, etc., by American cities. The Veterans of Foreign Wars and Rotary International have purchased and placed in foreign schools a 99-volume specially selected *American Bookshelf*. Local chapters of various industrial and advertising councils have been induced to undertake projects to inform peoples abroad of United States national aims and policies, and many magazine publishing firms have made unsold copies of their journals available for use by people abroad. In addition some American firms have been induced to see that these magazines reach a foreign reader.

The story of American participation in trade fairs abroad has been given separate treatment in this casebook, and therefore little need be added here. However, the employment of specially prepared exhibits is another matter. There have been exhibits established at these fairs, but the ones that have received the greatest acclaim have been those mounted on wheels and carried directly to the people. "Atoms for Peace" exhibits were widely shown in Yugoslavia, Colombia, Argentina, Brazil, the Dominican Republic, Uruguay, Japan, India, Pakistan, Italy, Germany, Greece, Turkey, and Denmark in 1955 and 1956.

A photographic exhibit, "Family of Man," selected and arranged by the Museum of Modern Art, was shown widely during the latter half of 1955 and 1956 in Germany, Mexico, Guatemala, France, Belgium, Holland, England, and Italy. The exhibit in Berlin is reputed to have drawn many visitors from the Communist-controlled East Sector. Along with television and trade fairs, exhibits are rapidly becoming an important channel for impressing foreign audiences with the peaceful intentions and non-warlike objectives of the American people and their allies.

SPRAGUE COMMITTEE REPORTS TO THE PRESIDENT ON U.S. INFORMATION ACTIVITIES ABROAD*

MANSFIELD D. SPRAGUE *was appointed by President Dwight D. Eisenhower in December of 1959 to conduct a comprehensive survey of the United States information system abroad. The committee appointed to assist him included* GEORGE V. ALLEN, ALLEN W. DULLES, GORDON GRAY, KARL G. HARR, JR., JOHN N. IRWIN II, C. D. JACKSON, LIVINGSTON T. MERCHANT and PHILIP D. REED.

On December 23 Mansfield Sprague, Chairman of the President's Committee on Information Activities Abroad, submitted to the President the Committee's conclusions and recommendations. On January 11 the White House released the following exchange of letters between the President and Mr. Sprague, with highlights of the Committee's recommendations and extracts from the Committee's report.

EXCHANGE OF LETTERS

PRESIDENT EISENHOWER TO MR. SPRAGUE

January 9, 1961

DEAR MR. SPRAGUE:

I have read with deep interest the conclusions and recommendations of the Committee on Information Activities Abroad which were submitted to me with your letter of December twenty-third.

I am impressed by the comprehensive nature of the study conducted by your committee and the breadth and vision which characterize it. As you know, I am asking that study be started on it at once by the departments and agencies involved in the matters it

* Reprinted from *The Department of State Bulletin*, Vol. 44, No. 1128 (February 6, 1961), pp. 182-195.

covers. Also, I am having it placed in the permanent records of the Government readily available for future use. With much of the report, and a great many of its conclusions and recommendations, I am in full and instant accord. Certain other conclusions and recommendations will of course require, and receive, further consideration. Altogether, I think it is a document of exceptional value to an informed understanding of this subject, and for this reason have determined to put as much of it as possible into the public domain. Your committee was not asked to make an unclassified report and indeed you have dealt with many things which must remain classified in the interest of national security. Even with these omitted, however, it deserves—and I hope will receive—wide attention. . . .

MR. SPRAGUE TO THE PRESIDENT

December 23, 1960

DEAR MR. PRESIDENT:

I am pleased to submit herewith the Conclusions and Recommendations of your Committee on Information Activities Abroad. During the past several months, in accordance with your letter of December 2, 1959, we have carried out a comprehensive survey of what we have called "The United States Information System." We have also considered the psychological aspects of United States diplomatic, economic, military and scientific programs which have impact abroad. Likewise, we have reported on several of the activities of private groups and institutions bearing upon foreign attitudes toward this country. . . .

As you will see from our recommendations, the Committee has formed three general conclusions:

a. On the whole, the United States informational system and efforts to integrate psychological factors into policy have become increasingly effective.

b. The evolution of world affairs, the effectiveness of the Communist apparatus, and the growing role of public opinion internationally confront us with the necessity of continuing improvement in this aspect of government, on an orderly but urgent basis.

c. This will involve the allocation of substantially greater resources over the next decade, better training of personnel, further clarification of the role of information activities, increasing the understanding and competence of government officials to deal with informational and psychological matters, and improvement in the mechanisms for coordination. . . .

EXTRACTS FROM THE CONCLUSIONS AND RECOMMENDATIONS OF THE PRESIDENT'S COMMITTEE ON INFORMATION ACTIVITIES ABROAD

I. INTRODUCTION

The 1960's may prove to be one of the most convulsive and revolutionary decades in several centuries.

Some of the underlying forces have been set in motion by scientific progress, and such progress can be expected to continue. Ninety per cent of the scientists who have ever lived are alive today; and the resources which will be devoted to research in the next ten years will equal the total for all past years since the beginning of history.

If progress is driving one wheel of the world transformation now underway, the consequences of backwardness are driving the other. Half the people on earth still live under conditions of hunger, disease and ignorance; but they have become conscious of the possibility of improvement and are now in active, often violent, struggle to improve their condition. In this vast awakening are infinite possibilities for constructive change and equally great potentialities of danger.

The Soviet Union, having now acquired great industrial and military strength, is pressing hard its drive for expansion and ultimate world domination. The prospect is for a period of protracted non-military conflict between the Free World and the Communist system. This conflict will reach into every portion of the globe. Its background will consist of the presence within the Communist Bloc of massive conventional military forces and the availability of great nuclear striking power. Its foreground will be characterized by the continuous employment by the Communists of economic, diplomatic and informational instruments as well as of subversive and conspiratorial action.

One of our basic problems will be to help in the development of forms of government in Asia, Africa and Latin America which will promote stability, discipline and economic advancement without undue infringement of individual liberties. It will be extremely difficult to accomplish this unless we can find more effective means to deal with the world-wide Communist apparatus dedicated to the destruction of free government.

The eventual outcome of the struggle, assuming that general war can be avoided, and that Communist subversion can be countered, will depend in considerable degree on the extent we are able to influence the attitudes of people.

The steadily mounting force of public opinion in world affairs is evident in all parts of the world, the developed and less developed countries, and to a degree even in the totalitarian areas. In the Sino-Soviet Bloc, where public opinion in the democratic sense is ineffective, it nevertheless cannot be wholly ignored by the regimes. If nothing else, it determines how far the screw of oppression can be turned without the outburst of revolt. Its rising force is explained by the growth of literacy and education, the introduction of new and wider channels of communication, and the spread of the democratic idea. The trend is perhaps most vividly symbolized by the United Nations, a diplomatic arena in which the economic and military power of the participants plays an important part in the outcome of issues, but in which world opinion is almost equally influential.

The changing styles of diplomacy also reflect growing concern with groups beyond official circles. From the formalized government-to-government communications of the classical past, we have now witnessed the advent of epistolary diplomacy, electronic diplomacy, summit diplomacy and unofficial diplomacy—not to mention undiplomatic diplomacy.

The United States is concerned with its general prestige in the world and its image as a dynamic and progressive society not out of national vanity but because the effectiveness of our leadership on crucial issues is involved. Today it is recognized that unless governments effectively communicate their policies and actions to all politically influential elements of foreign populations, their programs can be impeded and their security placed in jeopardy.

This Committee has addressed itself fundamentally to the question of improving U.S. performance in reaching and influencing opinion abroad. We have dealt with this question in two distinct but related parts: improving the effectiveness of information, cultural, exchange and educational programs as such; and improving our efforts to shape our foreign policies and programs so as to maximize understanding and support and minimize resentment, confusion and opposition.

Since World War II, the principal overseas information agency of the U.S. Government has been renamed six times and reorganized four times. It has in the past been subjected to great year-to-year variations in its appropriations, much to the disadvantage of long-term programs, effective planning, and needed personnel development.

A mere listing of some of the principal characteristics of the information system will indicate how heavy and difficult some of its problems are. It embraces a wide variety of mass media, cultural, educational and exchange programs. The scale of activity must be large enough to meet urgent requirements in every major region of the globe; no politically significant area can be ignored. Operating responsibilities must necessarily be distributed among several agencies, whose efforts in turn must be coordinated. The system must have affirmative as well as defensive capabilities—sound and vigorous programs in all media for the presentation of U.S. policies and programs, and facilities to counter the moves and expose the purposes of the Soviet apparatus. It must have strategic as well as tactical capabilities—the ability to build enduring relationships with foreign leaders and institutions and at the same time handle daily issues effectively. Yet it cannot be muscle-bound. It must accurately reflect the content of foreign policy, yet preserve the qualities of humanness, quickness, subtlety and lightness of touch.

In recent years great progress has been made in strengthening the U.S. information system. Staffs have been professionalized, effective media organizations have been built, and arrangements for coordinating information programs with foreign policy have been improved. Such progress must continue, for the demands placed upon the system will increase rapidly in the years ahead.

Although our informational and cultural activity will continue to play a valuable supporting role, it is American policies and actions, far more than official information programs, that will influence attitudes. "Actions speak louder than words" is a maxim which applies abroad as well as at home.

The Committee therefore believes that world opinion should be fully considered in the development of policies and programs—diplomatic, economic and military—which have impact abroad. There are cases in which opinion considerations are secondary; there are other cases when they are of great moment. The necessity is that they be considered along with and on the same footing as other factors in the formulation and the execution of foreign policies and programs. Within the government this concept needs to be more widely accepted and applied more vigorously and consistently. Inadequacy in dealing with the intangible elements in our foreign policies under present and prospective world conditions can be just as fatal to their outcome as inadequacy in dealing with the more traditional and tangible aspects.

This does not mean that foreign opinion considerations should determine or control U.S. policies or objectives, nor that our actions should be ornamented with public relations gimmicks, nor that we must solicit constant foreign approval and inevitably recede in the face of criticism. It does mean that we must show a "decent respect to the opinions of mankind" in what we do. Since our objectives must not be popularity but long-term and durable relationships of friendship, understanding and respect, we must stand firmly on principle regardless of temporary storms of dissaproval, and in doing so make our actions comprehensible to our friends and clear in their implications to our enemies.

In the long run, a nation like an individual achieves stature and exercises leadership not by avoiding criticism and seeking to please but by its character, strength and goodness of heart.

The United States must demonstrate by actions as well as by words that we are militarily invincible yet supremely devoted to peace; that we are zealous in our support of the aspirations of other nations and respectful of their sovereignty; and that we are a progressive society actively in support of progressive change, greater material well-being and social justice everywhere.

These purposes must be translated at the highest level of government into concrete, dramatic and timely form. This labor of giving active support to the ideas which will reach the hearts and minds of people around the earth is an important part of the task associated with the term, "leadership of the Free World."

II. Strengthening the U.S. Information System

The Committee has studied both the foreign informational programs of the U.S. Government (including mass media, exchanges of various types, cultural and educational programs) and those programs designed to expose and combat Communist attempts to sub-vert the countries of the Free World.

This broad spectrum of activities, which we have called the U.S. information system, constitutes roughly one per cent of the approxi-mate total of $50 billion spent annually for national security.

In *Western Europe* the scale of U.S. information activity has been substantially reduced in recent years. This process of reduction has gone as far as it prudently should, except in the case of certain exchange programs. It is of the utmost importance that the people of this area understand American objectives, have confidence in our leadership and cooperate actively in mutual undertakings.

In the *Soviet Bloc* we must take every opportunity to provide the populations with information in hope of lessening to some de-gree the hostility and aggressiveness of their governments.

Communist China presents a baffling and theatening problem for official information activity. Sustained government-wide action must be developed to prepare long-range plans, to mobilize available resources and to formulate new approaches to communicate with the Chinese people who are being subjected to the most massive "Hate America" campaign in all history.

In the *less developed areas* of Asia, Africa and Latin America, the United States faces certain common information tasks. In the face of the sweeping social, economic and political revolution now underway, we must: identify ourselves with the forces of progress toward stable and democratic institutions; expose and counter inso-far as possible the multi-faceted Sino-Soviet offensive against orderly development of these areas; provide effective close support through informational means to U.S. development programs; as well as ex-plain U.S. policies, objectives and way of life.

In *Africa,* the pace of political developments has outstripped our informational preparations. We lack basic knowledge of the processes by which information and ideas are communicated within these societies; we lack sufficient information specialists trained in the languages and cultures; we lack sufficient physical facilities; and we lack contacts. In the judgment of the Committee, Africa pre-sents the United States with a challenging opportunity to build friendly ties. The Committee recommends a drastic and prompt upward revision of all plans, estimates and preparations for infor-mation activities appropriate to the area.

In *Latin America* the immediate outlook is more disturbing

than promising. U.S. economic policy in the hemisphere has undergone recent modification and strengthening, but informational activities have not been equally reinforced. Greater efforts are needed.

Countering Communist Subversion

In addition to mass media activities, there is need for programs of action to counter the international Communist threat. We should continue and increase our efforts to aid those who are threatened by Communist subversion.

Budget

We have reviewed the requirements for informational activities abroad based upon our appraisal of the current world situation and estimates of probable developments over the next decade. In comparing these requirements with present informational programs, we have concluded that there is a growing need for greater effort generally, and an urgent need for substantially increased efforts in the critical areas of Latin America and Africa. These increases are over and above those required to meet the rising costs of current programs and to provide adequate representation in the newly independent countries of the world.

The extent to which information budgets should be increased in future years can best be determined in light of changing circumstances. However, it is likely that the scale of the total U.S. information effort will have to be progressively expanded for some time to come. The Committee urges that, if and when such expansion is contemplated, the Executive Branch seek Congressional approval for planned and orderly growth of these activities.

Because speed and flexibility of operations are essential to effective information programs, the Committee recommends that adequate contingency funds be appropriated. As a minimum, adequate flexibility to transfer between accounts must be provided.

American efforts to develop contact with influential elements abroad should not be diminished by niggardly allowances for official hospitality. The Committee recommends that renewed efforts be made to obtain Congressional approval for adequate representation funds.

In making recommendations for budget increases, the Committee has sought to find areas in which it might properly recommend reductions or eliminations of programs. With one exception, namely government sponsored educational exchange programs with Western Europe, there is no realistic possibility of providing for additional needs by cutting back present programs; nor is it feasible for the United States to stretch present resources by deliberately neglecting urgent needs in any major region.

Structure

Because it is outside the Committee's terms of reference, the structural relationship between the Department of State and the U.S. Information Agency has not been examined. However, the Committee believes that the present allocation of responsibilities has functioned reasonably well and that practical means have been worked out to insure necessary policy coordination.

Training and Personnel

The expansion of training programs is a fundamental requirement. Long-range efforts should be made to qualify more top officers engaged in economic, military, diplomatic and scientific work in the psychological aspects of policy, and to develop more information officers with adequate background in non-information fields of foreign policy. It is important that these matters should be dealt with adequately in the war colleges and the Foreign Service Institute. Training in these fields can also be improved through graduate study in universities for government officers and through seminars and discussion groups which periodically bring together governmental and academic persons and informational specialists. . . .

Research

Knowledge is lacking about some of the major factors which can determine the success or failure of informational efforts. The Committee recommends that the various agencies involved in foreign informational programs re-examine the adequacy of their research programs. In such re-examination, they should draw upon the best available advice from private sources.

III. EDUCATIONAL, CULTURAL, AND EXCHANGE ACTIVITIES

The Committee believes that great and as yet insufficiently realized opportunities are offered by educational, cultural, and exchange programs. Changing world conditions are generating a particularly rapid expansion of needs in these fields.

In developing these programs we have not yet adequately capitalized on our cultural and intellectual resources, our educational traditions and institutions and even our language itself. There is need for new emphasis and for substantial increase in levels of effort. We can thereby serve effectively several objectives. Educational, exchange and cultural programs over the long run can strengthen our political ties abroad, re-enforce our economic assistance programs, advance social development and stability, and add to our chances for peace and security.

Ultimately, the development of the human resources of the less developed areas through education and training may be the most effective form of economic assistance which can be given. At the same time strengthened cultural, exchange and education efforts will help correct a widespread distortion of the American image. Such action will put into perspective alongside our military, political, economic and technical programs our enduring concern for the individual and for learning. We will demonstrate meaningfully our understanding of the relationship between education, democracy and social progress.

The activities which can contribute to these ends are what much of the world wants us to provide. Our techniques are respected and sought. Increasing numbers of foreign students are attending our universities. English is increasingly recognized as one of the preeminent languages of this era and people seek by the tens of thousands to learn it.

Foreign Educational Development

Through various programs and agencies, the U.S. Government is already providing considerable help to education and training abroad, particularly to persons in the less developed countries. These programs, though valuable, are diffuse and frequently not readily identifiable with the United States. They are subordinate elements of agencies and activities directed principally to other things. They have no single voice or general leadership. They are not based on a coherent and avowed over-all policy or legislative enactment. They therefore fail in large part to realize their great symbolic value in identifying the United States clearly with one of the universal human ideals—education.

The Committee feels there is need to move with conviction in giving new accent to our assistance to foreign education. This should be made concrete in the form of a new declaration of policy in support of long-term assistance to foreign educational development by the President and the Congress. . . .

International Meetings and Awards

Most international scholarly gatherings take place outside the United States. Few of the major international festivals in the fine arts take place here, and even fewer of the major world prizes for intellectual and creative achievements are American. Our national capital in the eyes of many is regarded, from a cultural standpoint, as a provincial town.

Our achievements in the arts and in scholarship deserve better than this. The Committee recommends:

1. The establishment of a continuing series of international festivals and exhibitions of the arts in the United States, including if necessary governmental subsidy of transportation and facilities.

2. Development in Washington of a cultural center to include operatic and ballet presentations, symphony concerts, and special competitions in the arts.

3. A permanent increase in the number of major international meetings in the United States in the humanities, social sciences, philosophy, the exact sciences and the fine arts. In some instances, this may require selective relaxation of visa requirements as well as governmental and private assistance in lessening the economic obstacles involved.

4. The establishment of a series of major American awards for outstanding achievements by men and women of all nations in science, art, education, government and human welfare.

English Language Teaching

There now exists around the world a vast and spontaneous demand for learning English. The Committee believes that it would be both feasible and advantageous to intensify the governmental efforts now being made to teach English to people of other nations. In so doing we will facilitate the transmission of technical information and skills useful to economic development. We will widen our channels of communication with foreign leadership elements. We will expose increasing numbers of people to the social and political ideals of Western civilization. We will as a consequence of these benefits reinforce our ties throughout the world.

The Committee recommends that we explore the possibilities of more massive and short-term efforts—in parallel with long-term programs—to achieve a rapid increase in the number of foreign students and adults able to use English as a working tool. These might involve the use of new techniques of teaching by television, and the development of a large and dramatic program using gifted American college students and teachers of English to conduct "summer language camps" each year in selected foreign areas. We should also collaborate more closely with other English speaking countries in the extension and coordination of these efforts.

Exchange of Persons Programs

The U.S. Government is extensively engaged in exchange of persons programs and the training of foreign specialists and leaders in this country. These activities lack a clear framework of over-all policy and require better arrangements for the handling of exchangees once they arrive here.

The Committee recommends that official exchange of persons programs be progressively expanded (except for Western Europe); and that priority be assigned to exchanges of students, specialists and leaders from Africa.

To make possible more effective handling of exchanges, funds will be required:

1. To expand and strengthen our specialized agencies which administer foreign student and leader exchanges.

2. To create an adequate nation-wide system, based on the voluntary help of local citizens and groups, for hospitality to foreign visitors.

3. To provide special guidance and courses tailored to meet the needs (often very different from those of the American student) of students from the less developed countries.

Exchanges with the Soviet Bloc countries* and the programs of reciprocal exchanges as provided under the U.S.-USSR Exchange Agreement† should be continued, with such expansion and governmental financing as may be. appropriate.

IV. ECONOMIC AID, SCIENTIFIC AND MILITARY PROGRAMS

U.S. economic assistance programs, scientific research and development agencies, and the military establishment exert enormous influence upon foreign opinion as a result of their activities. The Committee has considered means by which the constructive impact of these non-information programs on foreign opinion might be increased.

Foreign Economic Assistance

In the decade of the 1960's, the demand upon the United States for economic assistance will undoubtedly increase. The need will be concentrated in the less developed areas, not in the industrially advanced countries as in the immediate postwar years. Aid will be concerned with modernizing total societies, not with the relatively simple labor of economic rehabilitation and reconstruction. Aid programs will pursue their objectives in a seething atmosphere of tension, turmoil and misunderstanding.

In many of the countries in which our aid programs will operate, we find practically none of the elements required for the development of the conditions we seek to promote. These countries in many cases are characterized by strong feelings of nationalism, impatience with the slow processes of economic growth, and lack of skills to deal with the technical and managerial functions of a twentieth century state. Omnipresent and alert to every possibility of disrupting constructive effort is the Sino-Soviet Bloc with its growing programs for subversion, economic warfare, propaganda and intimidation.

* For text of an exchange agreement with Rumania, see BULLETIN of Dec. 26, 1960, p. 968.

† For text of an agreement of Nov. 21, 1959, see *ibid.*, Dec. 28, 1959, p. 951.

It is therefore not only relevant but indispensable to give the most careful attention to public opinion and informational matters in the formulation and execution of aid programs. However, the purpose of such attention should be to facilitate the achievement of the goals of economic development, not to arouse extraneous sentimental manifestations. Informational targets must be set in accord with functional requirements, not out of sentiment or belief in publicity for its own sake. The attitudinal obstacles to the adoption of better methods of production and distribution should be understood. Procedures and policies which unnecessarily generate friction or misunderstanding must be modified.

In the long run, we can hope, by giving aid, to strengthen ties of mutual respect and cooperation. But it is naive to think that our aid programs—affecting as they do basic social and economic institutions in the recipient countries—will be or can be universally understood and applauded. . . .

Scientific and Technological Programs

A startlingly new development in recent years has been the increasing impact of scientific and technological achievement upon world opinion. Without question the launching of the first Sputnik gave the Soviet Union a psychological triumph which has profoundly affected its image as a technically advanced nation and as a great military power. Its feat in one branch of technology has been systematically exploited—and with considerable success—as evidence of the dynamism of the entire Soviet system.

The United States has had, and continues to have, over-all superiority in science and technology. Nevertheless, since the launching of Sputnik I there has been considerable evidence of a widespread belief that Soviet capability continues to grow relative to that of the United States and that the Soviet Union leads in certain important aspects of space technology. It will not be easy, short of some revolutionary scientific breakthrough, to re-establish the degree of American technological prestige relative to that of the USSR which existed prior to October 1957.

The Committee feels that, since throughout the world the status of the nation's science is increasingly taken as a measure of its power and dynamism, two things are indispensable: (1) that the

U.S. maintain its continuing stream of scientific and technological achievements; and (2) that these achievements be more effectively communicated to the world than has been the case in the past.

The Committee recommends:

1. That the scale and effectiveness of our overseas information efforts to communicate the facts of U.S. scientific achievements be increased. This will require particular attention to the recruitment and training of qualified information specialists who are at the same time competent in technical subject matter.

In stressing the need for more vigorous informational support of scientific programs, it is important also to caution that premature publicity and "leaks" that appear to promise more or quicker technical progress than can practically be realized can prove most injurious to U.S. prestige.

2. These increased efforts should be designed to improve our communications both with scientific elites and with the general public.

·3. Recent organizational measures to give new prominence to the role of science in our government have indirectly been of value to informational activities abroad. The Committee would like to cite particularly the establishment of the offices of President's Assistant for Science and Technology and of Science Adviser to the Secretary of State, and the appointment of science attachés at our principal embassies abroad. Further development of these activities can help improve understanding abroad of our progress in science and technology.

4. Where particular needs are identified, agencies of government participating in technical assistance should be asked to expand and intensify certain programs for teaching and transmitting American· technical knowledge. This is already being done on a large scale in the field of agricultural technology. Other possibilities would appear to exist in the field of medicine and in new teaching techniques such as educational television.

The dramatic and highly useful curriculum developments in the various fields of science education should be exported in a planned, coordinated program involving the several agencies concerned with foreign information, education and exchange of scientific knowledge. Making available developments in science education would have the twofold value of providing genuinely useful materials to countries that need them and at the same time demonstrating American advances in technical and scientific fields.

5. Joint scientific and technological programs with other countries of the Free World should be encouraged.

The best assurance of a continued flow of major scientific discovery which will serve the broad spectrum of human needs and thereby the nation's prestige abroad is ample unprogrammed financial support for basic research. At the same time, the Committee recommends that the President bring to the attention of government scientific administrators and those responsible for budgetary allocations to scientific research, the relevance, propriety and importance of taking world opinion into account in determining the relative emphasis to be given to various activities.

Military Programs and Policies

The American military establishment is a huge and powerful system to protect the nation in the event of war. In the course of protracted conflict short of war—which is the prospect—it will also exert enormous and continuing influence in every part of the world in behalf of the objectives of U.S. foreign policy.

It will exert such influences primarily by the reality of its military power—its forces and weapons—but also through many important side-effects: the presence of hundreds of thousands of service men and their families on foreign soil, its relationships with foreign leaders and military personnel, and its expenditures abroad. The Department of Defense and the armed services have made considerable progress in recognizing the importance of these side-effects. Measures which the Department of Defense has taken to deal with these matters should be continued and intensified, particularly among the lower echelons of command. . . .

V. New Dimensions of Diplomacy

In some historic periods deep shifts in the mission and style of diplomacy occur. We seem now to be in such a period. The changes taking place reflect technological developments in transport and communications, and the growing role of public opinion in world affairs. In addition, the persistence of the ideological, economic and strategic struggle with the Communist world imposes new challenges to our diplomacy. The whole Soviet system from the beginning has placed great stress on propaganda, both at home and abroad. In the next ten years, the conduct of our foreign relations and the organization of our diplomacy will have to cope with the various aspects of this encompassing struggle, including the propaganda and the psychological, particularly in its transference to new arenas in Asia, Africa and Latin America.

In both the new countries and the older ones going through the crisis of modernization, formal and traditional diplomacy of the predominantly government-to-government type often plays a limited role. This means that our diplomacy increasingly must understand public opinion in all countries, open and closed, old and new, and must give greater emphasis to this factor in the handling of conferences and negotiations, in the selection and training of members of the foreign services, and in our treatment of foreign visitors.

American diplomatic representatives abroad should make a greater effort to develop close and friendly contacts with all key leadership groups. Dealings with all major sources of influence in foreign societies will be of increasing importance in years to come.

Visits to other countries by the President or the Secretary of State can have extraordinary value in terms of impact on foreign opinion. The greatest care should be exercised in deciding the timing and detailed arrangements of such visits.

A renewed effort should be made to reduce the size of certain of our missions abroad, particularly in countries where elements attached to the embassy are disproportionately large.

Major Negotiations

Major diplomatic conferences and negotiations now require more careful planning and preparation than ever before, in part because our adversaries commonly try to convert them into propaganda jousts. Such preparations and negotiations now must be conducted simultaneously on two levels: the laborious, intricate process of negotiations between governments, and the continuous effort to build public support for our proposals.

The United Nations

Since the inception of the United Nations, debates in that body have dramatized major international issues and given an additional dimension to diplomacy. The UN has been important not only as a means of discussing issues and, on occasion, of settling disputes, but also as a sounding board.

The United States, in continuing its support for the UN, should make the fullest use of UN meetings, including those of specialized agencies, to launch major new plans and proposals and to state its position on issues of enduring importance.

In the makeup of delegations to the United Nations and of assignment of U.S. personnel to UN affiliated organizations, careful attention should be given to the ability of the representatives to deal effectively on the informational front. Experience in international conference work and training for it should be more widespread in our services, especially the Foreign Service.

Greater emphasis should be given to UN affairs by U.S. Government information media and to dealings with the press to explain U.S. positions.

Far greater attention should also be given to the responsibilities and opportunities of the United States as "host" to the UN. As the most recent session of the General Assembly has demonstrated, the impact on the delegates from the new states of their reception, housing and general treatment is a factor of real importance.

Arms Control

Today the world is on the threshold of an important new era in arms control negotiations. The Committee recommends that the U.S. make more timely informational preparations to communicate its proposals and objectives. Heads of U.S. delegations to such negotiations should provide full and frequent background briefings for the world press. All statements by government officials bearing on the question of arms control must be effectively coordinated, especially during a period of negotiation.

Visitors to the U.S.

The Committee believes that better arrangements are needed for welcoming both foreign dignitaries and ordinary visitors to the United States. In the case of the former, additional funds are required for protocol and official hospitality. Efforts must be stimulated to provide imagination and some pageantry in the reception of chiefs of state and high-level dignitaries. Consideration should be given to the utility of consultative citizens' committees for this purpose.

Measures should also be taken to improve the reception of tourists, businessmen, students and other ordinary visitors at U.S. ports of entry. Although somewhat lightened and humanized in recent years, the procedures of our various port authorities remain more rigorous than those in most other countries. We suggest that the sensitivities and reactions of the foreign visitors, whose image of America is sharply affected by their arrival experiences, be given greater weight in determining the methods, manners and procedures of our receiving officials.

VI. INTERNATIONAL ACTIVITIES OF PRIVATE ORGANIZATIONS

In total, the greater part of the influences emanating from the United States and affecting opinion abroad result from private, not governmental, activity. The free and uninhibited contact of an open society with the rest of the world contrasts sharply with that of totalitarian systems. The Committee believes that private activities abroad have importance in a generalized way to the world's image of America and that they contribute significantly to international understanding—and misunderstanding. However, private international activity is not a substitute for sustained and systematic informational activity by the government.

Business Firms Abroad

The climate of opinion for foreign investment is deteriorating in many areas where the need is greatest. To counteract this requires a determined effort by business and government. The necessary business associations exist, such as the Business Council for International Understanding and the International Chamber of Commerce, to give leadership.

Individual firms are commendably beginning to face their responsibilities for good corporate citizenship abroad. Such progress should continue at an accelerated rate. There should be more vigorous Government efforts to encourage the best practices by

American firms abroad. More companies should develop community relations programs abroad as they do at home.

Labor Organizations

American labor organizations provide a uniquely acceptable channel of communication with their counterparts abroad and they have become increasingly involved in world affairs. Whether their response has been adequate to the challenge is a matter of some dispute. However, what they have done in countering the spread of Communism in labor organizations abroad is to be commended.

Universities

As world affairs become more important to the nation and as our international involvements increase, the demands upon our universities for training, research and operational support for governmental programs likewise grow. The Committee feels that it would be highly desirable to clarify and strengthen the role of a single agency of the government to deal with our universities on the over-all and long-range policy questions presented by the requirements of the various governmental agencies working abroad. Likewise, it would seem desirable for the universities themselves to bring into existence a permanent council to deal with fundamental problems of government-university relationships.

Private Foundations

The international activities of private foundations provide an important and independent channel of American communication with influential scientific, cultural and academic leaders abroad. The Committee believes that foundations can make no more vital contribution to the national welfare than by activity abroad in their fields of special competence, and it urges the trustees of all foundations not barred by charter or other legal inhibitions to consider seriously such activity. The independence of action of foundations is to be valued and protected. However, effective communication and consultation between Government and the foundations working overseas is increasingly important.

International Sporting Competitions

The Soviet Union obviously attaches considerable propaganda importance to international sporting events. It spends large resources and marshals hundreds of thousands of its youth to dedicate themselves at governmental expense to become international sporting champions.

Some Soviet sporting victories have had certain propaganda value. But the Committee believes that the problem does not justify any fundamental departure from the established American practice of participating in the Olympic Games and other international competitions on a private and amateur basis. However, the situation does underscore the importance to our standing abroad of the work of the President's Committee on Youth Fitness and the role of the armed forces in the physical development of our youth. It would seem worthwhile if many of our institutions, including our schools, were to encourage development of greater skills in the athletic events in which the United States has a demonstrated weakness.

The News Media

The freedom and independence of U.S. news media are rooted in basic principles of our democracy. These private commercial enterprises are, however, clothed with a public interest and responsibility.

On a world-wide basis, the two main problems which the news media present are:

a. The needs of the less developed areas in building up the competence and objectivity of their media as literacy and political interest develop.

b. The obstacles which exist to the international flow of news, particularly between the Soviet Bloc and the Free World, but also within certain Free World areas.

The Committee recommends:

1. That, under the leadership of the Department of State, all Government agencies increase their assistance to foreign correspondents in the United States to enable them to report more fully on and to develop a better understanding of America, and that

private organizations and corporations be encouraged to do likewise.

2. That the United States continue to provide to the world an example of freedom in access to and the transmission of news; and that it demonstrate vigorous interest in promoting the rights of the news media to freedom of travel for correspondents and freedom from censorship.

3. That there be parallel efforts by private media, professional journalistic bodies, foundations and government to help strengthen the news media in the less developed countries, to develop standards of journalistic objectivity and the competence of personnel.

International Television

The Committee recommends that a coordinated government-wide policy be developed to guide and extend U.S. participation in the future overseas expansion of television broadcasting.

Also, it recommends that under the leadership of the State Department steps be taken now to develop policies to clarify the roles of the U.S. Government and private broadcasters in international telecasting and to plan international proposals for frequency allocations which would prevent chaos on the airwaves once international telecasting begins.

Books and Publications

In a time of new technical marvels of communications, the importance of the printed page in the transmission of information and ideas remains fundamental.

The Committee recommends the continuation of the Informational Media Guaranty program and, where feasible, its extension to cover additional areas where the shortage of dollar exchange continues to be a serious hindrance to the distribution of American books and publications.

VII. GOVERNMENT ORGANIZATION

Intra-Agency Organization

The Committee recommends that the President reaffirm to all departments and agencies the importance of adequately considering foreign opinion factors in the formulation of policies and the execution of programs which have impact abroad; that he request the Departments of State and Defense to continue and re-enforce the efforts already made to this end; and that he ask the heads of other departments and agencies to take whatever organizational or procedural steps may be necessary in this connection, leaving to their discretion the determination of the particular methods to be used.

The Role of the OCB

The coordination of information activities in the general structure of the U.S. Government is a formidable problem. They are conducted by a number of different departments and agencies, and they are both diverse in character and substantial in scale. Even more complex is the task of integrating psychological factors in substantive programs affecting opinion abroad.

The creation of the Operations Coordinating Board in September 1953 represented a major step forward in improving the effectiveness of U.S. psychological and informational activities. Although the activities of the Board have been the subject of continuing debate, there can be no question that it has performed and continues to perform a number of vital functions in the coordination of informational activities and the integration of psychological factors in substantive programs of the government.

The weekly executive sessions of the Board provide its members with a unique and high-level mechanism in the government for the expeditious and effective handling of a whole spectrum of inter-agency matters including those related to the climate of world opinion. Its working groups and committees carry on part of the continuing task of inter-agency coordination of information programs. Most important, the OCB is a point high in the governmental structure where security programs and policies are considered in relation to their public opinion as well as other aspects.

In the judgment of the Committee it is essential that, whatever changes may be made in national policy machinery, the functions now performed by OCB continue to be provided for.

We believe that the most effective means for insuring the continuation of these functions, particularly those related to public opinion and informational matters, is through the continued existence of the OCB.

If the OCB did not exist, it would have to be invented; its creation was the logical outgrowth of the increase in U.S. information activities up to 1953, as well as of the growing importance of public opinion and communications in foreign affairs.

Furthermore, we believe that the OCB not only should be continued but that its potentialities should be more fully recognized and realized. In accomplishing this, continuing strong Presidential interest in making the OCB effective is the crux of the matter.

The OCB should further stimulate and coordinate planning by the various elements of the U.S. information system. This requires greater attention to anticipating major opportunities and problems, identifying the requirements for trained personnel and physical facilities on the scale and at the time needed to deal with upcoming situations, and mobilizing all the informational assets of the government in support of national objectives.

In the areas of foreign educational development, exchange of persons, English language teaching, exhibits and trade fairs, and radio and television, there is need for increased integration and coordination of current efforts.

The Committee believes that it is important to achieve program evaluations of a more objective and critical character than has been the case in the past. There is some question whether such evaluations, given the understandable concerns and perspectives of operating agency representatives, can be most effectively accomplished through the committee approach. Nevertheless this Committee firmly believes that the responsibility rests with the Board itself, and that the Board members should give greater attention to meeting it. . . .

THE USA GOES TO THE FAIR*

J. D. RATCLIFF *is a prominent American author whose articles have appeared in* Time, Newsweek, Fortune, Reader's Digest *and many other publications.*

In Bangkok, Thailand, a 2000-seat theater was jammed day after day with people who came to see the wonders of Cinerama. In Bari, Italy, farmers listened fascinated while a six-foot wooden chicken, with egg-producing organs exposed, gave a tape-recorded lecture on modern poultry practice. In Bogotá, Colombia, throngs jostled around a stand offering free ice cream made from surplus powdered milk from Wisconsin. The United States was going to the fairs—the world trade fairs—and registering a smash success.

Each year there are something like 130 large fairs, ranging from the giant International Trade Fair in Paris, with nearly four million visitors, to the agricultural fair at Verona, Italy which attracts about 130,000. Totally unlike United States state and county fairs, the trade fairs are market places where new goods are displayed, where businessmen go to buy and sell.

Although United States businessmen long ago saw the wisdom of buying space and displaying goods, the United States government stood aloof until 1954, when President Eisenhower reviewed some disturbing facts. Since the war, Russia and her satellites had participated with spectacular exhibits in 133 fairs. Personable young Chinese sipped tea with German businessmen; Russians talked the virtues of Soviet tractors; Czechs demonstrated heavy machinery and spoke of booming production. The impression was left that the United States was too busy preparing for war to take part in such peaceful pursuits.

President Eisenhower decided to correct this. He earmarked $2,250,000 from an emergency fund to be spent at trade fairs to "put the United States in the best possible light overseas."

The Departments of Commerce and State and the United States Information Agency drew the planning job. There were two main objectives: to sell the idea that this nation's vast industrial production is the result of a free-enterprise system, and to stress trade as a two-way affair.

To direct the program, the Commerce Department borrowed Roy F. Williams, New England industrialist and executive vice-president of Associated Industries of Massachusetts, who recruited a team of architects, designers, idea men. With only three months to design and build an exhibit for the fair at Bangkok, where a year earlier Russia had taken first prize with a costly and elaborate pavilion, Williams chose *Fruits of Freedom* as the United States theme. The exhibit would emphasize ways and means by which United States industrial techniques could help lift living standards in the East. Cinerama was an added eye-catcher.

Russian had 242 crates of murals on the Bangkok fairgrounds—heroic representations of Soviet industrial might. Getting wind of United States plans, the Russians didn't bother to unpack them. They withdrew from the fair.

A similar situation arose in Paris last May. When it became clear that the lively United States exhibit was almost sure to be the hit of the fair, the Russians packed up and went home. Altogether, the Soviets have withdrawn from five fairs rather than face United States competition.

The United States exhibit, *America at Home,* was the outstanding success at Paris, drawing as many as 70,000 people a day. It included a five-room house through whose open windows visitors could look while "Mother" prepared meals in a model kitchen equipped with freezer, garbage-disposal unit, dishwasher, mixers and other gadgetry. "Father" puttered with the car in the carport, worked with power tools in the home shop, broiled steaks on the terrace. But the real delight was the playroom, where children of United States soldiers stationed in France concentrated on toys, oblivious of the crowds.

A similar display at the Vienna fair in September caused a newspaper to comment: "The Americans stole the show. They show us how we could live if we had plenty of money. But they do it in a way that makes us forget we do not have it."

When possible, exhibits are related to local problems. Italian farmers are keenly interested in United States agricultural methods. Hence, at the agricultural fair in Verona the United States exhibit included a small field of hybrid corn in which farm machinery was demonstrated. A model cow, cut away to expose internal organs, lectured on cow diets that increase milk production.

Spain has always had export difficulties with her valuable citrus crop. Fruit is often poorly sized and packed. Losses due to spoilage are high. For display at the Valencia fair the United States imported a citrus-packing plant from Lakeland, Fla. In a continuous, automatic operation the plant cleaned, sized and waxed oranges. (Waxing retains juice and cuts spoilage.) Another exhibit suggested a new market for the Spanish and a new market for United States machinery: it showed how orange juice is extracted, concentrated and frozen—all new to Europe.

Lately Pakistan, the world's largest producer of jute, has worried about the growing competition of other fibers. Jute is used mainly for burlap and coarse sacking. The United States exhibit at the Karachi fair included ingenious new machinery which converts coarse jute into a soft fiber—suitable for dress and other fabrics. Knitting machines, poultry-raising equipment, TV and a fashion show rounded out the lively display.

The Communists spread the story that the United States is planning to hydrogen-bomb the world. *Atoms for Peace,* which tells of our peacetime atomic projects, has been a key United States exhibit in a number of fairs. Including a 30-foot model reactor, mechanical hands to handle "hot" atomic materials, and other eye-catching displays, it presents the atom as a friend of man, the producer of medically useful isotopes, the source of curative radiations, a future producer of commercial power.

At the fair at Jakarta, Indonesia, last summer the United States exhibit included a glass-walled TV studio broadcasting to 24 receiving sets spaced around the fairgrounds—the first TV the country had seen. A model train built by Lionel, puffing and whistling its way through a maze of tracks, gave Indonesians an idea of what a modern transportation system looks like.

At the Berlin fair, hordes of people swarmed over from Soviet-controlled East Berlin to see the Western world on display. Two United States labor unions—the Amalgamated Clothing Workers and the International Ladies Garment Workers Union—provided a stirring rebuttal to the Communist story that the American worker is the slave of a capitalist economy. Pictures showed union health centers, camps, clubs; explanatory material told about the wage scales, pension plans and arbitration procedures.

In state-controlled stores in Communist East Berlin shoddy clothing brings sky-high prices. On living models at the Berlin fair a large United States clothing chain displayed a complete winter wardrobe for a family—mother, father, two children. A large tag carried the price of each garment. Total cost of outfitting a family: about three weeks' pay for an American carpenter. To East Berliners this was an impressive demonstration of the fruits of free enterprise.

The key part of every United States exhibit is a trade mission— a six-member panel (usually), drawn half from the Department of Commerce, half from industry. These men answer questions about buying goods from the United States and about exporting to the United States market. In eight fairs last spring such panels handled a total of 26,000 queries.

In Hanover, Germany, the woman owner of a linen shop seeks and gets information about importing the bath towels displayed in the model United States home. In Salonika a dealer wants the agency for a small tractor. He is put in touch with several makers. At Cologne a grocer wants floor plans of American supermarkets. Several United States firms can supply them.

Such advice often bears immediate fruit, advantageous to all concerned. At Milan an Italian was interested in exporting ceramics. Two Americans interested in *importing* ceramics happened to be present. They got together on the spot.

This American readiness to do business *now* has been impressive. At the International Trade Fair at Lyon, France, Red China had a lavish display of motorcycles, saxophones, heavy machinery— much of it clearly handmade. When asked about prices and delivery dates, the Chinese were noncommittal. It became apparent that the goods displayed were pure propaganda, not for sale. Meanwhile, the United States trade panel was doing a land-office business—a fact duly observed in the French press.

Trade panels occasionally get hecklers. A man with clear Communist leanings denounced the group in Hanover: the United States was interested only in war, he said, not in helping people. Panel members questioned the man about his interests. He was an out-of-work salesman of household appliances. It was arranged for him to get the agency for a United States refrigerator. The line went well, he prospered, and has altered his political outlook.

By next July 1, the United States will have been represented in 34 fairs. No one will hazard a guess as to how much trade has directly resulted, but Roy Williams is sure that the small investment has been repaid many times over. The business world apparently agrees. The year before official United States participation at Bangkok there were 47 American industrial exhibitors. This year there were 140. At Hanover the number increased from 13 to 47; at the giant Milan fair from 571 to 700.

Thirty million people are expected to see our exhibits this fiscal year. "They will all go away," says Williams, "with a new realization of what free enterprise in a democracy really means."

INDUSTRY COMMUNICATIONS
PROGRAMS IN SUPPORT OF
U.S. FOREIGN POLICY*

ROGER W. TUBBY

ROGER W. TUBBY, *government official and newspaperman, is Assistant Secretary of State for Public Affairs.*

I am delighted to be here today, to attend your workshop, to join in your discussions and profit from your ideas. We in government are of course also deeply concerned with communications and with the need to inform people and governments of the world effectively. Our problems are similar to many of yours. In

* Mr. Tubby's remarks were made before a film workshop for the Association of National Advertisers at New York, N.Y., on January 17, 1962 (press release 35 dated January 16). Reprinted from *The Department of State Bulletin*, Vol. 46, No. 1180 (February 5, 1962), pp. 213-215.

our effort to solve them we find that all the media of communications and especially films are playing an increasingly significant role.

You are asking yourselves how to get maximum results from business films. This involves a study of all the new techniques and component elements of production—writing, designing, musical scoring, visual effects, etc. As businessmen and advertisers you must have some way of gaging the effectiveness of these programs. Do they dramatize your products? Do they improve customer and stockholder relations? Do they train and build the morale of your employees? Do they expand business; if so, in what directions and with what implications for the future? You take into consideration whether the film material is treated realistically and yet with imagination, whether it will make a favorable impact on audiences to whom it will be shown.

I emphasize these points, well known as they are to all of you, for several reasons. American enterprise is increasingly directed to the overseas market. We are in a period of adjustment and great opportunity with respect to our trading relations with Europe and the developing areas of Asia, Africa, and Latin America. When we ask, "Do films expand our business?" we increasingly think of their impact abroad. Is their message always intelligible? Are we sufficiently aware of the opportunities which visual presentation of our enterprise and the workings of our society present? I think not.

Whether we are or not, your films, individually and in the aggregate, export an image of America. The higher their quality, the better the job they will do for you and for our country. Films produced by many such companies as Standard Oil, International Harvester, E. R. Squibb, Sears Roebuck, Caterpillar Tractor, the Aluminum Company of America, and many others have played an excellent dual role—effective salesmanship of product and, not so incidentally, of country.

Films, whether for TV or movie theater, for schools or civic organizations, whether news or documentary, can make more vivid and understandable AID programs, developments in Laos, Berlin, the Congo, and South Viet-Nam. They can illustrate the work of the Peace Corps, Alliance for Progress projects in Latin America, or strides being made in Europe thanks in part to the Common Market.

We must, if we can, establish the relevance to others of our experiment in freedom. To much of the world we appear too comfortable and conservative. Many erroneously think we are opposed to forces of change, though our society thrives on change. This is clearly evident in many of your films. But we need to do more not only to show what we are doing but how others can more rapidly develop their own farms, industries, schools, and other institutions. By doing so, developing and uncommitted nations may prefer to move forward in a free society, rather than in one imposed by the coercion of the Communists. I might say that the many pictures of the wall sealing off the people of East Berlin have characterized for millions the harsh meaning of Communist coercion.

HOW THE FILM INDUSTRY SUPPORTS U.S. OBJECTIVES

While I suggest we can and should do more, recognition should of course be given to what is now being done by the film industry in support of our broad American objectives.

For example, approximately 40 percent of the films which stock the overseas libraries of USIS [United States Information Service] are produced by U.S. companies. Your cooperation in granting rights to translate the pictures into the required languages and to narrate, reproduce, and distribute them abroad has made it possible for USIA to show many outstanding pictures around the world. A few examples are "Books for All" on U.S. libraries, "The Lady from Philadelphia" on Marian Anderson's tour of the Near and Far East, "Dark Interlude" on rehabilitation of the blind, and "The Face of Lincoln."

One can appreciate the potential for expanding this program when one considers the surge in distribution figures for business-sponsored films in the United States. For example, just one film distribution network delivered 16 mm. prints for its clients to over a million and a half group audiences last year. This means they reached nearly 68 million people as films. The same network reports that television's growing interest in educational materials led to 45,000 showings of this type film which, with an estimated audience of 40,000 viewers per showing, brings us to a total of 2 billion people for factual films.

When we consider the hunger for information on science and

technical subjects abroad, and the many ways of distributing it—in USIA libraries, homes, clubs, villages, and settlements, by mobile trucks and river boats—we have some idea of the opportunities at hand.

Figures from the Department of Commerce support this trend, particularly with regard to the export of 16 mm. films which has increased 100 percent in 10 years.

Aside from educational and informational films we have learned from international medical film exhibitions that there is much work yet to be done by governments to simplify procedures by which such films can be exchanged.

In the agricultural field I think American companies are now more aware than ever of the value of documentaries. One might cite as an example of farsightedness the film entitled "Seeds of Progress" sponsored by the affiliated Ford Motor Companies of Latin America. It is conceived as part of a broad inter-American communication program, with emphasis on the work of rural youth clubs. It is a story with Spanish, Portuguese, and English sound tracks which will reach millions of young people interested in exchanging ideas and techniques on improved farming and agricultural methods.

Of course, although we lay emphasis on motion pictures as a medium for increased understanding, other sorts of audiovisual materials are useful, such as filmstrips, kinescopes, recordings, slides, models, maps, and charts. One gets some idea of what is available from the fact that the USIA catalog on "U.S. Educational, Scientific and Cultural Motion Pictures and Filmstrips Suitable and Available for Use Abroad" has some 14,000 listings.

I think it helps us appreciate the dramatic possibilities of films if we consider that each USIA documentary, whether originally produced for a U.S. firm or for the Government, after it has been distributed in 40 languages and dialects has a potential audience of 500 million people each year. In this connection I would like to comment on the very useful function which *Business Screen* magazine performs in highlighting these programs and establishing the relation which they have to the basic aims of our foreign policy.

If we consider that in many parts of the developing world newspapers and radio are still limited, we can appreciate the value of films and other audiovisual materials in helping to provide basic educational and technical skills. If we can reach this audience with films of technical competence, imagination, entertainment, and know-how, we will be laying a base for expanding trade with vast numbers of the world's people.

EXPORT EXPANSION PROGRAM

In his state of the Union message [January, 1962] President Kennedy said, "Above all, if we are to pay for our commitments abroad, we must expand our exports. Our businessmen must be export-conscious and export-competitive." The President further stated that he will shortly send to Congress a new 5-year trade expansion act to make it possible for our major industries to compete with their counterparts in Western Europe for access to European consumers. "If we move decisively," he said, "our factories and farms can increase their sales to their richest, fastest growing market."

I would urge everyone here to examine every opportunity for extending the use of business and industry motion pictures abroad. Certainly among the 5,000 motion pictures annually produced by American business and industry there is a significant resource for assisting in carrying out the proposed new instrument of trade policy.

I should mention that the Department of Commerce is already exploring with a number of industrial firms the possibility of their making available for use by commercial attachés abroad business and industry films describing competitive products. They propose to do this through the relatively inexpensive new medium of 8 mm. sound films with magnetic stripping for foreign languages.

INTERNATIONAL FILM FESTIVALS

Before going on to more general observations, I would like to say that is not often that the competition between nations for the minds of men can be measured. But very much as the Olympic games provide a means of comparing the athletic achievements of individuals in most of the countries of the world, so do the international film competitions provide confrontation between nations not only in artistic accomplishments in motion pictures but also a comparison of ideologies and social concepts which relate to their production. I want especially to commend the business and industry community for their part in developing a method for selecting from their very impressive productions outstanding films to represent the United States in the international film competitions in Berlin, Cannes, Venice, and Edinburgh, and many other festivals around the world. I understand that many of you in this audience have contributed many hours to screening and selecting the finest examples of motion picture products to represent the United States in these international events. Since the United States Government is invited by foreign governments to participate officially in these events, this cooperation is very much appreciated by the Department of State.

The initiative and imagination which go into the production of these motion pictures brought into being CINE, the Committee on International Nontheatrical Events. And I understand that both the present and the past chairman of this organization have come from this audience. In 4 short years this organization has effectively represented the United States in the major international exhibitions and by its participation has increased and augmented the prestige of the United States in these events. Its regional screening committees function very much like selection boards in the Foreign Service. We want to be represented abroad by only the best ambassadors.

The programs I have summarized are among the programs which America adapts to a changing world. We change as we grow.

Communication, essentially, is an agent which facilitates change. It can channel it in the right direction by throwing light on societies that grow by choice, by observing those hobbled by coercion.

The historian Toynbee said: "Our age will be remembered . . . because it is the first generation since the dawn of history in which mankind dared to believe it *practical* to make the benefits of civilization available to the whole human race." If this challenge can be met in practical terms and if, in the process, communication can be extended between men, we will find that the American experiment has a mighty relevance for the world.

Our communication programs—whatever products, processes, or policies are involved—must help inform our citizens and the world of the direction in which our society is moving. We seek to inform, to have access to other peoples, to learn from them, to help them. We would help them, I believe, if there were no Sino-Soviet threat— help them because by doing so we help ourselves.

Information Agencies of the U.S.S.R. and Communist China

The same kinds of things which create images of America abroad also create images of the international Communist movement. Communist travelers, books, movies, newspapers and governmental actions are important ingredients in the international impact of communism. But there is a major difference in the organization of the things which make up the Communist impact. In the United States the degree of official coordination of American international contacts is a major public issue. In the Communist world it is the dominant fact.

Evron M. Kirkpatrick's article, which follows, gives a detailed description of the organization of Communist propaganda activities. It is included because it offers the reader an opportunity to evaluate the possible advantages of the totalitarian approach. It also gives a clear picture of the kind of operation with which opponents of communism have to cope.

COMMUNICATION MEDIA AS CHANNELS FOR THE COMMUNIST MESSAGE*

EVRON M. KIRKPATRICK

EVRON M. KIRKPATRICK *is an American political scientist and author who has also held several important positions in the* Department of State. *Among his books is* The People, Politics and The Politician *(1941).*

ORGANIZATION AND DIRECTION OF COMMUNIST PROPAGANDA

. . . Because propaganda, recruitment, and organizational activities are best conducted overtly, Communist parties struggle to remain

* Reprinted from *Year of Crisis* (New York: The Macmillan Co., 1957).

legal. Finances and legal aid also are easier to obtain through overt organizations.

The Central Committee of a national Communist Party appoints one or more of its members to guide the clandestine apparatus. This control body, the *Triad,* normally consists of a political adviser, an Agitprop adviser, and a cadre adviser; there is sometimes a fourth member, a technical adviser.

Clandestine apparatus is carefully hidden in the most innocuous groups and must not be exposed except where there is a chance for success of armed revolution or *coup d'état.* Normally, no member of the open Party is shifted to the clandestine apparatus; members are recruited "clean." Sometimes, however, a Party member is publicly anathematized and "expelled" from the Party so that later he may enter the clandestine operation.

A clandestine intelligence apparatus collects "information" to support Party and propaganda operations. A Communist Party must have information: (1) to make a reasoned estimate of its own capabilities in relation to its hostile environment and in relation to the organized forces it opposes; (2) to devise a practical plan of action in view of external conditions and internal capabilities; and (3) to dispose its forces in the most economical way to carry out its plans and to adjust its tactics to changing conditions.

AGITPROP

Agitprop is the central policy organization behind the propagation of the Communist doctrine throughout the world. . . . Agitprop operates directly under the Central Committee of the CPSU as one of the principal Party organs.

The Chinese Communist Agitprop, speaking under the instructions of Mao's Politburo, has assumed an increasingly responsible and authoritative role within the world propaganda organization. During 1956 Peking took several unusual steps to reinforce the authority of Soviet Agitprop and to ensure that other parties, like its own, would continue to accept Soviet leadership in policy and propaganda without major public qualifications.* Its most spectacular gesture of obeisance was to accept and retransmit without question Moscow's rationalization of its attack upon Hungary. . . .

* Editor's note: Mr. Kirkpatrick wrote before the developing independence of the Chinese regime began to be reflected in the public statements of the two Communist governments.

Within the Soviet framework noted above, the Presidium of the Central Committee of the CPSU, the small group which rules the Communist Party and thus the Soviet Government, directs the world-wide Communist propaganda network. Charged with combining revolutionary theory and practice to give strategic and tactical direction, it determines the tactical "line" of the Party on all major questions of current policy.

Once the line is determined by the Presidium of the Central Committee, Agitprop—a policy staff producing little propaganda material of its own—acts as planner, director, and "watchdog" of all Communist media engaging in propaganda dissemination. These functions are exercised both internally and externally. For internal propaganda the flow of direction is from the CPSU Central Committee directly to Agitprop to *Pravda*, thence to internal media—the Home Service radio, *Izvestia*, the Mosfilm Studio, and other domestic media. For external propaganda the flow of direction is from the Central Committee of CPSU through Agitprop, coordinating with the Foreign Section to "inform" Communist diplomatic and other missions of propaganda policy and to assure necessary administrative support.

Propaganda guidance reaches the "national" Communist parties and front organizations in several ways. Normal methods of "guidance" and "exchange of experience" (instruction) are overt. Moscow and Peking broadcasts are an increasingly important quick method of disseminating the line. Tass transmissions often contain propaganda instructions in the form of "news items." The CPSU theoretical journal *Kommunist* interprets the Party line on a monthly basis. *Agitator's Notebooks*, published every ten days in almost every language, interpret the Party line on timely subjects of both domestic and international interest—usually treating one or a very few themes. *Pravda* and *Izvestia* editorials also guide propagandists in determining the "correct" line on current issues, and Soviet delegations to foreign nations occasionally help in transmitting Moscow directives to local Party organizations in the countries they are visiting.

Each year on May Day and on the anniversary of the Bolshevik revolution, the Party publishes a long list of slogans, as does the Chinese Communist Party, on corresponding anniversaries, which in each case are action directives stemming from the Central Committee by way of Agitprop, and which are aimed at the lower echelons of Party leaders.

The Soviet Agitprop organization is elaborate, consisting of approximately fourteen subsections or departments, as follows:

Propaganda (administrative)	Publishing Houses
Agitation (administrative)	Films (Sovfilm)
Local (Provincial) Press	Radio
Central (Moscow) Press	Fictional Literature
Art Affairs	Science
Cultural Enlightenment	Party Propaganda—Mass Agitation
Schools	VOKS

Although VOKS (the All-Union Society for Cultural Relations with Foreign Countries) assumes the posture of an autonomous, and even public, society, it is included above as a department of Agitprop because for all practical purposes it is an integral arm of the propaganda apparatus subject to Agitprop direction and control.

VOKS is responsible for all cultural exchange matters and relations with the innumerable "friendship societies" throughout the world. Organizationally, it is an administrative department divided into geographic area sections. VOKS maintains committees of prominent Soviet artists and specialists from all fields of culture who act as advisers in the selection of representatives and cultural materials (for example, films, art, and literature) which are to be sent abroad by VOKS to illustrate Soviet accomplishment. Committees are established for the natural sciences and mathematics, history, economics, theater, literature, music, architecture, sports, films, and so on.

VOKS also produces a number of newsletters and bulletins and bi-monthly magazines, which at the beginning of 1957 became the monthly, *Culture and Life.*

FRACTIONS AND MASS ORGANIZATION: THE PARTY'S CONTACT WITH ELITE OR MASS GROUPS

The Communist Party itself is a highly restricted communications channel, generally serving to transmit straight doctrinal propaganda, or action messages. In communicating its disciplined commands to other organizations or to peoples at home or abroad it relies heavily on two devices, the fraction and the mass organization.

Within a Communist country the fraction, known as the Party group, is formed of Communist Party members in other political parties, organizations, and institutions. According to the 1952 statutes of the CPSU (Article 36), the Party group constitutes the agency of Communist Party communication and control over all other groups. Specifically: "The Central Committee guides the work of the central Soviet and public organizations through the party groups within them."

Within the Free World, fractions, generally concealed, comprise the agency through which the Communists control or subvert other organizations, or reorient and manipulate their programs and personnel to Communist interests. The old manual on organization of the Communist Party of the USA calls for fractions in all organizations boasting three or more Communist Party members:

> . . . , in all the unions and other mass organizations of the workers and in cultural, fraternal, sport and unemployed organizations of the workers and farmers, in all united front organizations. In all conventions and conferences of such organizations where there are at least three Communists, a Communist fraction must be organized. . . . In all questions in which there is a decision of the corresponding Party organization, the fractions must carry out these decisions. (J. Peters, *Manual on Organization*, New York, Workers' Library Publications, 1935, p. 99).

Fractions may exist at all levels, and come under the jurisdiction of corresponding regular Party organizations.

COMMUNIST RADIO PROPAGANDA

Radio has proved itself one of the most potent instruments of propaganda. No other medium can compete with its speed and reach over international boundaries. Whereas books, films, delegations, and others can be stopped at the borders of a country, radio waves cross in either direction unhindered by "curtains." In the majority of the newly developing countries, moreover, the spoken rather than the written word provides the most effective way to reach men's minds. This is true in spite of the fact that radio receivers are still considered a luxury in many of these lands.

The Communists have been quick to realize radio's advantages in the dissemination of international propaganda. They have found it to be the surest and quickest way to acquaint a potential worldwide audience with the glories of Communism and the perfidy of their opponents, and to carry the latest variations of the Communist "line" to their followers abroad.

The external broadcasts of the Soviet Union go back to 1933 when German-language broadcasts were initiated over the long-wave Moscow station. The following year several short-wave transmitters were placed in use, and by 1942, when the Voice of America took to the air, the Soviet Union was already making use of ten short-wave transmitters at Moscow and Kuibyshev to broadcast around 400 hours per week in 17 foreign languages. These facilities have been further increased and strengthened, so that today the Voice of the Soviet Union can be heard loud and clear in practically all countries of the world.

The Soviet International Service is a vast operation making use of an extensive transmitter network extending from Leipzig in East Germany to Petropavlovsk in Kamchatka. Radio Center Moscow beams broadcasts to six target areas, known as the North American, Latin American, European, Near and Middle Eastern, Far Eastern, and the South and Southeast Asian Services. In addition to Radio Moscow, several stations also originate broadcasts to foreign areas. These peripheral stations—Kiev, Vilnyus, Tallinn, Yerevan, Baku, Tashkent, and Stalinabad—are specially suited for broadcasts to selected audiences because of geographic advantages and linguistic facilities.

When the countries of Eastern Europe were taken over by Communist regimes, their radio installations were also put at the service of world communism. Though not on a scale comparable to the Soviet Union, the European Satellites individually carry on a substantial amount of international broadcasting, and also permit the Soviet Union to use their transmitters on a part-time basis to relay Moscow programs to the outside world. . . .

EXPANSION OF PEKING'S INTERNATIONAL PROPAGANDA BROADCASTS

Peking's propaganda broadcasts, including its International Service and transmissions to Taiwan (Formosa), increased by 55 per cent in 1956. With the addition of two powerful short-wave transmitters with beam antennas, Peking at the end of the year utilized nine short-wave and two medium-wave transmitters in its International Service. This was in addition to eight short-wave and eight medium-wave transmitters in its broadcasts to Taiwan—a total of twenty-seven transmitters beaming propaganda abroad. Furthermore, Peking's international broadcasts, beamed only to the Far

East and to Southeast Asia during 1955, in 1956 spread out to Europe, the Near East, and Africa. One of its English-language broadcasts to the Far East is also beamed simultaneously to North America. And with a 1956 year-end announcement that broadcasts to Latin America would begin soon, it appears that the voice of Communist China will soon be heard around the world, putting Peking in the ranks of the foremost international broadcasters.

DIRECT TELECASTING ACROSS THE IRON CURTAIN

Besides the cooperative presentation of television across the Iron Curtain, whereby each side voluntarily shows the educational, cultural, and artistic products of the other, there is another means of penetration in the field of international television, which does not depend on the consent of the recipient country. This is simply direct telecasts from one side of the Curtain into the border areas and population centers of a country on the other side. Only a few areas at present offer this strategic possibility.

EAST AND WEST GERMANY

Berlin is ideally located for this kind of activity. It is a unique case of an Iron Curtain within an Iron Curtain. Residents of Berlin actually have a choice of programs. Both East and West German transmissions can be received by the use of adapters on television sets.[1] In addition, two television stations on the East German network are located on high mountains close to the zonal border, and their telecasts can reach many big cities in West Germany.

This situation has caused serious concern in West Germany. The press has repeatedly warned the country against this "infiltration." One newspaper pointed out that "East Zone television has vast funds at its disposal and its rigidly centralized management adopts everything that makes West German television attractive. . . . The television stations on the Inselsberg and the Brocken mountains beam their programs into West Germany, and the Ruhr is expected to be brought within the range of East Zone transmitters

[1] Though different systems are used in East and West Germany, which has necessitated the adjustment of sets for reception of across-the-border telecasts, one of the East German stations in Berlin began to telecast on Western standards at the end of the year, thus making it possible for West Berliners to view Eastern programs without having to have their sets adjusted. This is a significant move to win West Germans to East German television.

in the near future. It will not be too long before East Zone television will be received in numerous areas of West, North, and South Germany as a 'second program.'"

The potential and the techniques are well suggested in another excerpt from a West German newspaper: "Soviet Zone television is being developed rapidly and with huge funds into an effective medium of propaganda. Responsible managers have understood that sledgehammer methods do not appeal to the German public. Therefore, Western forms are adopted. Jazz and sex appeal are no longer outlawed. Jokes are allowed; one smiles and charms. What to date was poured into the audience's heads by the bucket is now injected through thin needles."

A survey of East German television fare reveals, however, that occasionally the needle is put aside for the sledgehammer.

One of the Sunday evening programs (shown twice in a short period of time) presented a play called *Ethel and Julius,* based on a story by a Polish author. According to the program notes, "The author presents the tragic fate of the Rosenberg couple, executed by American justice. It is a play which none of our viewers ought to miss. . . ."

Another play, *Joe Hill, the Man Who Never Died,* was also presented over the East German network. According to the East German radio and television magazine *Unser Rundfunk* (Our Radio), the play conveys "a powerful picture of the fight of the American working class at the beginning of the century. . . . It affords an insight into the despicable methods of that American lynch justice, which again and again victimizes innocent men, especially members of the Negro race. . . . The aim of this television play is to erect a monument to this revolutionary leader of the American working class. . . ."

COMMUNIST USE OF FILMS

The motion picture, like all vehicles of public influence, is viewed by Communist theory and practice as essentially an instrument in the class struggle.[2] As such, it was held in high regard by both Lenin and Stalin. In fact, during the Stalin era, great efforts

[2] "Soviet cinema art has not and cannot have any interest or task other than the interest of the state and the task of educating the people, and the youth, particularly, in the spirit of the great ideas of Lenin and Stalin."—*Pravda,* September 11, 1946.

were made to produce all films in a didactic, orthodox mold. Artistic talent was regimented, strict Party specifications were imposed upon every step in production, and a complex of cumbersome and time-consuming censorship devices was employed to ensure compliance. However, instead of creating an effective instrument of the state, these restrictive methods resulted in the steady deterioration of the entire Communist film industry. In 1951 output in the Soviet Union was reduced to six feature-length films, and, as a rule, those which survived the close bureaucratic scrutiny were so stereotyped and so heavily laden with Communist didacticism that they had no propaganda value abroad, and offered little to interest the home audience.

After the death of Stalin in 1953, the tight grip of the Party was relaxed, and the industry made a new beginning toward a realization of the full potential of the motion picture. The film makers were allowed to operate with somewhat greater flexibility and latitude. There was, for example, less insistence on direct Communist instruction as a necessary element in every scenario, and entertainment as a purpose—either for itself or in conjunction with education—was permitted. In this atmosphere, the four post-Stalin years became a time of experiment. The fact that the 1956 total feature-film output of the major film-producing countries in the Soviet Bloc represents an increase of 250 per cent over that of 1953 is a clear indication that it was also a time of rapid growth. The artistic and technical qualities of some of these productions won critical acclaim in international competition and helped to open the world film market to the Communist countries.

Against this background, 1956 became clearly the most successful year in the history of the film enterprises of the Soviet Union and its Satellites. The continued expansion of the motion picture industry of the USSR was assured by the policy makers who, within the framework of the Sixth Five-Year Plan, committed the economy of the country to provide the studios, equipment, and trained workers necessary for large-scale production. The "new" film became a natural and important adjunct to the general "cultural offensive" as the Communists turned westward and sought recognition for themselves and their products. The technique of co-producing motion pictures with other nations was extended beyond the boundaries of the Orbit. By the year's end the Soviet Bloc had concluded an unprecedented number of private and official film sales and exchange agreements with foreign nationals and countries, and established itself as a new competitor in the international market. By learning to use indirection and subtlety, it finally succeeded in equipping itself with a propaganda instrument more effective in both reach and impact.

PRODUCTION

During 1956 the Soviet Union's film industry produced 85 feature-length films. This was ten more than the target figure set for it by the Ministry of Culture at the beginning of the year and was accomplished in spite of inadequate studio space, technical equipment, and staffing. In addition, numerous documentaries and newsreels covering a wide variety of subjects were turned out. Production was begun on a major film venture with India.[3] Another was being filmed with a Finnish company,[4] and several with film enterprises in other Free World countries were in the process of negotiation.

With the capabilities of the industry thus demonstrated, the Sixth Five-Year Plan prescribes no fewer than 120 full-length films a year by 1960, and contemplates substantial improvements in techniques, processes, equipment, and facilities. To attain these objectives, the USSR plans to double the amounts expended during the past five years for studio development. Remodeling and enlargement of the major Mosfilm and Lenfilm studios has already begun, and efforts are being made to perfect the Sovcolor process, to increase production of widescreen films, and to establish facilities for the manufacture of noninflammable film. This program marks the first recognition of the film industry as of sufficient stature to warrant inclusion in a five-year plan. . . .

CONTENT

Soviet films entered in the major international film festivals give some indication of the quality and variety of those which appeared most often on the foreign market.

[3] *Journey Beyond Three Seas (Pardesi)*, Mosfilm with Naya Sansar International Film Company, India.
[4] *The Cobblers of the Heath*, filmed in Sovcolor and developed in Leningrad laboratories.

For example, one of the Soviet films at the Cannes Film Festival was an adaptation of Shakespeare's *Othello,* which received not only the best direction award, but special mention for film production as well. How the Soviets consider presentation of a Shakespearian classic as supporting the Communist cultural offensive was indicated in an article written by its producer, who declared that as the Soviets filmed it, "people like Othello and Desdemona are the symbols of harmony," and, "under a capitalist society, are doomed to die." Iago is the symbol of chaos. He is not a murderer, but merely the "tool of the princes of primary accumulation."

Two of the entries at the 1956 Edinburgh Film Festival further illustrate both the wide range of subject matter being utilized by the USSR and the stress on personality and individuality rather than on ideology. The first, *The Rumyantsev Case,* is on the order of a detective story, and purports to show how Soviet justice protects the innocent against the unscrupulous and unprincipled within its own society. This film is an innovation in that it portrays to foreign audiences products of Communist society cast in something less than heroic role. The second, *Magdana's Donkey,* also concerns justice—this time in nineteenth-century czarist Georgia. Good fortune comes to a poor widow's family when a donkey, abandoned by a merchant because it was too sick to work, is found and nursed back to health by the widow's children. The owner then claims it. Despite the pleas of the entire village, the judge decrees that the donkey must be returned to the merchant.

Often the scenario of a joint film venture stresses a common historical or cultural bond between the co-producing countries. *Journey Beyond Three Seas (Pardesi),* undertaken during 1956 by the Soviet Mosfilm Studio in collaboration with an Indian film company, is based on the chronicle of a fifteenth-century Russian, Afasii Nikitin, who, the USSR claims, traveled throughout India in 1469. The Soviet contention is that until Nikitin wrote an account of his journey, Europeans had no reliable information about India and the countries of the Middle East.

Of the many documentaries produced in the USSR, those presenting the events connected with the visits of foreign heads of state are, in the opinion of many observers, of major propaganda value. During 1956, feature-length documentaries were made on the visits to the USSR of President Sukarno of Indonesia and of Shah Reza

Pahlevi of Iran. Both films stress the ovations accorded the visitors and the welcoming throngs constantly surrounding them. Both show a grand tour of the Soviet Union, including a visit to Tashkent, capital of the Central Asia Republic of Uzbekistan, where a majority of the population is Muslim. The Indonesian press commented, "The most impressive scenes were the President visiting Tashkent . . . the impression is that the Indonesian visitors felt very much at home there."

Typical subjects of the shorter documentaries are Soviet advances in various fields, such as atomic research and its peaceful application, hydro-electric development, and construction projects. Particularly designed to make the Soviet cultural campaign carry appeal to the susceptibilities of foreign audiences are art films like *Rembrandt*, which shows the paintings of the great Dutch master; *The Dresden Galleries*, a film tour of the Dresden collection; and *The Mystery of Matter*, a series of biographical sketches of the scientists of many countries whose work in chemistry and applied physics led to the ultimate release of nuclear energy.

A large number of documentary films are made for instruction in such fields as practical engineering and agricultural production. Although these are produced essentially for the home audience, the efforts of Communist countries to place instructional films with various foreign ministries of education may well give them a wider utilization, particularly in newly developing areas.

In June 1956, the Moscow Documentary Studios initiated a monthly newsreel, *USSR Today*, in thirty languages, the stated aim of which is "to help people to know more about life in the Soviet Union and its ties with other countries. . . ."

THE PRINTED WORD

The printed word is probably the most far-reaching and versatile of all conventional Communist propaganda media. The word can be a "fast" medium, reaching its target as quickly as TASS or NCNA wireless teletypes; or a "slow" one, as deliberate as a scholarly archeological work of the Soviet Academy of Sciences. It can carry a highly didactic message for party cadres, a subtly persuasive message for politically sophisticated government leaders, or a simple message for the barely literate and for children. It may take the form of a slogan painted on a wall or of a magnificently printed and illustrated volume on President Sukarno's art collection. It may stand on its own or be part of a concerted campaign utilizing radio, films, and fronts. It is limited only by the facts that it must have a literate audience and that its audience must be directly accessible.

The supreme importance of the printing press as an instrument for complex and precise propaganda was understood by Lenin. Through *Iskra* (The Spark), first Bolshevik organ, Lenin won the following of Bolsheviks who later made revolution possible. The printed word continues to be the main reliance, of course, of Communism's assault on the intelligentsia, not only in providing the texts for doctrinal persuasion, but in attempting to influence the whole range of intellectual life in both political and non-political context.

The function of defining and expounding the current orthodoxy for the parties continues to be a major one for Communism's publication effort today. But this task is not permitted to overshadow the other continuing functions of conditioning readers—wherever they can be reached—to draw conclusions favorable to Communist aims even when the subject matter appears far removed from dialectic arguments or political polemics.

BOOKS AND PERIODICALS: FROM PRINTING PRESS TO READER

The Soviet Twentieth Party Congress in one of its resolutions called for a further expansion of technical facilities, to provide printed material for its own people and for an international reading public:

> More books, magazines, and newspapers to be printed with special emphasis on further increasing circulation. General make-up and typography must be improved, printing facilities increased, the capacity of printing plants under the USSR Ministry of Culture to be expanded approximately 50 per cent. Printing shall be provided with modern equipment, new types, and better quality inks.

In order to implement these resolutions the USSR Ministry of Culture allocated 800,000,000 rubles for printing-plant expansion. Work was pushed on enterprises at Kalinin, Yaroslavl, Minsk, Kiev, and Saratov. When completed these plants will increase the Soviet printing capacity by over a hundred million volumes.

BOOKS

At the end of 1956, the release of Soviet publishing figures based on statistics from Moscow's publishing weekly, *Book Herald,* revealed that 613 new titles of full-sized books (over 50 pages) had been printed in Free World languages during the year. The total number of these volumes came close to thirty million.

In Communist China, too, book publishing continued to play an important role. Projections based on figures available for 1955 show that in 1956 Communist China's book production program may have reached a total output of close to 1½ billion copies including 28,500 titles. China's drive for additional printed material, like the Soviet Union's, required additional publishing establishments. The eight reportedly planned will bring the total number of State publishing enterprises in Communist China to forty-five.

A brief survey of the subject matter of books issued for foreign consumption by Moscow and Peking, however fragmentary, suggests the diversity and range of interests to which these millions of volumes tried to appeal. There were the multi-lingual editions of Communist "classics": Marx, Engels, Lenin, and Mao Tse-tung. There were, of course, both Chinese and Soviet books which portrayed the heroic proletarian struggle against the "class enemy," books which depicted in idealized terms the virtues and advantages of life under Communism. Although the stereotypes were still prominent in these publications, and a specific "mission" often detectable, the burden of propaganda appeared somewhat less insistent and obtrusive. There were also handsome editions of the traditional Russian and Chinese classics, implying that the cultural heritage of the past is both continued and respected by Moscow and Peking—the works of Tolstoy and Pushkin, or a poetic dramatization of a seventeenth-century Chinese love story in a royal setting. And, appealing to yet another segment of the world's intellectuals, Chinese, Soviet, and Satellite printing presses turned out books of high artistic quality in luxurious editions frequently offered at prices far below those for books of similar quality produced in the Free World.

But perhaps the most important single target of Communist foreign book publishing was the youth of the world. Possibly the largest share of Chinese and Soviet Bloc book production for non-Communist audiences was composed of books for young readers.

Generally speaking, young children's books published by the Bloc avoided strong propaganda overtones, although an anti-Western slant appears in books intended for older children. Like the universal classics provided by Communist presses for Free World adult readers, the dissemination of children's stories and fairy tales having universal appeal serves to depict Communist society as interested in preserving and perpetuating the universal and traditional values, and suggests a community of innocent interests. Textbooks—particularly for use in developing areas—are more direct in their ideological approach.

To make books palatable to foreign readers, expert translators are needed. There is evidence that the Communist Bloc was hard pressed during 1956 to secure enough of them. The Soviet Union in particular—publishing the greatest variety of foreign-language material—offered high financial rewards to foreigners to induce them to come to the USSR to translate Communist propaganda material from Russian into their native languages. In Burma a monthly salary of 4,000 rubles ($1,000 at the official rate) was reportedly offered. And the USSR claimed during 1956 to have achieved a measure of success in designing translating machines—eventually, another means of overcoming the language problem in producing masses of printed material, especially technical and scientific data for foreign audiences, as well as helping to make foreign materials readily available to its own people.

The Communist Bloc has energetically explored and expanded all channels for transporting books from source to target. Book exhibits, book fairs, lending libraries, local book clubs and exchange programs are all utilized for distribution and promotion of Communist books. Cultural agreements signed between Bloc countries and Free World nations frequently provide for book exchange programs. Library exchanges, a normal and welcome activity among non-Communist institutions, make it possible for Communist books to take a place on foreign bookshelves. Moscow's Lenin Library, for example, announced that it had exchanged books with over one thousand foreign libraries and institutions of learning, in fifty-five countries.

Bloc representatives have been extremely active in their attempts to enlarge the existing exchange arrangements for scientific works, thus both supplementing the information and research of

Communist scientists and technicians and providing a persuasive demonstration of the new "openness" and interest in other cultures.

The USSR, in particular, also supported an extensive book presentation program in 1956. Hundreds of volumes were given to various selected libraries as well as to Communist front groups abroad. Frequently, visitors to Communist Bloc countries received as gifts collections of books which thus found their way into the Free World.

Among notable Soviet gifts were thirteen crates of books presented to the Athens Library by the Lenin Library in Moscow, a collection of three thousand books presented to Helsinki University by the Soviet Union, two hundred volumes of Russian literature presented by the USSR to the Central Library in Mariehamn in the Aland Islands, and sixty thousand volumes given to the Academy of Arts and Sciences in Zagreb, Yugoslavia.

Communist China donated thirty rare Chinese volumes to the Royal Danish Library in Copenhagen. The Peking Library presented the Syrian National Library, the Library of the Arab Academy in Damascus, and the State University Library in Damascus sets of Chinese art books together with selected works of Mao Tse-tung. The Egyptian National Library and al-Azhar University in Cairo were other recipients of shipments including almost four thousand volumes.

Communist book exhibits and book fairs organized in non-Communist countries were highly successful in 1956 in bringing Communist books to the attention of the foreign reading public. Exhibitions were held in Paris, London, Leipzig, Copenhagen, Frankfort, Stockholm, Ghent, Mexico City, Tripoli, and Djakarta.

Communist Orbit presses, of course, were not the only source of printed material. Local Communist Party and front printing presses produced books, as well as other propaganda material. According to information available for 1956, close to 100 million copies of about 9,000 Soviet titles were produced outside the USSR; and although statistics are not available, a considerable part of Communist China's foreign book publishing also is done beyond the Chinese mainland.

Dissemination of Communist books abroad is further aided by various forms of subsidy. The cost of advertising campaigns, which small local outlets could not bear alone, was often financed by Communist sources. Subsidies in some cases permitted Communist publishers to sell books abroad at one-third of their estimated actual cost. Finally, Communist financing supplements the income of many bookstores owned or run by various Communist and front groups.

Communist diplomatic representatives also play an important role in the book dissemination effort, and many of the missions are equipped with reading rooms and libraries. Local friendship societies and front groups frequently sponsor libraries, and where no Communist diplomatic mission exists, or where the Party is illegal, such societies or groups may provide the chief reliance for assuring availability of Communist books.

MAGAZINES AND PERIODICALS

Although books may be regarded as having a more lasting value, magazines and periodicals, appearing regularly, have the value of fresh impact with each issue, and are more readily attuned to contemporary events. A magazine subscription, too, provides an opportunity for repeated, multiple exposure to the Communist message.

Communist Bloc magazines and periodicals aimed primarily at foreign audiences are on the whole well prepared and carefully tailored for a variety of specific targets. Perhaps most outstanding among Soviet, Satellite, and Chinese periodicals during 1956 were the increasing number of prestige pictorial publications which, usually appearing monthly, used text, illustrations, and typographical art in a combination designed to advertise the issuing countries' high living standards and cultural advancement. Sold by various outlets throughout non-Communist countries, they are normally priced considerably below production costs. The magazines in this class generally appear in various languages without changes in text or illustration. These publications are not all intended to reach world-wide targets; they appear only in those languages where the largest audience can be reached. Nevertheless, in 1956, as a result of, and in line with, expanding East-West cultural-exchange programs, the number of languages in which the prestige magazines appear registered an over-all increase. Among typical Soviet, Communist Chinese, and Satellite "prestige" publications circulating in 1956 were [those given in Table 32].

In addition to multi-lingual prestige magazines and periodicals, the Communist Bloc also disseminates publications which appeal to particular classes of readers or to specialists. To cite a few examples: the Soviet Union publishes an *International Affairs* monthly in English and Russian; a more "newsy" approach to international topics is contained in the Moscow-printed *New Times*, which appears weekly in Russian, Spanish, English, French, German, Polish, Czech, Rumanian, Hungarian, and Swedish. *Soviet Literature*, another monthly from the USSR, is published in German, English, French, Polish, and Spanish. A special effort to appeal to the interests of women marks the Soviet-edited *Soviet Woman*, a monthly circulating in Russian, German, Chinese, English, French, Spanish, and Polish.

Moscow News, a semi-weekly in English and French, was an important addition to the Soviet export press. Although published by VOKS, it is a general-interest paper which has already gained circulation in many parts of the Middle and Far East.

TABLE 32

Some Typical "Prestige" Publications Issued by Communist
Bloc Countries, 1956

TITLE		LANGUAGE VERSIONS
Soviet Union Monthly	USSR	In Russian, English, Chinese, French, German, Spanish, Japanese, Hindu, Urdu, Arabic, and Serbo-Croatian (the last four added in 1956).
China Pictorial Monthly	Communist China	In Chinese, Mongolian, Tibetan Uighur, Korean, English, French, Japanese, Indonesian, Spanish, Vietnamese, and German (the last two added in 1956).
Poland Monthly	Poland	In Polish, English, French, German, Russian, and Spanish.
German Democratic Republic in Construction	E. Germany	In German, Russian, Chinese, Polish, Czechoslovakian. (English version discontinued, Chinese added in 1956.)
Bulgaria 8 issues a year	Bulgaria	In Russian, English, French, German, Spanish, and Chinese (the last added in 1956.)

On the strictly "cultural" side—and closely related to the work of the various "friendship" organizations abroad—is the monthly VOKS *Bulletin*,[5] published by the All-Union Society for Cultural Relations Abroad. It is printed in English, French, Spanish, and a number of other Free World languages. . . .

. . . Communist-controlled news agencies have often employed bargaining tactics to get their material in newspapers which do not propagate the Party line. They offer to buy advertisements from these papers in return for publication of items favorable to the Communist cause. Frequently, they pay for advertisements, although the item or goods promoted have no ready market in a given area. Communist news sources may threaten to cancel their advertising as long as a newspaper insists on running articles unfavorable to Communist-supported causes.

Other economic incentives are sometimes offered to editors of foreign publications in order to get them to accept Communist-manufactured news and stories. They consist in some cases of "loans" extended to editors who follow the Party line—these "loans" to be paid on a regular monthly basis so long as no anti-Communist items appear in the organ edited by the recipient of the bribe. In other instances, when Communists were aware that certain editors had substantial business interests in Communist-controlled areas they offered them preferential treatment in the form of customs exemptions and sales privileges. In return, the Communists expected those editors to remove from the pages of their publications any item inimical to local and world-wide Communist policy.

Among other economic "incentives" provided by Communist countries intent on securing certain propaganda privileges in return for aid rendered were the supply of newsprint, either gratis or for a small fee, to areas and press organs where the paper scarcity was being felt. In 1956, for instance, Thailand reportedly received newsprint from Communist China; and Czechoslovakia allegedly supplied a Mexican publishing house with forty rolls of newsprint.

In order to receive wide dissemination for their product, TASS and NCNA* frequently make their services available without fee,

[5] VOKS *Bulletin* announced in its October 1956 edition that it would cease publication and be succeeded by a new monthly periodical, *Culture and Life*. The first issue of *Culture and Life* came off the presses in February 1957.

* NOTE: NCNA is the New China News Agency (Hsinhua) of the Chinese Communists.

particularly in areas where Free World agency prices cannot be paid by many newspapers. Communist news organs also install wire services in strategic areas and then offer free services to local non-Communist publications. They also distribute complimentary copies of news releases to newspapers and selected editors, or permit them to use their facilities.

TRAVEL AND EXCHANGE OF DELEGATIONS

During 1956 the Communist Bloc continued to make increasing use of exchange of delegations and other official and semi-official travelers for the purpose of promoting its propaganda aims. Delegation exchanges, begun on a small scale in 1950, expanded during the past year into a broad flow of world-wide contacts in the sciences and the arts. The Moscow-Peking Axis was apparently determined to drive home its contention that the Communist Iron Curtain was a fiction created by the Western world. In the words of Mme. Kislova, one of the leaders of USSR Society for Cultural Relations With Foreign Countries (VOKS): "Every honest and unbiased person will agree . . . that the Soviet Union has always stood for the widest expansion of cultural relations and contacts with foreign countries."

A number of important propaganda considerations made this emphasis on freedom of movement, on Communism's new "openness," appear desirable. For instance, the frontier Curtain was a grim monument and an embarrassing reminder of all that Moscow and Peking now claimed was part of the Stalin era. It drew uncomfortably heavy fire and too much attention from the Free World. The Bloc wanted to prove, and Free World peoples wanted to see, the changes so highly publicized by Moscow and Peking. Communist leaders believed they had a new opportunity to cater to uncommitted leaders by means of a red-carpet tour of carefully selected sites within the Bloc. The Communists believed, and with good reason, that they could use such visits as levers for obtaining counter-invitations and therefore access to Free World countries, especially those in Asia and Africa hitherto inaccessible to them.

Khrushchev, in his speech to the Twentieth Party Congress, cited one of the most important reasons for encouraging two-way contact: "We must study the capitalist economy attentively . . . study the best that the capitalist countries' science and technology have to offer . . . [and] exploit everything in foreign experience that is of use."

Thus, the curtain was parted at select points to allow seemingly unchecked admittance to and ostensibly free movement within the Bloc. Even the barbed wire along the Austro-Hungarian border was, for a time, removed. The results were impressive.

Travel to and from the Bloc during 1956 was 44 per cent higher than in 1955. Communist Bloc delegations increased in number by 69 per cent, while the number of Free World delegations increased by 28 per cent. There were 4,555 delegations and groups traveling between the Bloc and Free World in 1956 as against 3,104 during the previous year.

INTERNATIONAL TRADE FAIRS

Communist participation in trade fairs is not primarily a matter of business or trade. Far more important are the political or cultural purposes typified in the following:

To foster the idea that free intercourse between countries is hampered only by Western restrictions;

To create the illusion that the Bloc is a rich market for foreign products, especially raw materials;

To convince developing countries that the Bloc is a rich source of equipment and advisers;

To give select urban groups in other countries a chance to come into direct contact with the products of "advanced" socialist culture, including its consumer goods;

To spread abroad visual evidence of the long, profound heritage of the Bloc countries, noting their strength, degree of "civilization," sense of scientific adventure, and desire for links with other countries and peoples.

In pursuit of these purposes the Communist countries in 1956 sponsored official exhibitions at 93 international fairs. This was an increase of 25 over 1955 and of 47 over 1954. These exhibitions in 1956 cost the Communist Bloc approximately $50 million as compared with $38 million in 1955 and only $10 million in 1954.

Although the magnitude of this increase is inspired in part by the Sino-Soviet desire to keep one jump ahead of the United States in trade fair competition, nevertheless, a careful study of Communist statements or literature concerning trade fairs suggests that they fit into two long-term facets of Communist strategy.

The first is to build up to the breaking point pressures among friends, allies, and trading partners of the United States for realignment of trade and cultural relations away from the United States to the Soviet Bloc. In the words of the acting mayor of Leipzig, speaking at the opening of the Leipzig Fair in February 1956:

> Interference with, and hampering of, international economic relations is still being caused by the United States embargo on East-West trade. The embargo policy serves only the intentions of the aggressive imperialist circles who are not interested in world peace, and is contrary to a policy of peaceful coexistence. It is therefore no coincidence that on the question of an embargo policy, diverging opinions appear in the United States on the one hand, and Great Britain and France on the other.

The second Communist hope is to create conditions within the "new" or backward countries for ultimate transformation to a Marxist-type society. The initial stages in this process may be seen in a Soviet description of the capital of Afghanistan, contained in an article of October 25, 1956, in *New Times* concerning the Kabul exhibition:

> The exhibition showed us once again that in the Soviet Union the Afghans see a friend who is always ready to share his knowledge and experience. The buses in the capital are Soviet-made; Soviet technicians directed the paving of the main streets in Kabul; and Soviet experts are helping build a grain elevator and mechanized bakery to improve its bread supply. Relations between our two countries are developing favorably, especially after last year's visit of N. A. Bulganin and N. S. Khrushchev. Further evidence of growing Soviet-Afghan friendship is the current visit to the Soviet Union of Prime Minister Mohammed Daud. There need be no doubt that these friendly relations will continue to develop for the good of our two peoples.

Here Soviet products and technicians may be seen not only as infiltrative agencies but more importantly as instrumentalities which can help reshape Afghan political and economic development along Soviet lines.

Cultural and sports activities in connection with trade fairs play a role in both facets of the strategy by making the Sino-Soviet institutional pattern appear to offer further palatable and even desirable social benefits. At the Kabul Fair in August a troupe of sixty Chinese dancers performed. A Soviet football team from Tashkent was also present and displayed a high skill by defeating all its opponents. At the Pakistan Industrial Fair at Lahore in March through May 3, the USSR organized a distribution center of its books and publications. The Muslim culture of Red China and reproductions of Sung dynasty paintings adorned the Communist Chinese exhibit at Djakarta Fair in September.

The Communists have been exerting every effort to improve their techniques of exhibition. In 1955 the United States staged a closed circuit television demonstration at the Djakarta International Fair. In 1956 the Soviets had closed circuit television demonstrations at fairs in Djakarta, Damascus, Kabul, and Milan. The Soviets also openly imitated United States "Atoms for Peace" exhibits with their version, "Atomic Energy for Peace."

The Communists, however, often seem to be unwilling to compete on an equal basis. At the Kabul Fair, for example, the Russians and Communist Chinese expanded their pavilions after examining the completed United States stand. Their final pavilions averaged four times the size of that of the United States. At the Paris Trade Fair the USSR canceled its plans to participate after it was announced that the United States planned to exhibit, in spite of the fact that both powers were allocated equal areas.

Trade fairs, like delegation exchanges, frequently provided occasion for a two-way exchange of information. At the International Foundry Trade Fair in Düsseldorf last September, the Russians took pictures of American machinery and offered cash payments for immediate purchase of some of the equipment. At a New York television show a Soviet delegation went on record as being willing to purchase "one of everything" displayed.

The Chinese Communists had the most lavish display at the Paris International Fair, which was held in May, but none of the exhibited commodities were offered for sale and no orders were taken. Neither Moscow nor Peking evidenced any interest in selling its products at the Damascus Fair.

In sum, international fairs and exhibitions offered a way to present in concrete terms an image of Communist society which particularly suited current propaganda designs: the image of a producing society, interested in the expansion of peaceful trade regardless of differing economic systems, and amply able—especially to the eyes of underdeveloped areas—to supply consumers' needs and to develop industrial resources. This society, moreover, it was implied, was both interested in raising its standard of living and capable of creating an exportable surplus. That image frequently was well received. A West German newspaper reported on the Kabul Fair: "The Soviet Bloc countries produced a convincing impression . . . of their peaceful efforts." An official of an Asian government commenting on the same fair reportedly said, "Our great American ally has been beaten hollow by the Soviets and Chinese." And the Milan Fair's Communist exhibits caused a Swiss correspondent of *Tribune de Genève* to expatiate on the "peaceful intentions" of the Soviet Bloc participants.

III

Propaganda Activities of the Superpowers

As we have discussed the information and propaganda agencies in each of the major cold war countries we have also studied their activities. Both Daugherty and Kirkpatrick have reported extensively on the work of the various agencies about which they have written. We have not, however, studied actual samples of either American information or Communist propaganda. They are easily available and they cover numerous subjects. It is not possible within the brief scope of this book to present more than a few examples of even the major types of propaganda. A visit, phone call or a letter to the consulate, embassy, or information office of almost any government with which the United States has diplomatic relations is sufficient to provide further material for study in this field.

Publications

By mutual agreement the United States and the Soviet Union allow each other to market information magazines in their respective countries. The United States publishes a Russian language illustrated magazine entitled Amerika which is circulated in the So-

viet Union. The Russians publish an English language monthly entitled USSR *which is sold in the United States. Occasionally these publications have become temporary victims of the cold war and their circulation has been restricted as retaliation for some unfriendly action on another front. They are, however, generally available.*

In addition, several Chinese Communist publications in English are allowed to circulate in the United States. These include China Pictorial *(described below), the weekly newsmagazine* Peking Review *and the monthly journal* China Reconstructs.

The following article from the New York Times *describes the American publication which is sent to the Soviet Union. It is followed by an excerpt from* USSR *in which the Russians describe their newspapers to American readers.* USSR's *format is similar to that of* Life *and* Look. *The same issue which carried the article on Soviet newspapers also included: a feature on the Soviet chess champion; biographical sketches and pictures of selected scientists from various parts of the USSR; an American-style "day with an average citizen" picture story; a serious article about the war against the Nazis; a discussion of Soviet school law; and a description of Soviet films available for international exchange.*

The concluding selections in this section are taken from China Pictorial. *This Communist version of the* Life- *or* Look-*type magazine is published fortnightly in Chinese, Mongolian, Tibetan, Uigur, Korean, Chuang, English, Russian, German, French, Japanese, Vietnamese, Indonesian, Hindi, Spanish, Arabic and monthly in Swedish. It carries beautiful photographs in black and white and in color, and brief articles on the arts, travel, education, agricultural and industrial developments and the like. The readings reprinted below have been selected to illustrate the propaganda impact of this publication in four vital areas of information: (1) Chinese internal developments—particularly the success of the commune system; (2) China's association with overseas Chinese; (3) China's relations with other developing states; and (4) the world image of the United States.*

AMERIKA ILLUSTRATED*

First copies of *Amerika Illustrated,* the new U.S. propaganda magazine for distribution in the Soviet Union became available yesterday.

Comparison of *Amerika Illustrated* and *USSR* shows many similarities but several sharp differences. Both magazines rely heavily on attractive pictures.

But where *USSR* emphasizes the "official" approach, featuring a message by Premier Nikolai A. Bulganin to the American people and a picture of Premier Bulganin and President Eisenhower, *Amerika* stresses the low costs and practical benefits of the American way of life.

"Changes in the U.S. economy in the past 20 years," *Amerika* tells its Russian readers, "have been nothing short of revolutionary, resulting in what amounts to a new kind of economy, a new pattern of efficient production and the equitable distribution of goods."

Implicit in *Amerika's* presentation is the startling contrast between the bountiful production of U.S. consumer goods, their variety and low prices and the comparative paucity of such products in the Soviet Union.

Explaining the basis of present day America to the Soviet public, *Amerika* declares:

"Higher wages have improved the standard of living for the lower income group. For both the rich and the poor the inexorable pressure is toward the middle class which now includes well over half the population."

Amerika documents this thesis with such features as a 5 page spread of colored silhouettes of automobile models from the 1956 production lines. The pictures and descriptions are accompanied by a price chart giving the prices of the 48 illustrated types of cars. The prices range from $1642 for a Rambler to $9507 for a Lincoln Continental.

Appended is a convenient conversion table based on the official exchange rate of four rubles to a dollar. Use of the table enables a Russian reader to discover that he could buy a Rambler for 6568 rubles, somewhat less than half the price of the POBEDA, a comparable Soviet machine.

* Reprinted from the *New York Times* (July 24, 1956), pp. 12-13.

There are articles about culture and science (Eugene Ormandy and the Philadelphia Symphony, the Palomar telescope, architecture in San Francisco) and homelife.

There is even home medical advice for Russian readers—an admonition to try cold water for burns, descriptions of a new kind of hearing aid so small that it is connected to the rim of eyeglasses.

General reaction to the magazine was favorable. The automobiles apparently made the greatest impression.

SOVIET NEWSPAPERS*

MARK ARKADYEV

MARK ARKADYEV *is a writer in the Soviet Union.*

More than 62 million copies of newspapers come rolling off the presses in the Soviet Union. They are read by a great many more people than that, however, for besides newsstand and subscription sales, copies are posted on bulletin boards in towns and villages and are freely available at clubs, libraries, theaters, railway stations and other places where people gather.

The biggest of the Soviet dailies is *Pravda (Truth)*, the official organ of the Central Committee of the Communist Party, with a circulation of 5,650,000.

At the end of the last century, when a Marxist workers' party was just beginning to emerge in Russia, Lenin proposed that a national political newspaper be founded. It was to replace the local leaflets which had been used to spread word of the party's program. The paper founded then was *Iskra (The Spark)*. It was superseded in 1912 by *Pravda*.

From its very first issue *Pravda* has spoken for Russia's working millions. In czarist days it was printed by hand in a changing succession of cellars and hiding places, in ever-present danger of suppression. Traced by the police to one spot, its type confiscated and staff imprisoned, the paper popped up in another, sometimes under

* Reprinted from *USSR*, No. 5 (June 1959), pp. 24-25.

a changed masthead but always unalterably dedicated to the struggle for a better way of life.

Although the *Pravda* of those days before the Revolution left much to be desired for quality of paper and ease of reading—it was supported entirely out of the hard-earned pennies contributed by factory workers and poor peasants—and although its circulation was small, it spoke with an infinitely more powerful voice than the heavily financed press of the czar. To be caught reading an illegal paper meant a prison term, but every copy passed through hundreds of eager hands until the paper was so worn through that the type was no longer legible.

A reflection of *Pravda's* prestige is the fact that May 5, the date of the appearance of its first issue, is commemorated throughout the country as Soviet Press Day.

Almost 10,000 Newspapers Published: Today *Pravda* is one of the world's biggest newspapers. Its editorial offices are in Moscow but it is printed simultaneously in many cities from matrices flown in from the capital. *Pravda* newsmen cover every part of the Soviet Union and are stationed in many foreign countries.

Izvestia (News), the official government organ, is another of the big dailies with a large national circulation. So is *Trud (Labor)*, published by the USSR Central Council of Trade Unions. *Komsomolskaya Pravda*, published by the Central Committee of the Young Communist League, has a circulation of 2,500,000 which sells out as soon as it hits the stands.

These and many others of the nationally-circulated papers are published in Moscow. Each republic and every town of any size has its own newspapers in addition. Besides those published in the Russian language, there are 2,500 papers printed in sixty of the languages spoken in the country. All told, the Soviet Union has 9,936 newspapers. In addition, there are 858 magazines published with a total circulation of 26 million copies.

Papers for Special Audiences: Aside from those which appeal to the general reader, there are numerous papers oriented to a particular audience. *Literaturnaya Gazeta (Literary Gazette)*, published by the Union of Soviet Writers, has many hundreds of thousands of readers. As the name indicates, it is primarily concerned with problems of literature, but it devotes considerable space to a much wider range of topics and takes vigorous positions on all of them. It covers the more important domestic and international affairs from the viewpoint of the Soviet writer.

There are 16 newspapers devoted to economics, industrial construction and related fields. These have a reading public much larger than their special character would seem to indicate. A paper such as *Promyshlenno-Ekonomicheskaya Gazeta (Industrial and Economic Gazette)* is required reading for plant directors, engineers and other people at the managerial levels, but it is not at all uncommon to find the paper in the home of a worker in one of the skilled trades.

Soviet railroad men, with the professional loyalty that workers in that field seem to have the world over, will go through their railroad paper first thing at the breakfast table. There are nearly 90 railroad newspapers, from *Gudok (The Whistle)*, the big nationally-circulated daily, to those put out by local lines.

Selskoye Khozyaistvo (Agriculture) is the farmer's paper, but it has many readers in the towns. So does the teachers' gazette, *Uchitelskaya Gazeta*, among parents and *Meditsinsky Rabotnik (Medical Worker)*, among nonmedical people.

There are papers published for army readers, for university students and for many other groups with common interests. Many of the local papers for young people are patterned on the bright, topical *Komsomolskaya Pravda*. Sports newspapers like *Sovietsky Sport* are immensely popular with old and young readers.

Both the nationally-circulated dailies like *Pravda, Izvestia* and *Trud* and those published regionally by local governmental divisions or public organizations give major space to national and international affairs. The problems they deal with are likely in many cases to be the same but the slant will be quite different, depending upon the special interests of the locality as reflected in the letters sent in by readers and the individual emphasis of the editors and staff writers.

Newspapers are on the stands early, five or six in the morning. The evening papers, mostly regional, carry more local news, less of the very thorough-going analyses than the morning papers and more lighter material generally—stories, poems, humor, cartoons and feature articles.

The bigger papers have their own publishing setups. The smaller ones have joint facilities for editing, printing and distribution.

Forums for Public Opinion: Newspapers are not commercial enterprises in the Soviet Union. It is not their function to publicize the point of view of the individual publisher or to serve as a medium for profitable advertising. Nor is their primary obligation to entertain. The job of the newspaper is purely and simply to inform and educate and to serve as forum for the freest expression of public opinion.

Just as there are no privately-owned industrial plants in the Soviet Union, there are no individually-owned publishing houses, whether for newspapers, magazines or books. A Soviet newspaper, regardless of its size, does not reflect the viewpoint of any single person. It is the community viewpoint and the community interest which is always represented. Its publisher will be one of several public organizations—a republic's or a city's Soviet, a local division of the Communist Party, a trade union, a particular factory, a student organization, or an administrative body.

This is in keeping with the socialist concept of public ownership and cooperative living. The constitutional guarantee of freedom of the press is not merely a paper proviso, but one which provides the people of the socialist society with the printing presses, the stocks of paper and the distribution facilities through which this freedom may be exercised.

The publishing house does the purely technical work of getting the paper out. All editorial work is in the hands of the editorial board headed by the editor-in-chief. The board is made up of writers, specialists in various fields and esteemed community people.

The editorial board is chosen by and is responsible to the organization that publishes the paper, but the final authority is always the reader. Editorial boards are very sensitive to public sentiment and Soviet newspaper readers are great letter-writers. Readers' conferences are held frequently and are by no means cut-and-dried affairs. Comment at these conferences is inclined to be very direct and, on occasions, vitriolic.

The editorial board plans the paper collectively. The latitude on controversial questions is unlimited in the planning and discussion stage but the article when it appears will most usually represent the composite judgment of the board as a whole.

Guardians of the Public Welfare: The popular soil which

nourishes the Soviet press makes for journalism which is forward-looking and creative. It mirrors the optimism of a country which has continued growing in these past four decades and a people certain of its direction of movement.

The Soviet press reports the news, it does not have to sell it. It does not go in for sensationalism to attract readers. Nor does it give space to gossip, scandal or the more intimate details of people's lives. The personal lives of Soviet citizens are private, except as they affect the public welfare.

A Soviet newspaper is for serious informative reading—the important national and international news of the day; current developments in industry, farming, science and the arts; contributions made by individuals in one or another field of endeavor.

In addition to current news, the paper will carry articles on aspects of economics, art, politics, science and education that are of more than immediate interest. Some of these, written by eminent scholars in the field, are of long-lasting significance and are clipped by many readers for future reference.

The Soviet daily is not a bulky newspaper. It averages four closely-printed pages and carries little or no advertising.

Criticism is a very basic function of the Soviet press, as it is of such other guardians of socialist standards and ethics as the party, the unions and all other public organizations. No one is exempt from objective criticism in the Soviet Union, whether in high position or low, whether a government minister, high party official, a novelist or a plain ordinary worker.

The press has the very responsible duty not only of informing and molding opinion but of promoting further progress of Soviet society. Its first and abiding criterion is the social welfare and it spares no effort in bringing to light unserviceable practices and in pushing for correction of errors that impede progress. Its tone is often sharp, its criticism does not mince words. If changes are necessary, it pounds away until they are made.

Letters to the Editor: At least half of the items that are printed in Soviet newspapers each day are written not by professional newspapermen but by contributing readers of all trades and callings—industrial and farm workers, specialists in a variety of fields, artists, educators and so on. This is traditional in Soviet journalism and has a history which stems back to the earliest days of the illegal

Pravda. The editorial backbone of any Soviet paper has been material from worker-correspondents.

Every morning mail bags crammed full with letters from readers are delivered to the editorial offices of the larger newspapers. This is the basic material out of which subsequent issues are worked.

It is from these readers' letters—the concentrated thoughts, feelings, critical remarks and suggestions of the community—that the paper makes up a considerable part of its issue. They supply the subjects for many articles, editorials and, of course, for the ever-present "Letters to the Editor" column.

These letters from readers are not literary masterpieces, but that is a minor consideration. By virtue of their individual slant, their spontaneity and their fresh outlook on a problem, they very often strike a note that elicits a public reaction very much wider than the better phrased staff-written articles.

The letters are most diverse. Some will merely comment favorably or unfavorably on some current matter, whether local or national. Others will be vociferous complaints about errors or negligence on the part of a plant management or administrative agency. Many will suggest improvements.

Those that have more than purely individual importance will be printed in the paper's column, allowing for space limitations. But all letters that cite abuses, that make reasonable complaints and that offer sensible suggestions result immediately in proper investigation and swift action. This is standard procedure, very conscientiously adhered to. It becomes the responsibility of the newspaper to follow up and see that the appropriate agency moves on the matter with energy and dispatch.

These letters to editors have more than once initiated national movements of large scope. A comment by Yevgenia Andreyeva, chairman of a collective farm in Tambov Region, that appeared in *Selskoye Khozyaistvo* was instrumental in sparking off the campaign by Soviet farmers to overtake the United States in per capita production of milk, butter and meat within the next few years.

To show the mass of these press contributions by readers: During the nationwide discussion of the seven-year plan which went on for some months before the Twenty-First Party Congress met in January, newspapers, magazines, radio and TV received over 650,000 communications from readers, listeners and viewers. About 300,000 of the letters and comments with the suggestions and amendments they offered were published by the press.

Professional Standards: Standards of Soviet journalism are high and the ethics of the profession demanding. Soviet newspapermen are respected by the public, and the profession is well represented among the deputies elected to city, republic and national legislatures.

Most Soviet newsmen are graduates of schools of journalism. There are many, however, who turned to newspaper work from other trades and professions.

The Union of Journalists is the professional organization. There are, besides, press clubs in many cities where newspaper people meet to relax and to talk over professional matters. These press clubs often play host to outstanding Soviet personalities and to visitors from abroad.

More Papers Each Year: In the past few years there has been a large increase in the number of factory, student and farm papers published. The local farm papers are a relatively recent development. There are about 200 of them now being published by the bigger collective farms.

More regional newspapers are constantly being published. Sverdlovsk, Novosibirsk, Gorky, Riga and other cities are now issuing evening papers besides morning dailies.

Some picture of the growth of newspaper publishing in the Soviet Union may be gathered from this fact: While before the 1917 Revolution only one newspaper was published in what is now Chelyabinsk Region in the Urals, today there are about 100.

With its millions of contributing writers, both professional and lay, the Soviet press plays an important part in the country's life, serving as an effective tribune of public opinion.

PEOPLE'S COMMUNES TAME
THE WATER DRAGONS*

CHU CHI-MIN

CHU CHI-MIN *is first secretary of the Linyi Regional Party Committee.*

The people of Linyi Special Administrative Region, Shantung Province, started to build six big reservoirs in the autumn of 1958. By raising high the red banner of the Party's general line for building socialism and relying on the mighty force of the people's communes, they finished the job in 1959. The dams of these reservoirs have a total length of 7.5 kilometres and block the torrential flow of six big rivers. With the completion of the reservoirs, 34,000 hectares of arid soil was changed into good arable land and a population of 900,000 was freed from the threat of floods. The aggregate storage capacity of the six reservoirs is close on 1,400 million cubic metres, providing a source of hydro-electric power with an annual generating capacity of 22 million KWH. Eventually, 140,000 hectares of land will be brought under irrigation and the reservoirs themselves will be used for raising fish and ducks and growing water-chestnuts and lotuses.

During the past years the local people have done a lot in the way of harnessing rivers and reclaiming barren mountains for cultivation under the leadership of the Party. At first they built small reservoirs with a capacity of under 1,000 cubic metres. After the coming of the agricultural producers' co-ops, they built bigger ones of several hundred thousand cubic metres. From 1954 up till the emergence of the people's communes in 1958, they built 4,317 reservoirs with an average capacity of 67,000 metres.

The forming of the people's communes gave them the chance of organizing their manpower and material resources in a·more rational way. In building the six big reservoirs, a 150,000-strong construction corps was formed by 110 people's communes of the

* Reprinted from *China Pictorial*, No. 1 (January 5, 1960).

administrative region. This still left enough people to bring in the magnificent harvest of 1959.

The people's communes pooled 81.5 per cent of the total investment in building the reservoirs. They provided 70 per cent of the materials. The rest came from the government. The people's communes set up repair shops on the construction sites which did a grand job in keeping the implements in good repair and so raising the working efficiency. During the course of construction, the people's communes and even counties co-operated with one another in a fraternal way. In striving to complete the Hsuchiayai Reservoir in Feihsien County before the National Day of 1959, for instance, the people's communes of six other counties sent over everyone they could spare as well as a number of tractors. This unselfish co-operation speeded up the job and enabled this reservoir—the biggest of the six—to be finished within a year. Furthermore, it fostered a communist spirit among the commune members, as was vividly shown by the way people moved out of the villages which would come within the future reservoirs. The secretaries of the county and commune Party committees gave a direct lead to the workers on the construction sites in going all out to vie with each other.

At present, the construction of four key water conservancy projects is under way. Within a short period these projects will be completed together with 16 medium-sized reservoirs and close on 1,000 small ones. In all, they will hold 2,300 million cubic metres of water.

Alongside the water conservancy, the commune members are planting trees and terracing the barren mountains. Before long, they will have completely changed the local natural environment.

OVERSEAS CHINESE*

China, the mighty socialist country, has always been deeply concerned about her sons and daughters living abroad. All overseas Chinese returning to China of their own free will are

* Reprinted from *China Pictorial*, No. 2 (January 20, 1960).

warmly received and proper arrangements are made for them. In recent years, no small number of Chinese nationals in Indonesia have come back to China of their own accord. They have been given proper jobs and taken good care of.

The moment they set foot on the soil of their motherland, overseas Chinese receive a warm welcome from the Returned Overseas Chinese Service Centre, the Overseas Chinese Hostel and other organizations. Those who want to go back to their native villages can do so to take part in agricultural production. Those who know one kind of technique or another and want to work in an industrial department are given suitable work. Those who are homeless and know nothing of technique are provided with every opportunity to learn it by the government. Students can either go into schools, colleges and universities through the normal entrance examinations, or first enter schools and institutes exclusively for the returned overseas Chinese. The government set up in Taishan, Kwangtung Province, a relief centre for the aged, weak, maimed and sick. It pays particular care to the livelihood of those in need and grants them relief.

Over 50 of the overseas Chinese who recently returned from Indonesia are now working in the Canton Heavy Machinery Works, some as lathe turners and fitters, and some as apprentices. Those having difficulty in supporting a large family are given special subsidies for food and clothing by the works. Cheng Hsiang had been wandering about Indonesia for scores of years. He returned to China with his 11 sons and daughters last April. In no time the whole family were taken care of; his five elder children are working and the younger ones are at school. They are getting along pretty well.

Many of the overseas Chinese experienced various difficulties abroad—unemployment, being unable to go to school and, sometimes, serious discrimination. Now back once again in their prosperous motherland and working for the rapidly-developing socialist construction, they cannot but feel the warmth of their homeland.

Certain reactionary forces in Indonesia have recently whipped up a campaign of discrimination against the Chinese nationals. The Chinese people are deeply concerned about this. They fully support Foreign Minister Chen Yi's proposals to the Indonesian Foreign Minister and warmly welcome overseas Chinese in Indonesia to return to China to take part in construction. Preparations are well under way in Kwangtung Province to receive large numbers of returned overseas Chinese. New reception hostels are being built and several farms are being set up or expanded. We are ardently looking forward to the return of our dear ones to our motherland.

FOREIGN GUESTS*

On October 3, Premier Chou En-lai attended and spoke at the grand reception given in honour of visiting youth and student delegates from 24 Asian, African and Latin American countries by the Central Committee of the Chinese Communist Youth League, the All-China Youth Federation and the All-China Students' Federation. He said that the peoples of the Asian, African and Latin American countries are awakening with each passing day and standing up heroically. This is a world event of great significance and is worthy of our warm celebration.

Premier Chou said that since the Second World War, and especially since the Bandung Conference, more and more countries in Asia, Africa and Latin America have rid themselves of colonial rule and won independence. We believe that many more countries in these regions will achieve their independence. He pointed out that it will still take a certain period of struggle before the various countries of Asia, Africa and Latin America are able to secure complete independence. Therefore, we must be closely united and carry on a common struggle.

Premier Chou said that now more and more people in the world are talking about the national independence movement and the struggles of the peoples in the colonies. Even the United Nations is discussing these questions. But what we demand is the genuine recognition of the national independence of the various countries, genuine non-interference in their internal affairs, and genuine recognition of a position of equality for the various Asian, African and Latin American countries, no toleration of either na-

* Reprinted from *China Pictorial*, No. 21, 1960.

tional oppression or discrimination because of colour. We believe that only a handful of persons are practising national oppression and colour discrimination. The great majority of the people, however, are our friends. We have friends all over the world. More than 90 per cent of the population of the world are or may become friends of the movements against imperialism and colonialism, to safeguard and secure national independence. Colonial rule will certainly be ended and the movement for national independence will certainly be victorious.

Time and again Premier Chou's speech was punctuated by stormy applause from all present. . . .

MARK TWAIN—EXPOSER OF U.S. IMPERIALISM*

LAO SHEH

LAO SHEH is Vice-Chairman of the Union of Chinese Writers.

Mark Twain, outstanding American writer and exposer of imperialist aggression and U.S. capitalism's sham civilization, died fifty years ago. But his criticism of U.S. imperialism, after the lapse of half a century, is still strongly true to life.

The time in which Mark Twain lived and wrote was a time in which the United States passed from free capitalism into imperialism. Seeing with his own eyes the piratical actions of British and U.S. imperialism in invading Asia, Australia, Africa and Latin America, he was highly indignant against their injustice. It was this righteous indignation which lent his outwardly mild and humorous works a sharp, sarcastic sting against the U.S. ruling class.

Today, when the war forces of imperialism are attempting a futile last-ditch struggle and flames of national liberation movement

* Reprinted from *China Pictorial*, No. 19, 1960.

are spreading all over Asia, Africa and Latin America, Mark Twain's castigation of the imperialist aggressive forces of his day and his sympathies with the Asian and African peoples in opposing colonialism are especially significant. These are among the most cherished legacies of Mark Twain's literature that have been handed down to us. Mark Twain never ceased taking the United States to task ever since the 1890s when it grew into an imperialist power. He ridiculed the U.S. careerists who attempted to conquer the whole world; he angrily stripped bare the "civilization" the white aggressors had brought to the colonial countries, and gave many instances to show how they brutally slaughtered the colonial people.

Mark Twain also expressed warm support of the Chinese people's heroic struggle against imperialist aggression. In a letter to a friend written on August 12, 1900, the day before the combined forces of the eight imperialist powers invaded Peking, he said: "My sympathies are with the Chinese. . . . I hope they will drive all foreigners out and keep them out for good." In November of the same year, he openly declared: "I am a Boxer. The Boxer is a patriot . . . and I wish him success." Mark Twain held that the invasion and occupation of the Philippines by the United States had sullied the U.S. national flag which was now properly one "with the stripes painted black and the stars replaced by the skull and cross-bones." He also caricatured the "peace-loving" aggressor as one with "the banner of the Prince of Peace in one hand, and its loot-basket and its butcher-knife in the other." This extremely realistic symbolic portrayal brings to mind Eisenhower's recent trip to Asia.

Mark Twain was the enemy of the entire hypocritical civilization of U.S. capitalism. His view of the American civilization, as he expressed it in a letter, was that it was replete with cruelty, bustle, brazenness, meanness and hypocrisy. He severely denounced the American bourgeoisie for their discrimination against and enslavement of the black race, and angrily called the United States the "United States of lynchdom."

Mark Twain undoubtedly was an outstanding writer, although, owing to the limitations of his world outlook, his protest against the society was only the voice of an individual rebel. In his later years, because he could not see humanity's bright future, he betrayed a feeling of despondency and pessimism. All these could not but influence the profoundness of his thinking as reflected in his works.

Mark Twain is a favourite American writer of the Chinese readers. Nearly all of his major representative works have been translated into Chinese. We hold his literary legacies in high regard because they give a clear reflection of the American people's fine tradition—ardent love of peace and democracy and opposition to imperialist aggressive war and colonialism.

In the half century since Mark Twain's death, U.S. imperialism has become increasingly more decadent and brutal, and has long become the most ferocious enemy of the people of the world. Today, in Japan, the Congo, Cuba, south Korea, Turkey, as well as in many countries of Asia, Africa and Latin America, the people are waging heroic struggles with great militancy against U.S. imperialism, its partners and its lackeys.

Mark Twain was on the side of the American people; he was on the side of the people of the whole world. In commemorating him today, we feel as if he were still standing among us and fighting by our side against U.S.-led imperialism.

Radio Propaganda

Radio broadcasting differs quite markedly from an exchange of printed information. While the printed word from the United States cannot circulate widely in the Soviet Union without official approval (and thus must be positively pro-American rather than negatively anti-Communist) a radio broadcast is harder to control. Each of the two countries receives broadcasts in its own language from the other. Americans with short-wave sets can pick up English-language newscasts from Radio Moscow, and Russians—if they can get a radio set and if it isn't jammed—can hear the Voice of America in Russian.

The following are excerpts from broadcasts of the two stations. The Radio Moscow broadcast is a Russian eyewitness account of the Hungarian revolt in 1956. It is followed by an "objective" account of the same incident published in the American news magazine, The Reporter.

TEXT OF VOICE OF AMERICA
BROADCAST TO THE USSR*

The sound of celebration salvos has died down. The band trumpets blare no longer. The planes have returned to their airfields. The regiments of Red soldiers have marched back to their barracks. The columns of marchers who walked past the tribune with quickened step have broken up and the marchers have hurried to their homes. Red Square is deserted. Night has come down over Moscow.

Then, in the night mist, another parade started, invisible to the human eye. Following the same route, across Red Square, countless columns of ghosts came marching along. Those in the columns had flown, trudged, or crawled from all parts of the boundless land. They marched in serried ranks, turning their faces to the tribune, shaking their fists in the air, and hurling curses at those who were standing there, also invisible to others.

At the head of the procession were the fighters of the civil war who believe in a bright new world, a world of plenty and justice, of equality and free labor, which had been promised them. They were the children of the generation which was captivated by the vision of communism, unable to foresee the flesh and blood this vision took on when it turned into reality.

Marching in the columns were soldiers and sailors whose bodies supplied the bridge over which enemies of the people, hiding behind the red cloak of communism climbed to power. Following them walked countless victims of famine in the Volga region and the Ukraine. Then came columns of peasants who died facing firing squads when they dared to bring up the promise of "Land to the people." There were marching columns of workers turned into state slaves; of idealists thrown into the dungeons of the Secret Police, who lost their lives in inexpert struggle with the careerists surrounding the throne of Stalin; columns of city dwellers whom the Communist local satraps left to the tender mercies of the invading Nazis.

* Reprinted from the statement of Alexander Barmine, *Overseas Information Programs of the United States, Hearings, Before a Subcommittee of the Committee on Foreign Relations, U.S. Senate,* (Washington, D.C.: Government Printing Office, 1953), Part 2, pp. 1458-1459.

Column after column they marched: Hordes of "bezprizorniki," those parentless children whom the Communists tried to reform at the point of the gun; poets and artists who dreamed of finding created freedom under the Communist rule; scientists who believed that the new rulers were bringing them freedom of thought; millions of prisoners from jails and slave labor camps whose bones line the country's roads and canals, gold-mines and lumber camps; the fugitives who even abroad could not escape the vengeful arm of the dictator.

They all marched in silence. But every gust of wind seemed to sound the curses uttered by the millions—the cries about the great lie which was used to dupe them and is being used to dupe mankind. As they turned their wrathful faces to the tribune, they saw the men who stood there a few hours earlier, who stood there arrogantly every May Day and every seventh of November. They saw them there, their executioners. On Lenin's mausoleum they stood, motionless—crushed by the weight of the hatred of generations, pale with fear, under triple guard, reviewing the parade in the night.

REMARKS BROADCAST ON RADIO
MOSCOW, NOVEMBER 10, 1956

E. M. BAZARINA

E. M. BAZARINA *is a Russian news commentator.*

We arrived in Hungary on 19 October with other Soviet tourists. We spent four days touring this beautiful country and were everywhere given a most cordial and hearty welcome. On Tuesday, 23 October, on our way to a theatre we saw crowds of people in the streets of Budapest. They were lined up in ranks and carried placards, many of which bore the inscription "Long Live Hungary!" . . . The students together with members of the intelligentsia and workers were demanding the redress of errors and omissions committed by the Hungarian Government. They were legitimate demands. . . .

On that first evening I saw from the hotel in which we were staying a man with a rifle appear on the deserted street. He took up a position in one of the drives and, taking careful aim, began shooting out the street lamps. The lamps went out one by one and darkness enveloped the street. What prompted the marksman to do this? Just hooliganism? Hardly. I think he was one of the bright sparks of the reactionary underground who wanted to create confusion and chaos in the city. Quite soon afterwards there were flashes of gunfire and sounds of battle and we saw wrecked and burning buildings in the streets of Budapest, overturned tram-cars and other vehicles. Firing would die down and and then flare up again. Hostile elements were aiming at paralysing the city's life but the workers of Budapest were repelling the rebels. Detachments of armed workers tried to restore order in the streets and prevent looting. In many places, including the area around our hotel, workers' patrols were posted. . . .

One member of our hotel staff, a middle-aged man with grey hair, told us: "Our workers cannot have had a hand in this looting and rioting. It is fascism raising its head." And that is what it was. The counter-revolutionary underground was in action in Budapest. Fascist reactionary elements had arrived there from abroad. The hostile venture was gathering momentum and the Hungarian Government asked the USSR Government for aid. In response to this request Soviet military units stationed in Hungary under the Warsaw Treaty entered Budapest to help to restore order. The overwhelming majority of Hungarians welcomed this move in the hope that life in the city would quickly return to normal. I myself saw in one street how the people were welcoming the Soviet tanks.

One Hungarian, a member of the hotel staff, described the following incident to us. Firemen-volunteers, absolutely unarmed, were putting out a fire in one of the public buildings. Suddenly, from a small house opposite, shots were fired by fascist louts who opened fire on the unarmed firemen. Several of them fell. Our tank was stationed in the street. The tankmen immediately aimed their gun at the house where the bandits were entrenched. This was sufficient to make them run into a side street. Several firemen ran up to the tank and shook hands with the tankmen. This episode gives a good testimony of the attitude of the Hungarians towards the Soviet troops. However, reaction did not cease its activities. When we walked along some of the streets we saw that the walls of houses were thickly covered with counter-revolutionary posters. . . .

When Soviet troops began withdrawing from Budapest an unbridled White Terror started in the Hungarian capital. We Soviet tourists recall this time with horror. It is difficult to describe the chaos which reigned in the city where public buildings were destroyed, shops looted, and where crowds of armed bandits, obviously fascists, walked along the streets committing bestial murders in broad daylight. I shall never forget what I saw with my own eyes. I think it was on 30 or 31 October. A man in a sports suit walked along the Lenin Boulevard. He might have been one of those who tried to restore order in the city. Several armed ruffians wearing counter-revolutionary tricolours ran up to him. A horrible inhuman cry was heard. A whole crowd of bandits appeared from somewhere. I was unable to see what they were doing with their victim, but in a few minutes he was hanging on a nearby tree with an eye gouged out and his face slashed with knives.

Some time ago I read how the fascists in Germany burnt progressive literature on bonfires. We saw similar things. . . . A group of some hooligans looted and set fire to the House of Books. Thousands and thousands of books were smouldering in the muddy street. We were there, witnesses of this barbarity. The works of Chekhov, Shakespeare, Tolstoi, Pushkin, and other famous authors were lying in the mud, black smoke rising. We saw an old man who lifted a few books, then carefully wiped the mud with his sleeve, pressed them to his breast and walked slowly away. Many people did the same.

In the Hotel "Peace" the atmosphere in those days was extremely tense. The counter-revolutionaries tore the red star from the front of the hotel and trod it underfoot on the pavement. We were told that the Hotel "Peace" from now on would be called Hotel "Britannia." The person who told us about it looked around and added quietly: "It doesn't matter. It will only be temporary."

More than once we were witnesses of acts which manifested the friendly attitude of the Hungarians towards the Soviet people. This friendly attitude was felt by us Soviet people, when we were leaving Budapest. . . . In small groups of two or three people we made our way along the devastated streets towards the Danube in order to board a Red Cross steamer. We were accompanied by a worker . . .

a young girl. She led us from one cross-road to another, fearlessly seeking the safest way. At the pier we heartily embraced her. She said: "Some one in the West wants us to pull their chestnuts out of the fire. Don't believe them, dear friends. We Hungarians are for socialism, and we are with you." When we were in Czechoslovakia on our way home, we learned that the counter-revolution in Hungary was routed and that life was becoming normal in the country. Now we are at home in Moscow. We shall not forget that Hungarian girl who said that the Hungarians were for socialism and that they were with us.

HUNGARY: THE FIRST SIX DAYS*

LESLIE B. BAIN

LESLIE B. BAIN *was in Budapest during the first six days of the 1956 revolt. He cabled this story to* The Reporter *from Vienna.*

The first people who found themselves in the field against the Communist regime in Hungary were those whom that regime had pampered the most: writers, journalists, engineers, athletes, students, artists, and the like. Nine-tenths of those who started the demonstrations were students whose tuition and living expenses were paid by the government and who had been picked from the families of workers, peasants, and Communist Party officials. Yet they marched into the open to make their demands and then, when these were refused, stayed in the streets to fight. The first blood on the fateful evening of October 23 was shed by men of this kind.

Down with Stalin! After the first demonstration that Tuesday in Parliament Square, half of the two hundred thousand demonstrators went home. The other half broke into several groups and marched through the streets. One of these went to Kossuth Radio House to broadcast its demands. These had been published earlier in leaflets; and while each university group had a slightly different

* Reprinted from *The Reporter,* Vol. 15 (November 1956), pp. 20-21.

set, which varied to include specific grievances at different schools, the main political demands were the same as those that had been drawn up two days earlier during a mass meeting of students at Szeged. They included the extradition and punishment of Matyas Rakosi, the dismissal of Erno Gero, the appointment of Imre Nagy, as Premier, the removal of Soviet shields as Hungary's emblem, and the adjustment of taxes, wages, and working hours.

A deputation of three students followed by thousands more arrived at the radio station, which had been heavily occupied by the AVH, the hated and dreaded security police. The AVH ordered the demonstrators to disband, then brought out tear gas and fire hoses to halt the masses of students pouring in from all sides.

The students attacked with pots and pans and pieces of coal they had picked up at a nearby restaurant. The AVH began firing—first into the air, later into the surging students. Another group of students raced to an arms plant, where more shooting developed. A third group of students went to the Stalin Memorial, and there a detachment of police joined forces with them. Stalin's statue came toppling down before a happy, dancing crowd.

But at the broadcasting station the situation rapidly deteriorated. A Hungarian Army detachment arrived and demanded a cease-fire. The students obeyed but the AVH refused to evacuate the building. When two army officers were shot, the army retaliated instantly, and so began the first pitched battle between the army and the AVH. New army detachments arrived and began distributing weapons to the students. By eleven o'clock, several thousand students had arms, and the first round of the battle was won. The army received orders to withdraw.

During the night more guns were acquired by the students, who had by now developed a taste for fighting. The city police either joined them or gave up their arms willingly. Even so, the students were not much of a fighting force.

Workers, Arise! It was 4 A.M. when the first Soviet tanks and armored cars arrived in the city. Overnight another series of events had occurred. Workers in the suburbs had held meetings and drawn up demands generally in line with those of the students. To these had been added several specific points about factory-management councils and general increases in wages. At dawn the workers began marching into the city. Only about fifteen hundred of them were armed. All the rest had nothing but their bare hands and flags. No one was in command. Whoever spoke the loudest or made the most sense was obeyed. Impromptu committees and delegations formed, but the general impression was of huge convergent masses chanting slogans such as "Down with Gero!" "Punish the murderers!" "We want Nagy!" Later in the morning, another cry was taken up that was heard all through the subsequent days: "Out with the Russkies!"

All through this second day furious battles raged. On one side were seventy Soviet tanks, fifty armored cars, and small arms and automatic weapons. On the other were twenty-five thousand students and nearly two hundred thousand workers steadily pouring in from outlying districts. The rebels had at this time about four thousand small arms. To escape the wildly shooting Soviets and AVH men, the insurgents broke into small groups and occupied strategic corner buildings. Some entrenched themselves in military barracks. But still there was no central command, and each rebel unit operated on its own. This lack of organization contributed largely to the heavy casualties. No one plotted this revolt. It just happened.

The second night brought great changes in the situation. Nagy became Prime Minister. The rebel groups disbanded. Only a few remained manning the barricades. The night was quiet.

At this point it did not seem likely that the revolt would continue. It probably would not have gone on but for the tragic events that occurred between ten and eleven the next morning. A peaceful and unarmed demonstration arrived before the Parliament Building to shout for another set of resolutions. There were Russian tanks in the square but the drivers were smiling and friendly. Seeing a crowd numbering ten thousand arriving, the Hungarian security forces opened fire. The Russians also started shooting. More than a hundred persons died within ten minutes.

Within an hour the people's rage was beyond control, and the rebellion spread. Groups poured from all over carrying Hungarian flags. They defied Soviet and AVH fire during the rest of the day and the night following. Ceaseless firing broke out in all parts of the city. This third wave of revolt included nearly everybody. Among the bravest were both Communists and anti-Communists. There was still no command. The rebels had about five thousand rifles and nearly two thousand automatic rifles. However, the army units (which participated in the opening battles alongside the people but later went back to their barracks) had a number of heavy machine guns and grenades.

Gero's removal was announced during the night. The unarmed rebels went home and now the fighting against the Soviet troops and the AVH was carried on solely by diehards.

On the fourth day, peace seemed near. Nagy had guaranteed amnesty. The last remnants of the first student bands surrendered. They considered that their demands had been met. So too, with some minor exceptions, did the workers from the surburbs. Practically all the citizens' groups that had been engaged in the fight started preaching and practicing cease-fire.

Up to then, at the height of battle the Soviet forces numbered 310 tanks, half of them heavy, 250 armored combat vehicles, and ten thousand men. What there was of the rebellion in the provinces was confined to meetings passing resolutions that were sent to Nagy and organizing local administration. One exception was Magyarovar, a small township between Gyor and the Austrian border, where the local AVH opened fire and the ensuing massacre claimed eighty-five lives.

Popular pressure exacted more and more concessions from the government, and the price of peace continued to rise. There was still some firing by groups fighting independently of any line of command. By Saturday, the fifth day, accurate counting was possible. The rebel army could still count on about eight thousand fighters, while another thirty thousand could be mobilized on short notice. Still the rebels had no leaders and not much of a program beyond "Out with the Russkies!" and "Down with the AVH!"

The Gentle Rebels: It is difficult if not altogether impossible to convey any notion of these people's fighting gallantry. Wherever the rebels were students and workers, there was not a single case of looting. Shop windows without glass were filled with desirable goods, yet nothing was touched. An incident I saw will illustrate this. Windows from a candy store and an adjacent flower shop were smashed and the sidewalk was littered with candy boxes. All these boxes were replaced in the glassless windows, but the flowers strewn about were gathered and placed on the bodies of dead rebels.

The masses of embattled students and workers never became a mob, but from time to time there appeared a few groups of marginal characters who gathered on street corners and started yelling "Exterminate the Jews!" Several cases of hard liquor were freely distributed and many people got drunk.

Nothing like this happened where students or workers assembled, but there was enough anti-Semitism around during the first night as well as during subsequent days to present a distinct danger signal in a country which only recently had gone through several years of intense Jew hating and which had maintained an official anti-Semitic policy since 1919. During the fifth and sixth days I saw four people attacked and beaten because they may have been Jews. Not severely, but nevertheless their clothes were torn and they were bleeding. The slogan was that Rakosi, Gero, and Mihaly Farkas—three Jews—were responsible for all the misery that had descended on the country. Still, during the first six days of the revolt these episodes could be considered both sporadic and exceptional.

Rising Nationalist Tide: Here and there, wherever a group started rioting, a few individuals seemed inclined to strike a note of extreme nationalism. I even wondered at times whether these nationalist elements had a supreme command. I did my best to find it, but I never succeeded in obtaining any convincing evidence. Yet the nationalist tide kept rising. A close associate of Nagy admitted on Saturday, the fifth day, that the revolt was beyond the control of those who had started it. Nagy decided that a final bid should be made. He advanced a program: The revolt was to be declared a national patriotic uprising and was to be handled as such. Again, he proposed an amnesty for all rebels and dissolution of the AVH, and promised the early withdrawal of all Soviet troops from Budapest and negotiations with Moscow for removal of all Soviet troops from Hungarian soil. The next day he appointed non-Communists Bela Kovacs and Zoltan Tildy to Cabinet posts. Two days later he announced the formation of a new Cabinet ending the one-party system and promised that free elections would be held.

The Nagy government kept floundering. The insurrection drifted. Then on Sunday, November 4, the Russian tanks that had been ringing the city opened fire.

IV

Proposals for Government Action on the Psychological Front

It is not difficult to find suggestions for government action in the United States. We are a nation of armchair strategists and we count it as one of our strengths that we make a constant stream of recommendations to our elected officials. Eight of these recommendations are presented below. They represent many different viewpoints on various questions we have raised so far in this book.

Although it is not possible to draw a strict line between evaluating what has been done in the past and recommending what ought to be done in the future the following readings are roughly divided into these two categories.

All of the questions discussed in this section have already been covered to some degree by the Sprague Committee's report, which was quoted at length in an earlier section describing existing agencies.

Evaluations of Present Agencies and Activities

How do the Americans and the Russians, working in very different ways, compare on the psychological front? Which of our ac-

tivities have succeeded and which have failed? If the outcome of the cold war depends largely on successful information or propaganda activity, which side is winning? Although they do not stop at the boundaries of these evaluative questions the four writers whose comments follow all attempt to assess the results of the psychological cold war so far. Their comments are included so that the reader may sample a variety of viewpoints before coming to some conclusion of his own about the present state of the nation's nonphysical defenses.

WHY WE ARE LOSING THE PSYCHOLOGICAL WAR*

ARTHUR KROCK

ARTHUR KROCK *is a prominent United States journalist and commentator. His articles have appeared in the* New York Times *for many years.*

The emergence of the United States as a nation began with the assertion of "These truths we hold to be self-evident." Yet the failure of the United States Government, for the larger part of the last twelve years, to give unremitting recognition to the most self-evident truths of the atomic age has allowed Soviet Russia to take from this nation the lead in the struggle that will determine whether international communism or governments of free men will dominate the future.

These truths are:

(1) In the contest between totalitarianism and democracy, propaganda as such is a toy pistol unless it exploits actual deeds by which mankind is favorably or fearfully impressed.

(2) The degree of propaganda effect of such deeds depends on their timing, and, among democratic governments, on their consistency with all other acts and all other professions of policy.

* Reprinted from *The New York Times Magazine* (December 8, 1957), pp. 12, 91.

(3) A democratic government must prove the deeds for the purposes of effective propaganda, and to remain in political power. Moreover, it cannot conceal its failures.

(4) An autocratic government must prove its deeds for effective world propaganda, but it can and does conceal its failures without danger of overthrow. And its policies can both be inconsistent with its professions and be reversed overnight.

(5) The "national superiority" cult which led the American people firmly to believe that the subjects of a totalitarian regime—particularly Russians—could never match us in scientific or any other achievements of craftsmanship (no matter how many more hours they worked and no matter how much of our gross production consisted of luxury goods) is a delusion which could reduce the United States to the status of a second-rate nation.

(6) The national folly of the United States by which the preceding truth is disregarded in these times invites common disaster beyond any comprehension of which man heretofore has been capable.

Not only are these truths as self-evident as those recited in the Declaration of Independence; they have been regularly stated by high American officials ever since post-war Soviet Russian policy produced the "cold war." President Eisenhower recited them specifically on Oct. 8 at San Francisco in his 1952 campaign in the form of a criticism of the Truman Administration for disservice to these facts. Eisenhower said:

"The present Administration has never yet been able to grasp the full import of a psychological effort put forth on a national scale. What would such a peacetime of 'cold war' national strategy mean? It would mean, in the first place, the selection of broad national purposes and the designation within these purposes of principal targets. Then it would mean this: Every significant act of government should be so timed and so directed at a principal target and so related to other governmental actions that it will produce the maximum effect. It means that our government in this critical matter will no longer be divided into airtight compartments. It means that in carrying out a national policy every department and every agency of government that can make a useful contribution will bring its full strength to bear under a coordinated program. We shall no longer have a Department of State that deals with foreign policy in an aloof cloister; a defense establishment that makes military appraisal in a vacuum; a Mutual Security Administration that, with sovereign independence, spends billions overseas. We must bring the dozens of agencies and bureaus into concerted action under an overall scheme of strategy. And we must have a firm hand on the tiller to sail the ship along a consistent course."

Yet it is disservice to the self-evident truths by Eisenhower's own Administration that has:

Continued to make the informational service of the United States cost far in excess of its demonstrated worth (almost $900 millions in the fiscal-year period 1951-1958);

Enabled Soviet Russia with two launched satellites to score over the United States the greatest psychological triumph in a contest of this sort between nations throughout history;

Enabled Soviet Russia successfully to imply, and induce all other nations, including the United States, to fear, that it will in time attain the military superiority with which it can rule the world on its own brutal terms.

This "final" consequence creates the influence on world public opinion which is the objective of national policy. The prevailing flaw in the informational machinery of the United States, ever since the first unit of this machinery was set up after the second World War, is the accent on mere propaganda as such instead of on the reason for its existence—to influence public opinion. Here again is an instance of a self-evident truth that was disregarded—or forgotten, since it was the basic principle of George Creel's Office of Public Information in the first World War.

This principle comes into play with the use of diplomatic, economic and military means by a government to promote national objectives. But it is ineffective unless it is wholly coordinated with these other means, and they with it. To attain this two-way coordination certain rearrangements of the Executive Department are required that successively for years have been recommended, praised and jettisoned. The most important set of such recommendations was formulated in 1953 by the President's Committee on International Information Activities.

This group, headed by William H. Jackson of Princeton, was

directed in effect to study all aspects of the "cold war." Among its key proposals, the result of much intensive study and personal consultations, was this:

"The directive which created the Psychological Strategy Board [1951] assumes that in addition to national objectives formulated by the National Security Council, there are such things as 'over-all national psychological objectives.' P.S.B. is indeed charged with the formulation and promulgation of these. The P.S.B. directive also speaks of 'psychological policies' and the board has been working to develop 'a strategic concept for psychological operations.'

"We believe these phrases indicate a basic misconception, for we find that the 'psychological' aspect of policy is not separable from policy, but is inherent in every diplomatic, economic or military action. There is a 'psychological' implication in every act, but this does not have life apart from the act. Although there may be distinct psychological plans and specific psychological activities directed toward national objectives, there are no national psychological objectives separate and distinct from national objectives."

The committee also made these points:

Our military strength must be continuously maintained. No foreign policy or promise to other peoples should exceed our capabilities. The United States will be judged abroad not only by what it is able to do and does, but by the gap between these acts and announced policies. Aspirations should always be carefully distinguished from policies. The primary and overriding purpose of an information program should be to give evidence to all the world peoples that their aspirations for freedom, progress and peace are the same as our own and that they are supported and advanced by our policies.

The program should deal strictly with facts and avoid the note of propaganda, emphasizing spiritual over material values, and not suppressing objective writings simply because they include criticisms of the United States. The wartime candor of the British Broadcasting Company in conceding early military errors and defeats led the world to believe its later announcements of the victories by which the second World War was won. The haphazard and diffuse information units should be consolidated. Thus far the United States has registered abroad "no single set of ideas." Above all, the American people should be kept closely and regularly informed of all the government's information activities.

This statement of principles was accepted with the usual expressions of approval. But the steps necessary to put it in practice were not taken; among them:

An Executive set-up of officials pervading all departments and agencies, with facilities to learn in advance all impending government acts and policies that would have a psychological impact on public opinion, and to calculate their relation to fixed and professed national policies. These officials to be headed by one whose accessibility to the President is immediate, and whose representation of the President is undisputed. The others to have similar accessibility to the heads of their own departments, and all to be consulted on projected acts and policies before taken or asserted.

Instead, the Administration continued to maintain the illusion that a single man can supply the psychological ingredient in the policies and actions of the Federal Government. The reference is to a White House job which, with greater or lesser scope, has been occupied in this Administration by C. D. Jackson, Nelson Rockefeller and William H. Jackson himself, and now in the minimum by Arthur Larson.

What W. H. Jackson's committee had proposed instead was the meshing of this White House function with the activities of an Operations Coordinating Board that would have the advance participation in the formulation of acts and policies which have a psychological effect on world opinion.

The board was duly established, and with this name. But though its chairman is the Under Secretary of State, and its personnel includes the highest secondary officials of the departments and agencies concerned, plus the White House representative, the O.C.B. does not perform the larger function essential to relating, whenever possible, government acts and policies to the world objectives of United States information services.

It does some useful coordinating, to the end that the routine administrative policy of one agency or department will not conflict with another and all will hew to the policy line laid down by the President. But it has neither the power nor the prestige to make its voice heard, or to have its "psychological" judgment weighed in advance of higher official activities that have badly damaged American world influence.

There are several examples of these activities that illustrate the abiding deficiencies of the system.

An example in the early Forties was the sound military conclusion, taken shortly after the Allies landed in North Africa in the second World War, to use the French Admiral Darlan to block French resistance and obtain the fullest measure of French cooperation. When announced, this act evoked a storm of criticism in the United States and Britain for which no propaganda defense had been prepared. This was also the situation when President Roosevelt, at the Casablanca conference in 1943, proclaimed the formula of "unconditional surrender."

More recently, Secretary of State Dulles referred to Goa on the Indian subcontinent as "a Portuguese province." This was popular in Lisbon as an evidence of the loyalty of the United States to its NATO partner. But to India it was a proof of American "imperialism" and support of "colonialism"; Soviet Russian propaganda made the most of this; and the phrase, true though it was, proved costly in world opinion. A government information official in the innermost councils could have foreseen this effect of the Secretary's words and advised him against them with the prestige of responsibility.

The same was true of the State Department's refusal to validate the passports of American reporters for professional surveys in Communist China—this despite constant State Department urgings that the Communist nations lift the ban on free gathering and free exchange of information. An information agency with an important voice on policy in the making could at least have pointed out the inconsistency of this action, and how adversely it would be taken by the American people, before the department got firmly stuck with it.

It was to assure greater coordination of policy with favorable public opinion that William H. Jackson a year ago endeavored to raise the status of the O.C.B. to an official level where this would be the result. Accordingly, he proposed that Vice President Nixon instead of the Under Secretary of State—present or future—act as chairman of the board.

Nixon's prestige as the second elected officer of the United States, and his close relations with the President that have brought him assignments as the President's deputy in the highest Administration councils, were precisely suited to Jackson's objective. The Vice President was willing; the President was favorably disposed. So was Christian A. Herter, the heir-apparent to the Under Secretaryship whenever the incumbent, Herbert Hoover Jr., decided on the date to execute his already made decision to leave government.

But Hoover viewed the proposal as a personal criticism; Secretary Dulles was similarly persuaded—also that it denigrated his department and that Hoover, who planned to remain in his post several months longer, would instantly resign if it were put into effect—and on this show of opposition the President turned down the plan.

But even with these administrative handicaps, and the native distaste for anything that can be given the name of propaganda, the effect of the information program of the United States would not be at its present low ebb in the world if the Truman and the Eisenhower Administrations had not failed so signally on the psychological as well as the material aspects of the missile and satellite programs. This is aside from any estimate of whatever lead Soviet Russia may have assumed in the race for first operational command of missiles as weapons from outer space—and surely in the launching of the two Soviet Russian satellites there is an implication of superiority over the United States in the military element of rocketry power.

Since the late Forties the development of missiles and satellites has been pressed on the American Government by persons within and without. It cannot be said that the vast official complex did not move at all in response to the pleas and warnings of scientists, military men, prescient administrators and studious politicians. It did move on both programs. But on missiles the advance was diffuse and afflicted with lapses. On satellites it was given greatly inferior priority. And where domestic welfare programs were proposed and undertaken in growing scope and at increasing expenditure, considerations of balancing the budget and reducing the national debt were given top priority over both outer-space projects.

By 1950 the undertaking for ballistic missiles had been temporarily diminished because the problem of a viable war head was stumping the experts. Whereupon John A. McCone, Under Secretary of the Air Force, wrote two memoranda for Secretary Thomas K. Finletter in which he outlined a vigorous construction program for guided missiles, to be started at once and without stint of essential cost, which he estimated at a budget increase of $2 to $3 billion. He proposed a project similar to the "Manhattan" which had produced the atom bomb in the second World War, and a "czar" with full Presidential authority over all concerned, especially the rival armed services.

Submitted by Finletter to Secretary of Defense Louis A. Johnson, the substance of these memoranda was conveyed by Johnson to President Truman. The President acknowledged the urgency, approved the plan and agreed with Johnson on the choice of K. T. Keller of the Chrysler Corporation as "czar." Keller, explaining he worked best as an analyst and coordinator and therefore wanted no administrative responsibility, took the Presidential commission on those terms.

He labored effectively within their limitations, under Secretaries of Defense Johnson, George C. Marshall and Robert A. Lovett, and had some results to show the incoming Administration. The wasteful rivalry among the armed services persisting, President Eisenhower then renewed the "czar" proposal, which Keller again turned down. But he remained in his self-limited role, at the President's urging until late 1953.

Then the continuing diffusion of missile production among the armed services which Keller felt he had coordinated fairly well, provoked the struggles for budgetary and other priority that McCone's proposal of a "czar" was designed to subdue. In addition to the annual waste of millions of dollars, this condition subordinated the work on earth satellites to the minor place of which Soviet Russia took such disastrous advantage.

So relegated was this program in the official mind that there seems, until the event was imminent, to have been little discussion in the National Security Council of the psychological hazard involved if Soviet Russia put up the first satellite. And, when our intelligence reported that the launching was at hand, a proposal that the United States informational service soften this by announcing that the feat was impending was rejected in the N.S.C. on the argument that the Soviet balloon might not go up after all.

Even when the actual launching of the satellite shocked the American people, and displaced the confidence of our allies and uncommitted nations in abiding American supremacy in industrial and military science—hence in the ability to protect the free world—the Administration at first seemed to dismiss the achievement as a scientific stunt of no military potential. Moreover, the official comments, until Vice President Nixon spoke to the people with harsh realism, indicated total unawareness of the immense "cold war" propaganda value of the achievement to the Kremlin.

This attitude quickly disappeared in a show of the urgency that animated the McCone memoranda of seven years before and now infused the alarmed American people. In a conversation with the President, McCone, updating his 1950 proposal, recommended three moves that shortly were translated into official action :

The investment of a Defense Department official with the Secretary's full powers to speed and coordinate the missile experiments of the rival services; the appointment of a Presidential aide with authority to direct the whole scientific and technical phase of the effort; the decision to place new contra-missile missiles that might show promise under a Manhattan-type project with a "czar."

But seven years were irretrievably lost. Soviet Russia had fitted the impressive deed to the word—which is the essential base of propaganda that the United States again had failed to supply. And the world psychology of ultimate victory in the "cold war"—which a flock of U.S.I.A. directors, with a personnel that is now about 12,000 and the expenditure of almost a billion dollars, had been employed to create—was sharply turned against this nation, with consequences yet to be computed.

The immediate consequences, of course, will be tempered by American achievements in outer space. And their military significance is but speculative, as contrasted with the restraining facts of American dominance in strategic air power and industrial might. But the consequences—immediate and potential—are real and alarming. And they would never have appeared if the Government of the United States, by whichever party controlled, had faithfully serviced the six "self-evident truths" set down at the beginning of this article.

Is all this a reflection of the American popular attitude, ever resurgent despite bitter experience with its penalties? And therefore are our mores, and the political, democratic government imposed by our constitutional system, helpless to break the hold of this historic popular folly?

The first may be true. If the second is, more than the psychological advantage will be lost to the United States in the rapid approach of the most perilous time in the annals of freedom.

BALANCE SHEET IN THE
WAR OF IDEAS*

ANDREW H. BERDING

ANDREW H. BERDING *is an American journalist and federal government official. He was Deputy Director of the United States Information Agency (1953-1957), and was Assistant Secretary of State for Public Affairs during the second Eisenhower Administration.*

A little over a year ago a rocket roared into outer space. It entered into orbit around the world—Sputnik number one.

Instantly the whole world reverberated to what was termed a great Soviet victory not only in the scientific but also in the psychological field. Since then the attention of Americans and many other peoples has centered as never before on the war of ideas going on between the free world and the Sino-Soviet bloc.

Perhaps the time has come to take a reading on this contest and see where we stand and where we are going. Frequently the question is asked, who is winning the cold war? Let us take a look and try to come up with at least some observations, if not absolute conclusions.

First, a caution. The battlefield of ideas is not described or delimited solely by words. The battle itself is fought in far greater part by actions which express ideas. I would give a factor of only 10 to 15 percent to words, 85 to 90 percent to actions.

Sputnik number one demonstrated that the Soviets know how to combine actions effectively with words. As soon as the satellite was successfully in orbit they began a barrage of information material to all parts of the world. They sought to prove to other peoples that Soviet science was superior to that of the United States in all fields, not solely in rockets—that the Soviet Union possessed better intercontinental ballistic missiles and therefore military superiority—that it was the Communist system which could produce such achievements—that the Communist system was the wave of the future—that

* Reprinted from *The Department of State Bulletin* (December 15, 1958), pp. 955-959.

it behooved other peoples to climb aboard the bandwagon while there was still time.

It is not without significance that the Soviets announced on the same day that Sputnik would pass over two cities—Bandung in Indonesia, and Little Rock in the United States. Bandung was the site of the Afro-Asian conference of 1955, which the Soviets have widely utilized in their attempt to win over the African and Asian nations. Little Rock they have used repeatedly against the United States.

Thus, in evaluating success or failure or stalemate in the cold war, account has to be taken of all actions and all use of informational media which produce an impact on world public opinion.

Too often we in the United States tend to ascribe successes to our opponent that he has not achieved or to exaggerate those he has. With the analogy that distant pastures are greener, the actions of our opponent seem to us more dramatic and effective than our own.

Nonetheless, I should like to begin with Soviet successes.

Clearly in front of them all was Sputnik number one, followed by Sputnik number two. It is doubtful if any action on either side came near to this in its overall effect. The impact was increased by two factors. One was the previous claim of the Soviets to have developed an intercontinental ballistic missile. The success of Sputnik seemed to confirm this claim. In the eyes of large portions of the world the Soviets had acquired military superiority over the United States. And the other factor, which built up this impression still further, was the much publicized failure of the initial American attempts to put a satellite in orbit.

Subsequently the Soviets have sought to take advantage of this impression through a series of propaganda approaches.

First, they went back to the Suez crisis of two years ago this month. They have asserted again and again that it was as a result of their threats to use missiles against Britain and France that those two countries withdrew from Egypt. Thus, said the Soviets, they had used their superior military force to keep peace in the world.

Second, after having built up a supposed threat of invasion of Syria by Turkey in the spring of this year, they asserted that their threats against Turkey had prevented the invasion. And again their superior force had kept peace in the world.

Third, after having created the fiction that the United States and Britain intended to invade Iraq after we had landed troops in Lebanon and Jordan respectively, they broadcast to the world that their threats had prevented the invasion. Once again their superior force had kept peace in the world.

And finally, only a few days ago, they declared that their threats of coming to the aid of Communist China had caused the United States to back away from its support of the Republic of China and had lowered tension in the area. Once more their superior force had kept peace in the world.

It is difficult, if not impossible, to measure the success of this effort. All four claims were fraudulent. But there will always be some people, sometimes many people, who will believe a claim if it is often enough staked out.

This series of efforts is significant because it ties in neatly with one of the basic objectives of Soviet propaganda—to show that the Soviet Union is the prime protagonist of peace, that the United States and the major Western powers are the advocates of tension and of war.

The Soviets scored a second important propaganda success when in March they announced the unilateral suspension of nuclear testting. Nations the world over had come to believe Soviet propaganda and likewise statements from other quarters that the air was being poisoned by nuclear fallout from tests. Hence when the Soviets announced their suspension of testing many people credited them with wishing to contribute to human welfare. It is interesting to note, however, that this was regarded as a much greater victory by the American press than by the foreign press. Many foreign newspapers saw the loopholes in the Soviet announcement—one being the fact the Soviets had just finished an extensive series of tests themselves; another the fact we had already announced we were about to start a series of tests; and finally the fact the Soviets said they would resume testing if we tested.

A third area of gain for the Soviet side in the cold war lies in the economic field. The Soviet offers of aid and trade to many nations in the last two years have won them wide recognition. Even though the offers often require looking the gift horse in the mouth, the Soviets have made extensive propaganda out of them. Their economic assistance program now totals about $2 billion. This is only a small percentage of our economic aid total, but their propaganda gain is out of all proportion to this amount.

While frankly acknowledging Soviet victories in the cold war, let us not forget the fact we have won some notable ones ourselves. We have learned well the old, old lesson that actions speak louder than words—and we have taken the requisite actions.

We proposed an Arctic inspection and control zone to prevent surprise attack. This was a positive step taken after the Soviets charged American planes were making provocative flights toward the Soviet borders in the Arctic. Instead of merely being negative and saying, no, we didn't do it—which was a fact—we made a positive proposal and took it to the United Nations Security Council. The Soviet veto of this proposal showed they were not interested in removing the causes of distrust.

We likewise took a positive stand toward a summit conference. At the end of last year the Soviets thought they had us on a bad propaganda wicket, with themselves apparently promoting a summit conference and ourselves apparently rebuffing the idea. But Secretary Dulles' wise handling of this issue proved we were willing to have a summit conference if it gave promise of leading to substantive agreement and not be a propaganda show staged by Mr. Khrushchev. And at the same time he uncovered their hand. Thereupon, instead of putting their cards on the table they literally threw them into the air by publishing all the secret correspondence on the matter and calling off the preparatory ambassadorial meetings in Moscow. The game was over because their game was up.

Other actions on our side have cut down the size of initial Soviet successes. The fact we were able to put up earth satellites markedly diminished the pristine impression of Soviet superiority. Our own discontinuance of nuclear testing, plus our proposal for the Geneva conference to reach an agreement on a control system to monitor a suspension of nuclear testing, darkened the skies of their earlier success in this field.

But the balance sheet of the cold war is but in minor part computed if it takes into account only the actions initiated by one side or the other which were likely to have a favorable effect. Now let us take a look at actions taken that have had bad, even disastrous effect.

First, as to ourselves. A democracy by its very nature contains certain inherent disadvantages in the cold war. Our strength is in our diversity. But at the same time differences of views, such as public statements and editorials criticizing the Government, can be made by Soviet propaganda to seem like overwhelming opposition to the Government. Our press services send out the seamy as well as the good side of American life—and the seamy leaps into the headlines. Not so in the Soviet Union, where the seamy side is seldom revealed. Little Rock can—and is—built into major campaign proportions by Soviet output.

But there are also disadvantages in the Soviet and Chinese Communist systems. These disadvantages are so great that I say with confidence: The Sino-Soviet bloc cannot in the long run win the cold war. The defects of their system which require them to take certain disastrous actions are too great. They may, and will, win battles in the war of opinion, but the ultimate victory will escape them.

Two years ago this month the world was shocked by the brutal Soviet repression of the Hungarian people. The Soviets had to take this action to keep their satellites in line.

Nearly three years ago came the devastating revelation by Khrushchev himself of the barbaric enormities of Stalin. Khrushchev had to take this action to pave the way for his own leadership.

The Kremlin rulers broke with Tito of Yugoslavia because they could not permit independence of thinking in the ideological field.

The Kremlin had to permit Poland a partial movement away from Soviet control because they did not dare risk another Hungary.

Then the Kremlin aroused world public opinion by executing former Premier Nagy of Hungary and several other Hungarian leaders. They had to as an example to other satellite leaders.

More recently Moscow has lost heavily in the psychological realm by resuming nuclear testing and particularly by continuing testing after the start of the Geneva conference 12 days ago.

And around the neck of the Kremlin hangs the fact of no fewer than 85 Soviet vetoes in the United Nations. These vetoes have prevented the United Nations from fulfilling the function of keeping the world's peace assigned to it by its founders. The Soviets wonder why they do not get more votes in the U.N.; they charge it is dominated by the United States. They have only themselves to blame.

The Soviets encounter adverse public opinion in Europe by

continuing to resist the reunification of Germany and to insist on the inhuman division of that country.

The Soviets cannot escape the fact—or explain it away—that every year scores of thousands of persons flee from the Communist system and take refuge in the West. A high percentage of them is made up of professional people and intellectuals.

Though we may suffer from the picture often conveyed abroad of dissension because of the variety of voices raised in our land, the Soviets suffer as much or more from the fact of their censorship and their control of thought. Many instances, including the expulsion of two American correspondents in recent weeks, prove that Soviet censorship is tightening up still more.

Seldom have the Soviets brought upon themselves anything more disastrous in the psychological field than their harsh treatment of Boris Pasternak, Nobel Prize-winning author of *Doctor Zhivago*. This misguided attempt to stifle original thought has resounded throughout the world. It will go on echoing for months to come.

The Chinese Communists, too, are not without their failures. They stand before world public opinion as opponents of the reunification of Korea and of Vietnam. The world knows they have executed myriads of people who did not conform. How many no one knows; that it is in the millions no one doubts. And now the world is becoming aware of the latest horror—the communes. In the communes being established throughout the China mainland men live in barracks, women in other barracks, children in still other barracks, workers are marched to work, all people eat in canteens, the family is shattered, the individual is crushed—regimentation is breathtaking.

A few days ago I talked with John Strohm, the American correspondent who toured Communist China for three weeks after having been in the Soviet Union. He emphasized the contrast between China, where the people are being forced into more regimentation, and Russia, where the people are gradually evolving toward a little more liberty.

In their recent actions at Quemoy the Chinese Communists have suffered sharply in world opinion. Their shattering of their own cease-fire and their indiscriminate off-again, on-again shelling has again revealed them as utterly regardless of humanity.

If we add together the outstanding acts by the Sino-Soviet bloc which I have cited, we cannot fail to see the inner compulsions imbedded in the Communist system which drive them to do the very things that hurt them, that help us. They will continue to do these things until they change their system, until they embrace what President Eisenhower pleaded for in his last General Assembly address—a world of open societies.

We cannot, however, remain idle. We must continually seek to make known to the world, through actions and words, the ideals for which we stand. The cold war is as active as a shooting war. The battlefield of this war is strewn with the corpses of the unwary, the unalert, the "unfarseeing."

All of us, as Americans, can do something to help in this struggle.

We can, for instance, get to know our own system better, so that we can explain it to other peoples if we go abroad, or to foreign visitors who come to see us. Can we capably explain to others our political life, our social structure, our economic system? Can we effectively explain the new American capitalism, which is as different from the capitalism against which Karl Marx railed a hundred years ago as the Equator is from Antarctica? Are we sufficiently informed of the widespread participation of the American people in the ownership and management of capital, of the relations between labor and management, of the potency of private enterprise? Can we effectively illustrate the fact that our economic society is a living refutation of Marx's theory that capitalism means the exploitation of the many by the few?

We can, for instance, use more the positive approach of setting forth our own ideals—those great fundamentals bequeathed to us by our Founding Fathers—and use less the negative anti-Communist approach.

We can, for instance, know and understand foreign affairs better. Our position in the world now is such that our people must know more about our relationship with other people. We must acquire a greater understanding of other nations if for no other reason than our own security.

We can, for instance, go out of our way to be hospitable to foreign visitors. Among them are the 43,000 foreign students now studying in the United States. . . .

We can, for instance, cease so often regarding our opponent as omniscient and all-powerful, even though we must not underestimate him. Too frequently we see a beam in our own eye and not a mote in his.

We can, for instance, cease regarding the cold war as a bilateral struggle between the United States and the Soviet Union. In this respect I have probably erred myself in this very speech, in the effort to highlight the balance sheet in the war of ideas. But it is essential to understand that this is not a conflict between two colossi. It is a clash between two worlds, the world of independence of nations and the freedom and dignity of the individual, and the world of conformity of nations and the submersion of the individual. However much peoples of the free world may differ in thought and structure among themselves, there is no difference in their desire to retain their own system and in their abhorrence of the other.

We can, for instance, acknowledge the help we receive both from our allies and from the other members of the free world in this war of ideas. We owe much to them, and it is helpful to all of us to let them know it. Examples: BBC and the British Council are doing an admirable work of great help to the free world. Australia is carrying on several valuable information activities in South and Southeast Asia.

Ladies and gentlemen, the war of ideas may well continue for decades to come. It calls for unremitting alertness and determination to continue the fight to victory. We can no more relax on this battlefield than on a field of battle. Given that determination, and with confidence in the fundamental ideals upon which our nation was founded, we can do no other than win.

PSYCHOLOGICAL WARFARE AND FOREIGN POLICY*

SAUL K. PADOVER

SAUL K. PADOVER *is Dean of the School of Politics at the New School for Social Research in New York City. He has taught at the University of Paris, the University of California, and at Stanford University. He also served in the Psychological Warfare Division during the Second World War.*

We can now attempt to evaluate the whole psychological warfare program from the point of view of its effectiveness as a foreign policy instrument. In other words, does it achieve what it attempts to do?

One must emphasize that psychological warfare in itself is not a policy, but an instrument. There are things it cannot do. It cannot, in the long run, get away with systematic falsehoods. It cannot impose an alien system of values on one that already exists. It cannot alter basic institutions or satisfy physical needs or permanently substitute words for deeds.

But properly used—which means always in coordination with action—it can encourage friends and discourage enemies. It can undermine and disrupt. It can neutralize the potentially hostile or wavering. Tied to military action, it can help to confuse the enemy, damage his morale, put him on the defensive. In wartime, for example, it can make systematic appeals to the latent nationalisms in the Soviet orbit and stimulate discontent that would lead to disruptive action.

Looked at from the foreign policy point of view, the American psychological warfare program has not been effective. Indeed, quite the contrary. Two chief misconceptions are largely responsible for the failure. One is the idea that psychological warfare or propaganda is just like advertising. The other is that foreigners think, or wish to think, like Americans.

There is a widespread belief that, since Americans are smart advertisers, all that the government needs to do is hire a few high-

* Reprinted from *American Scholar* (April 1951), pp. 158-161.

pressure hucksters and fast-talking public relations counsels and, bingo, they will "produce the goods." Even Dr. George Gallup seems to hold such a belief. Recently he proposed a five-billion dollar propaganda department to be staffed, he said, "with the best brains . . . drawn from the fields of publishing, broadcasting, public relations and advertising." But this is precisely what the situation does *not* require. This is exactly the kind of staff that could easily lose us the world politically, no matter what happens militarily.

For it cannot be emphasized too strongly that political propaganda is not the same as selling soap or tissue paper. It is not a job for slick "operators," trained in the art of "putting over a sales campaign." We are not dealing with that kind of campaign. We are dealing with a world revolutionary situation involving races and cultures and aspirations totally alien to the experience of advertising executives. Advertising men have their function—on the American scene and inside the American economy. But the world situation calls for totally different types of professionals. Political propaganda, a task of extraordinary complexity, requires intellectuals, scholars, specialists and—in the final analysis—political philosophers.

All world-political signs indicate that we are in for a long conflict on ideological grounds, and one that will continue whether there is general shooting or not. In fact, it would be wise to act on the assumption that even if a general war should break out and should end in an American military victory, there will be a prolonged political aftermath of global proportions. Postwar upheavals all over the earth will require the ablest, the steadiest, the most skilled and sophisticated American political guidance—if this country is to survive as a world power.

This leads us to the second American misconception, namely, national ethnocentrism. There is in the United States a tendency to disregard the basic interests and outlooks of the foreign audiences to which America addresses itself. The American inclination is to assume that what is good for the United States is good for everybody. Effective propaganda, however, must take into account the hopes, demands and expectations, not of the propagandist, but of the audience. Instead of telling a Malayan, for example, about the daily life of a worker in the Ford factory, or a Turk about the Christmas spirit in America, it would be more fruitful to inform him of his own plight and what American democracy is ready to do for him.

Even in Western Europe, American propaganda fails in its

effects when it describes—truthfully, to be sure—the gleaming kitchens, labor-saving devices, and assorted gadgets which the middle-class housewife of the United States has at her disposal. Since the overwhelming majority of European housewives could not possibly afford or ever hope to possess such equipment, the result is either disbelief or resentment. This is particularly true in our propaganda to the Russians, whose standard of living is so low compared to that of the United States that they simply cannot conceive the vastness of the difference. Consequently, statements of American superiority in material things sound to the Russians like sheer lies. The Russians plainly cannot imagine that such things as carpets in every home and cars in workingmen's garages could possibly be true. This is clearly brought out by the comment of Moscow's *New Times:*

> What the Voice of America has to say about worker's housing conditions is no less phony and unconvincing. . . . He [the commentator] wants to assure us that Americans—all Americans!—live like princes. Here is the rosy picture he paints: "The American worker," he says, "lives either in a separate house or in a separate apartment with kitchen and bathroom. Very many married people prefer to live in the suburbs in a detached cottage with a garden." And he further asserts that the 25 per cent of earnings paid in rent includes gas and telephone and even carpet-cleaning. Carpets, of course, are mentioned here not by chance. The Voice of America wants to insinuate the carpets are as common a thing in America as gas rings.

Even the most truthful statement can boomerang, if it is not geared to the range of the audience's beliefs and expectations.

All reports from Europe and Asia indicate that the United States has failed to win over the masses of the people in those parts of the world. This is notably true in Asia, where our policy-makers have failed to take into proper account the revolutions that are now convulsing that continent. Leadership of the revolutionary movements there has been virtually abandoned to the Communists. Despite all that, as Reinhold Niebuhr pointed out, "The American nation is grossly overestimating its moral standing in Asia." The truth is, the United States has little prestige left there. Washington's psychological warfare program has hardly made a dent among the masses of the colored and undernourished peoples.

It is clear that the best radio transmitters in the world and the most far-flung organization of information specialists are no substitute for policy and leadership. United States policy has been singularly deficient in this moment of world crisis. It has been largely negative: *against* communism, *against* Sovietism, *against* dictatorship. But *for* what? To a world in fear and in need, a humanity in the agony of upheaval, the rich and powerful United States has offered no inspirational ideal or positive social program. As Maury Maverick once said: "You cannot fill the baby's bottle with liberty." Faced with a Communist-led ideological challenge, we have offered no Wilsonian Fourteen-Points program, no Rooseveltian Four-Freedoms appeal. And it is an axiom that you cannot beat something with nothing.

In consequence, our psychological warfare, even as our foreign policy, which it reflects, suffers from intellectual and spiritual emptiness. Perforce it must continue to do so until such a time as the United States shall have formulated a positive program for action, an ideal around which to rally men. Short of that, we are in danger of talking only to those of our friends who already share our expectations, and of losing the great majority of mankind that is still searching for a hope and a vision.

CAN PROPAGANDA MAKE FRIENDS?*

VICTOR LASKY

VICTOR LASKY *is an American newspaperman and author. He is editor of the* American Legion Journal *and co-author of* Seeds of Treason.

Only recently has it begun to dawn on Americans that despite the noblest of intentions Uncle Sam is hardly the world's most popular character. This troubles us. We don't like handing out billions of dollars in foreign aid only to get kicked around.

A leading Italian political writer, Indro Montanelli, sympa-

* Reprinted from *Saturday Review*, Vol. 38 (September 17, 1955), pp. 19-49.

thizes with American resentment towards the seeming ingratitude. He would resent it too, he wrote, "if I were an American who had lost, let us say, one son in Normandy to save France."

One reason for Europe's attitude, he said, is a basic defect, "of which there isn't the slightest hope that Americans can be cured, because it is in their blood. . . . It is the craze for improving us [Europeans], for making us try to be in every way kinder to each other, juster, richer, happier."

Moreover, Europeans are "envious of America, envious of her power, her well-being." They are also suspicious of our motives in aiding them. For centuries Europeans were "trained . . . to look for evil behind the mask of innocence, and to oppose it with malice even more subtle and perverse."

Still another kind of resentment towards the U.S. was expressed last January by a youthful Iranian at the annual *Herald Tribune* Forum for High Schools. Our aid, the youth said, often helped Communist propaganda, in that it provided big salaries to a few Iranians while leaving the unemployment problem unsolved. The U.S. consequently is not as popular in Iran as commonly believed.

In the face of rising anti-Americanism abroad we look for simple solutions. If only we'd pour money and energy into our propaganda! The fact is we have spent more money on so-called information services than any other Western nation. Yet we are more widely misunderstood than any other nation.

Is Congress to be blamed for our propaganda failures? Is Congress the villain because it is forever curtailing appropriations for the U.S. Information Agency?

That's the thinking of a new group formed by the noted publicist Edward L. Bernays. Unfortunately, it fails to occur to the National Committee for an Adequate U.S. Overseas Information Program that the trouble is not lack of Congressional and public support, but the justifiable suspicion most foreigners feel towards propaganda from any source.

Moreover, Mr. Bernays at a press conference said that one of the USIA's major problems in presenting U.S. policy abroad is that "anyone can shoot off his mouth in the United States. This makes it difficult for people abroad to know what the U.S. stands for."

Mr. Bernays, of course, is more accustomed to advising large corporations, which can speak with one voice. But there is no one voice in America. There are as many voices as there are Americans. The fact that Americans, unlike enslaved people, are unregimented is perhaps the best propaganda we have. It should be capitalized upon, not frowned upon.

Moreover, our propagandists cannot be accused of not trying. They are trying—too hard. But they don't have much to sell. The USIA was assigned by the President the "mission" of "explaining and interpreting to foreign peoples the objectives and policies of the United States Government." But what are those "objectives and policies"?

Who can really say—when the Administration talks about "massive retaliation" one day and invites a deal the next with Red China to settle the difficulties in the Formosa straits?

It's not that our propagandists are not trying. In fact, so eager are they to make a showing that frequently their well-meaning efforts backfire to U.S. disadvantage.

Item: Last March they sought to glorify a Russian juvenile delinquent as a courageous anti-Communist defector. In trouble with his parents, Valery Lysikov, seventeen, had run away from home. Turning up in West Berlin he declared, "Communism stinks." Immediately the USIA put its propaganda trappings to work. Press conferences, newsreels, a spread in *Life,* the Voice of America—all these trumpeted our superiority to the world. It was a perfect propaganda coup—except for one thing. Having savored of our soft drinks and juke boxes young Lysikov returned home. The Kremlin, naturally, had a field day. One West Berlin newspaper observed, "Perhaps it would have been better if the Americans had let this unripe fruit remain on the tree."

Item: In Burma our propagandists, hoping to whip up anti-Communist sentiment, secretly subsidized a Buddhist conference. When news of the subsidy leaked, according to Worldover Press, considerable bitterness was aroused. A leading Buddhist declared that, while Buddhists have no quarrel with Americans, "we may have if they persist in trying to use Buddhism as a weapon against Communism."

Item: In India USIA activities have aroused tremendous resentment. In fact, some months ago the Foreign Ministry officially protested publication in a USIA weekly of a sharp attack on Red China on grounds, as reported by the *Herald Tribune,* that "India did not want to become a battleground for propaganda disseminated by power blocs." A top Indian diplomat, asked what could be done to improve Indo-American relations, replied: "Stop pressuring us. . . . Take your U.S. Information Service out of India. We don't like propaganda agencies."

True, the diplomat is not known as a friend of the U.S. But India happens to be his country. If New Delhi had sent a team of propagandists to preach "neutralism" in the U.S. the resulting protests would be loud and angry, indeed. Americans don't like propagandists. We require their registration as foreign agents. Why should foreigners feel any different towards us?

Edward L. Bernays once observed that for the Government, as for private enterprise, "good public relations depends on making and keeping friends."

Obviously, the USIA isn't making friends in India. Good public relations would call for the USIA to curtail sharply its activities there.

It would be absurd to contend that the anti-Communist cause would suffer as a result. There are many vociferous anti-Communists in India. India's free press has published even sharper attacks on Red China than the USIA's. Books exposing Red China have enjoyed success. But they were written by Indians and since they do not carry any propaganda label they are that much more effective.

It isn't, as Roscoe Drummond, of the *New York Herald Tribune,* infers, a problem for our propagandists to be heard. And as James P. Reston, of *The New York Times,* declared last February, the problem is being believed.

"So great is the mistrust around the world of our Government propaganda," says Mr. Reston, "that the voices of our officials are often discounted because they are official voices. The readers in Paris are more likely to believe the report of their own correspondents in Washington than the statements of our officials. . . ."

If what Mr. Reston says is true then what is needed now is, as Roy Howard suggested, a Congressional investigation. Such an investigation should not be undertaken to pillory. It should be directed towards a thorough reappraisal of our already swollen USIA establishment to determine why our propaganda is so lamentably ineffective.

That it is ineffective, even USIA director Theodore C. Streibert concedes. But in asking Congress for additional funds Mr. Streibert recently declared: "You can't afford just to sit back and say, 'There isn't anything we can do about it.' "

True enough, we have to do something. But what?

Mr. Streibert's program for the coming fiscal year hardly is inspiring. For example, he asked for a large appropriation "to saturate some areas with books . . . areas that the Communists are saturating, and it takes money."

About $250,000 is earmarked for overseas distribution of an anthology entitled "Profile of America." The House Appropriations Subcommittee balked on this one, one solon calling it "a dangerous book." But the Senate Subcommittee approved the appropriation after Emily Davie, the anthology's editor, protested the House action.

"If such treatment goes unchecked," she asserted, "the USIA book program will have been hopelessly crippled and no writer in America is safe."

Although Miss Davie's indignation was justified her statement was not. Congress does have the right to decide how to spend public moneys. If funds for a book are at issue some Congressmen inevitably will turn literary critics—and poor ones at that.

Actually the issue was not "bookburning," as Miss Davie contended. The real issue, overlooked in the ensuing editorial uproar, was whether USIA distribution of such books as "Profile of America" could do any good.

Books, of course, are most important weapons in "the battle for men's minds." All too often foreign intellectuals prove susceptible to Communist propaganda.

But the kind of books is important; and the distribution even more so. Excellent as "Profile of America" is for domestic use, it is doubtful whether any book so laudatory of U.S. life would find ready acceptance among suspicious foreign intellectuals, particularly when distributed by the USIA. Whether justified or not, anything bearing the USIA imprint invariably is dubbed propaganda.

It can also be asked whether the indiscriminate dumping of U.S. publications abroad—"saturation" is Mr. Streibert's term—does any good.

According to Worldover Press, the U.S. sends free two daily newspapers and a "strongly anti-Communist weekly" to British

Labor members of Parliament. "The stuff is all right," one M.P. said, "but it seems rather obvious."

According to Roy Howard, the USIA's "giveaway stuff has the same value as anything you get for nothing—and that's nothing." The publisher cited one nation where "the USIA is directed by an intelligent newspaperman, trying to do the best job possible. Every day he is deluged with thousands of words—most of it more than thirty-six hours old and which has already been completely covered by U.S. news agencies."

The A.P., U.P. and INS, he added, already do "a magnificent job of telling America's story."

Roscoe Drummond, however, maintains that thousands of foreign newspapers cannot afford U.S. wire services. Which is true, of course. But, he added, "Obviously the USIA cannot afford to leave the field to Tass."

Mr. Drummond apparently is unaware that the Soviet news agency, Tass, rarely, if ever, gets its stuff published outside the Soviet orbit. The reason is simple. The stuff is obvious propaganda. Unfortunately, the USIA's material similarly is suspect. Since, as Roy Howard contended, few foreign editors ever use our "give-away stuff" why should it be assumed things will be different in the future?

Too much consideration has been given to ways of telling our story. Too little consideration is given to the story itself. Therein lies our biggest propaganda failing.

Writing in the *New Leader* recently on his experiences in Austria as a teacher at the Salzburg Seminar in American Studies, Philip W. Bell, assistant economics professor at Haverford College, reported: "If there was one unanimous criticism of our foreign policy by the participants collected there from all over Europe it was that we talked too much, that we preached to the rest of the world but failed to practice what we preached."

As Adlai Stevenson once stated, "There is nothing wrong with our foreign policy that a good case of lockjaw wouldn't cure."

Whatever the merits of our foreign policy, our compulsion to keep sounding off at all times, even when the golden qualities of silence are most obvious, does us harm.

There were no U.S. propagandists at Bandung. Yet things turned out so well for us that, despite their earlier fears, Secretary

Dulles and Mr. Streibert actually congratulated themselves on the outcome.

It may be a humbling thought, but if there were no USIA or State Department the anti-Communist statesmen of Asia still would fight the battle of free men. The peoples of the world do not need to be told the truth about Communism. Given a choice few would voluntarily accept Red enslavement.

In fact, the closer people are to Communism the more they hate it. In Austria, for example, our propagandists, according to a recent *Baltimore Sun* dispatch, have had an easy time of it. "They did not have to aim any of their efforts at wooing the Austrians away from the Russians," according to correspondent Howard Norton. "The Red Army took care of that when they sent Mongolian troops to seize and occupy Vienna. . . . And by the time they had finished ravishing, robbing, and terrorizing the city they had created a legacy of hatred that even the current Soviet expenditure of about $25,000,000 a year on propaganda in Austria alone has been unable to counteract to any visible degree."

But excellent as Austrian-U.S. relations are, there are a few dark spots, Mr. Norton reported. "One of these—the one causing the most worry—is the inability of Austrians to understand the relative luxury in which Americans live in their midst. The abundance of big American automobiles shipped here at Government expense for the diplomatic, military, and propaganda missions makes the American luxury vastly more conspicuous."

According to Mr. Norton, many Austrians are bitter over the contrast of their impoverished way of life with that of Americans.

Mr. Norton quoted a long-time American resident in Vienna as suggesting "that one of the best possible strokes of propaganda so far as Americans are concerned would be to cut down the amount they spend on propaganda—or at least the amount they spend keeping the propagandists comfortable."

If this is the case in Austria, imagine the feelings of Asians as they view our overseas profligacy. A prime fact of Asia is its poverty, so pervasive few Americans can quickly understand it. We should ponder the warning of Canada's Foreign Minister, Lester B. Pearson, that the West should offer more than plumbing to the East and not try to substitute "Coca-Cola for Confucius" in dealing with Asians.

The mere presence of Americans in overwhelming numbers in world capitals has become bad propaganda in itself. Foreigners, unfortunately, have grown to resent our presence. The Communists know how to exploit resentment. In Paris even anti-Communists talk of the American occupation. One Frenchman, pointing to United States-occupied buildings in Paris, recently observed to an American friend, "Even during the Nazi occupation there were never as many Germans here as there are Americans today."

Good public relations, obviously, require the immediate slashing of our huge overseas establishment. Unfortunately, however, the bureaucratic mind insists on empire-building. For example, Theodore Streibert not only is insisting on diplomatic passports for key USIA officials (against State Department opposition), he even is asking for uniforms for foreign personnel.

Congress, typically, approached this request from an economy viewpoint. One solon asked Mr. Streibert, for example, how uniforms would "help our President balance the budget?" A more important consideration is how uniforms could possibly help our propaganda. If anything, uniforms, replete with caps bearing the letters USIA, will only emphasize our propaganda, when less emphasis so obviously is in order.

Mr. Streibert testified uniforms were a "necessity" because State Department employees have them. His testimony brought into focus the incredible bickering and jealousies existing among dozens of our overseas agencies. In itself the resultant confusion has caused the U.S. to lose "face." So much so, a White House spokesman admitted, that "this friction lowers U.S. prestige abroad."

There are basic reasons why the United States is misunderstood abroad. They can be summarized as follows:

1. All too often our propaganda is viewed as an end in itself. Propaganda must be backed by deeds. Otherwise the words lose their impact.

2. Our propaganda appears dedicated to making others see us not as we really are but as we wish them to see us.

3. Our propagandists amateurishly attempt what professionals already do on a private enterprise, cash-on-the-line basis. The USIA press service can hardly compete with legitimate news agencies. The $6,000,000 it costs obviously could be put to better use elsewhere.

4. Our top propagandists are selected primarily because they

are excellent technicians or administrators. But other, more important qualifications are needed for psychological warfare. For example, a key Voice of America executive at a recent staff conference was unable to name the countries behind the Iron Curtain. Yet this executive has much to say about what we broadcast to the enslaved people. Obviously, an electronics expert is needed in the Voice operation. A Soviet-affairs specialist is more necessary, however.

What the free world needs is not more propaganda but dramatic victories against Communism. Such victories cannot be achieved by propaganda. In the late forties, when China was falling to the Reds, the U.S. conducted a full-scale propaganda program in China, replete with plush offices and book-crammed libraries in principal cities. Why should it be assumed that the USIA can accomplish in Southeast Asia what its predecessor organizations failed to do in China?

That dramatic victories against Communism can be achieved only by a firm foreign policy was the generally-overlooked premise of David Sarnoff's widely-publicized memorandum to President Eisenhower. General Sarnoff called for the expenditure of several billions annually for a "political offensive against world Communism." But his "offensive" could be based only on the kind of no-compromise foreign policy advocated by Senator Knowland. Which makes the President's indorsement of the plan all the more surprising.

General Sarnoff noted that our current diplomacy, while aimed at soothing world tensions, is essentially defensive. That gives it the appearance, at least, of weakness. The Kremlin, by its phony peace offensive, its recent Austrian settlement, and its recent arms offer, is outscoring us propaganda-wise.

General Sarnoff's plan also called for the cooperation of our Allies, whether they like it or not. "We need their help in this field," he said. "We are fully justified in asking for such help and ought to receive it." True enough, but suppose England, as would be likely, doesn't want to play ball. What do we do?

Questionable as are some of his specific proposals, General Sarnoff's basic thesis can hardly be argued.

"While the Kremlin has suffered some setbacks," he wrote, "its record in the Cold War has been strikingly one of success piled on success. This trend must be reversed to hearten our friends, dismay the enemy, and confirm the fact that Communist power is a transient and declining phenomenon."

When a golden opportunity to strike back presented itself, as during the June 1953 East German uprisings, our psychological warriors were caught off guard. Not knowing what to do, they did nothing. And the revolt fizzled, enabling the commissars to warn the enslaved peoples, in effect, "The U.S. cannot be counted on. Why rebel?"

If the peoples of Asia have lost faith in the U.S. no amount of picture books, films, and other USIA paraphernalia ever could recover that faith.

More concretely, how can the USIA be expected to "sell" U.S. support of British and French colonial policy to Asia? Or even North Africa?

Our changing Formosa policy highlights our basic propaganda problem. When Washington "unleashed" Chiang Kai-shek that policy could not be sold to Europe no matter how hard the USIA tried. Now that our policy is reverting to "containment" of the Nationalists no USIA is needed to obtain a better press in London or Paris.

But in Taipei there is such bitter, and justified, resentment, towards Washington that, obviously, the best the USIA can do under the circumstances is to keep quiet. One Nationalist newspaper commented, "The U.S. is undoubtedly the most respectable nation because of her lofty ideals. But the trouble is that she can hardly translate those ideals into a dynamic and inflexible policy." This resentment has spilled over into the Philippines. *The Manila Chronicle,* editorializing on "the ever-changing American policy" towards Formosa, deplored Washington's habit of "altering policies without previous notice, without benefit of consultation (and, much less, agreement) with her weak and trusting allies."

Sheer humanity calls for propaganda which can be backed by deeds. As Stewart Alsop has pointed out, the U.S. encouraged some 700,000 refugees to flee to Southern Indochina from the Communist North. "The eager hucksters and public-relations officers in Washington even portrayed the fearful human tragedy of this mass flight as an inspiring, reassuring event—almost indeed as another Administration success in foreign policy. . . . What then is to happen to these refugees if Southern Indochina is also to fall to the Communists? They cannot be transplanted a second time. . . . Are they to be left to their cruel fate? Or are the Marines to be sent to rescue them and hold the south?"

If the U.S. is anxious to obtain the confidence of other peoples, particularly in Asia, this dilemma must be solved. No amount of propaganda will sugarcoat the immense tragedy of these refugees if all Indochina falls to the Reds.

Obviously, the reason the U.S. has been unable to sell itself abroad is we have little to sell. The U.S. happens to be foremost in the arts of public relations and advertising. But, no matter how good soap advertising at home may be, it is valueless if soap isn't available in the stores.

The time has come for our top policymakers to take a fresh look at what we're trying to sell abroad and how we're trying to sell it. Obviously, too, a thorough revamping of our propaganda is in order. Perhaps, until we have something to sell our propagandists should keep their mouths shut. And, above all, we should operate on the premise that the best propaganda is not fashioned of words but of deeds.

Suggestions for Changes in Government Programs

Just as the preceding commentators have been tempted to add suggestions to their evaluations so have the following presented some evaluations as bases for their suggestions. However the emphasis in the next four readings is on recommendations for action—or, in some cases less action—by the United States Government.

OPPOSITION TO THE UNITED STATES INFORMATION PROGRAM*

EUGENE W. CASTLE

EUGENE W. CASTLE, *a film executive and journalist, was a contributing editor to* American Mercury *magazine until his death in 1961.*

One of the most misleading notions that has entrapped the official American mind since V-J Day has been the belief that propaganda can do in peace, or even in the Cold War, what it did in the late shooting war.

The whole rickety structure of foreign information, into which we have poured our hundreds of millions, is erected upon this baseless conviction. An urgent duty of the American people is to reexamine their concepts of propaganda, and to reassess them.

Actually, propaganda has a necessary role in war, as both World Wars I and II demonstrated. Skillfully directed, it saves lives and shortens hostilities. It is an agent of demoralization when turned against retreating or losing enemy troops: it is an agent of defeatism when turned against the home front. It is in the nature of such propaganda that it needs to have little relationship to truth: indeed, the most effective propaganda coups in both wars have been variations of the "Big Lie" technique—the British atrocity stories and pictures in World War I, or OSS's "Operation Annie" in World War II. Such war-time stunts are feints and hoaxes, cynically designed to throw enemy troops and populations off balance.

But the fact that such operations have been sensationally effective under war conditions is no analogy for peace. In normal times the only function of a good information program is to tell the truth, not falsehood—to sell goodwill, not dissimulation. Probably the greatest mistake of our costly post-war information program has been its attempt to carry over, into peace times, the fabulous mentality of war.

* Reprinted from *Billions, Blunders and Baloney,* by Eugene W. Castle. Published by the Devin-Adair Company, New York.

Regardless of how jaundiced the reader's opinion of the man's controversial place in the world of journalism may be, the fact cannot be ignored that William Randolph Hearst knew the power of the press and how to exploit that power. He also knew the difference between fact and fiction. He wrote:

> President Roosevelt is entirely and emphatically right when he tells the conference of pressmen that propaganda should not be printed in newspapers as fact. Propaganda is not fact. It is falsehood. It is, in truth, willfully distorted out of all resemblance to truth, in the interests of one or another party to a dispute or conflict.
>
> Propaganda is, at best, an opinion, and opinion should not be printed as fact even if it is an honest opinion. And propaganda is neither honest fact nor honest opinion. It is essentially dishonest. (Quoted from *Newsmen Speak* by Edmond D. Coblentz.)

The disastrous impact of current American propaganda upon traditionally friendly people abroad was strikingly pointed out to the author by a prominent French businessman and firm anti-Communist.

"The naked truth is," he declared, "that all Europeans hate propaganda in any form because they have, and for many years, been propagandized to death. They don't believe propaganda when it comes from their own government: they won't believe it from yours. Your hordes of busybody press agents in Paris and throughout France actually harm Franco-American relations, and more than you would believe."

When the present Administration assumed power, there was reason to expect a new and effective approach to the information task.

President Eisenhower, in setting up the USIA in October, 1953, specifically stated that the "new agency" would present factual reports without attempting to imprint American culture on other nations. And Theodore C. Streibert, in assuming the Directorship, defined as his intended policy: "Avoiding a propagandistic tone . . . we shall, therefore, concentrate on objective factual news reporting and appropriate commentaries."

These were reassuring intentions, but how disillusioning has been the follow-up. A few perfunctory changes involving the reshuffling of the top command. A temporary reduction of the vastly overstaffed personnel—these things were done with maximum promotional fanfare. But the vitally important transformation of the program from a vehicle of noisy and often provocative propaganda to an honest, thoughtful and intelligent presentation of America's aspirations and hopes to the world—this has not been done.

The USIA continues in its obtuse course, making enemies and critics for America instead of friends. The fine and bold resolutions of 1953 have withered away into disappointing non-fulfillment.

Our present Information Agency will never be effective for Americans because its chief operators are too busy catering to the administration which happens to be in power. They are too busy over-promoting politicians in countries where there are no votes for them. Moreover, they are too busy with never-ending campaigns for more funds to enlarge their already too big and unmanageable global establishment for press agentry. They therefore have no time to pinpoint a job of good press relations for Americans and to confine that job to the countries and places where our Government requires such efforts.

The tragedy of the situation is that what ought to be done is perfectly obvious. We are the victims of our own overorganization. We have erected a much too costly and complicated superstructure to do a job which can be done with vastly greater effectiveness by a relatively simple and inexpensive agency administered from within the Department of State.

Instead we have built, and the American taxpayer is unknowingly supporting, a cumbersome bureaucratic machine with thousands of employees constantly seeking to justify their existence with blown-up radio projects, propaganda-slanted motion pictures, ineffective and totally unneeded cabled news reports, elaborate libraries often far removed from the native population centers, subsidized newspapers, magazines and anti-Communist slick books and pamphlets. The books and pamphlets are distributed almost exclusively to specialized intelligentsia groups with little or no influence at all in the countries where they reside.

Also, there are highly questionable religious "inspirational" programs, synthetic propaganda for free enterprise, etc., all of which grinds on and on globally and planlessly by sheer force of the bureaucratic pressures behind it. In reality, we find ourselves in the unfortunate position of maintaining these ineffective and all too often harmful promotional knick-knacks merely because we have them on our hands!

It is a tragic fact that no ruthless and thoroughgoing overhauling of this costly and inherited apparatus has yet been made by President Eisenhower and his advisers.

When it was pointed out to the present Administration that a whole segment of waste could be eliminated by abolishing the $4,612,177 worldwide propaganda film service, the President's budget estimates asked for $6,964,000 for fiscal 1955 to continue this ridiculous and unnecessary program.

When, in passing the 1955 appropriation, the House voted a cut of $8,000,000 in the over-all USIA appropriation, direct White House pressure caused the Senate to add $12,000,000. Only in conference with Congressional leaders was a final budget of $77,000,000 approved. This was $20,000,000 less than the first White House demand. And this was $40,000,000 more than is actually required to pay for a properly conceived and directed overseas information effort.

For more than twenty years during the administrations of Presidents Roosevelt, Truman and Eisenhower, the American people have been conditioned to accept government expenditures and deficits in the billions. Now, as in the past, the President and his chief spokesmen and advisers insist that only millions are spent for propaganda abroad in terms of government spending, that this is only a drop in the Atlantic Ocean. That is true, but what remains unsaid is that in terms of potential damage to our country and all our citizens, the impact of the USIA on most foreigners may, in the end, prove to be as dangerous for peace and security as the force of a Texas tornado at the height of its destructive fury. . . .

Certainly we need and should have a "Voice of America," but beamed only to countries where its effectiveness could be depended upon. And only in the form of a terse, strictly factual news program confined to interpreting American foreign policy and to nailing anti-American lies. To render such overseas radio service we do not need to maintain nearly 1,000 government broadcasters in Washington, D.C., alone! Instead, and to keep its contact with reality, the over-all policies and direction of the Voice might well be placed under the supervision of the major American radio and press associations. . . .

The three American press associations—the Associated Press, the United Press and the International News Service—daily send many thousands of words throughout the world. This professional, unbiased and full coverage of what is happening throughout the United States every hour and every day is the best and only kind of propaganda that should be issued from a land of free people. The USIA's 6,000 word overseas news cable is a costly and totally unnecessary duplication of the services maintained by the American press associations. Our government's propaganda news cable should be taken off the backs of the American taxpayers at once. . . .

The USIA is worse than useless to the American people as their voice abroad as long as this over-staffed and over-zealous agency substitutes needling and crisis talk for sensible and effective informational efforts abroad. The present policy boils down to spending still more tens of millions of dollars in stepping up wasteful and harmful policies that result only in challenging the Soviets to competitive contests of ill-will and abuse.

PROPAGANDA VS. DIPLOMACY*

THEODORE SANDS

THEODORE SANDS *was formerly with the Office of Research and Intelligence of the Department of State. He now teaches history at Illinois Normal College.*

Diplomacy, which once was a whispered secret, has now become the favored subject of radio, television and newspapers; daily we are bombarded with the moves and proclamations of national leaders. Now, as the season of Summitry approaches, we might with profit make a distinction between diplomacy and propaganda, ask ourselves in the weeks ahead which we are witnessing, and ponder the proper place of both in the conduct of our foreign policy.

* Reprinted from *The Nation*, Vol. 188 (May 30, 1959), pp. 488-489.

The current crisis is not likely to be the last; nor should we anticipate a liquidation of the cold war at the coming Summit meeting. But although the substance of the issues may not be greatly affected by the meetings now in the headlines, the procedures employed deserve close attention. For how we use the techniques of diplomacy and propaganda may weigh as heavily on the scales of peace as the substance of the issues themselves.

Much of what passes today for diplomacy is not diplomacy at all; it is propaganda. Yet unless the practice of proper diplomacy is protected and preserved, the means required to find future solutions of current problems will not be available. The tragedy of the next Summit meeting might be less any failure to agree than the further erosion of the pattern of diplomacy by the winds of propaganda.

Diplomatic discussion has traditionally supplied the materials out of which the cement of agreement and understandings have been made. Discussion implies an exchange of views; it implies listening as well as talking. Propaganda can be clothed in the forms of diplomacy, such as an exchange of notes between Heads of State, but its functions and purposes are very different. In propaganda there is no exchange of views or explanation of the reasons for them. There is no listening, for the intent is not mutual understanding or agreement, but the presentation of a position.

The Soviet Union has largely discarded the art of discussion for the art of propaganda. It has used diplomacy to talk to peoples over the heads of their leaders and thereby influence world opinion. Thus, Russian-style diplomacy has become more an instrument for extending conflict than for reconciling differences. The United States, on the other hand, has attempted to cling to the traditional practices of diplomacy, but not to its spirit. Rather than accommodation and compromise, it has stressed inflexibility. And when confronted with Soviet propaganda disguised as diplomacy, it has responded with diplomacy disguised as propaganda.

While the initial responsibility for the corruption of this traditional instrument of peace into one of war lies with the Communist world, the United States shares responsibility. For the use of propaganda in the guise of diplomacy is as much the result of American indecision and confusion as it is of Russian guile and ambition.

The difficulties we now find ourselves in may well stem from a lack of understanding of the differences that currently exist between the nature of diplomacy in the Soviet Union and in the United States. In this country, diplomatic procedure has required that discussion and negotiation be carried on among duly accredited representatives of the state. Our diplomacy has been geared to the sober and serious atmosphere of the conference room. At the same time, we have allowed the Soviets to conduct their diplomacy via the marketplace and for purposes other than a compromise of official differences. This situation carries with it a double jeopardy. It inhibits the proper investigation of areas of accommodation, and it leaves the initiative with the Soviets.

The task of diplomacy in this nuclear age is to provide a means of discussion, negotiation and agreement between governments. In the final analysis, the atom is no respecter of ideology; it recognizes neither the class struggle nor the immutable workings of the dialectic. And unless we are willing to abandon completely a rational frame of reference, we must assume that in the foreseeable future the Soviets will recognize (if they have not already done so) the limits the atom has imposed on their ambitions.

When this stage of mutual fear and respect for the atom is reached, it will be necessary to have available the means by which the required communication, negotiations and agreements can be worked out. That instrument is already at hand. It is the practice of conventional diplomacy.

Thus it would be the height of folly for the West to abandon the practice of diplomacy merely because, as currently practiced, it seems ineffective in the face of Soviet propaganda tactics. The trouble is not with diplomacy, but with our improper use of it. We are trying to use diplomacy, for a task for which it has never been designed: propaganda and psychological warfare. If we wanted to attract a crowd to a carnival side-show, we would certainly not use the language of the lawyer or the university professor. Yet in effect this is what we are currently doing. The result has been that we have been carrying on neither fruitful diplomacy nor successful propaganda, while the Soviets, on the other hand, have captured the initiative in diplomacy and control of the field in propaganda.

It is within our initiative to force a separation of diplomacy from propaganda. The accomplishment of this task is not one of legalism, but of action; it is not a matter of rules, but of process. There is already a sort of rule of thumb in our State Department to the effect that any Soviet proposal accompanied by publicity is propaganda. On the other hand, a proposal made through regular diplomatic channels and unattended by publicity is worth considering. This is a sensible approach and deserves to be applied more fully than it currently is. Our current dilemma is that although we spot much of Soviet "diplomacy" to be propaganda, we feel constrained to counter it with a diplomacy that is neither good diplomacy nor good propaganda. What is required, it would seem, is a clear and definite divorce between the two instruments. Western diplomacy could restrict its activities to sincere attempts at reaching agreements of mutual benefit. It could abandon completely the practice of "open diplomacy" and treat any proposal which is given publicity in the exploratory stage not as diplomacy, but as propaganda. Any violation of the confidential discussions and negotiations prior to agreement could be treated as an official act tantamount to a breaking-off of negotiations.

At the same time, the West could begin to wage propaganda on the same terms as the Soviets. However, before this could be done there would have to be a clarification of what we were trying to do with propaganda. It would seem that there should be two main objectives: (1) to create conditions within the Soviet bloc which disrupt and weaken the functioning of the Communist system; (2) to immunize the non-Communist states to the blandishments of the Soviets and to create an ideological and emotional attachment to the West.

There is no reason why the United States could not embark on an all-out propaganda campaign to convince the world that we are a peace-loving nation and that we are constantly working to ease the danger of nuclear war. This cannot be done by explaining the necessity of an adequate inspection system as part of an atom-test ban; it can be done only by a skillful manipulation of the stereotypes and symbols by which the mass of men can most easily be influenced.

What is to prevent the United States from inviting the Soviet bloc to join us in a pact of re-dedication to the principles of the U.N. Charter? Why could we not start a world-wide disarmament movement in which the goal would be a petition of 100 million signatures calling for the Soviet Union to reopen disarmament talks?

Our official attitude towards this approach is that it is useless and therefore immoral. This judgment is true in the framework of diplomacy, but completely invalid in terms of propaganda. One must keep in mind the difference in objective. In this case, since the objective is to convince others of our peaceful intent, we must take actions that are symbolic of this intent and at a level that will be understood by all. While it may be true that the signature of the Soviet Union on a pact of re-dedication is not going to strengthen the U.N. materially, or even ease the tensions between East and West, it would create the impression that the United States is desirous of peace. At the same time it would in no way prevent us from pursuing more realistic goals through normal diplomatic channels.

What would happen if the United States not only accepted the bid to the Summit, but countered with a meeting of "Peoples for Peace"? What would happen if the United States not only accepted the Soviet bid to outlaw atomic warfare, but countered with invitations to outlaw conventional warfare, forced labor and one-party elections? The current position of the United States is that such agreements would create a false impression in the free world, that they would indicate that the cold war had been liquidated and there was no further need to maintain our defense. This line of reasoning is open to serious question. It assumes that the West can stay armed and vigilant only under a psychology of crisis. It assumes, too, that the peoples of the NATO alliance would be so naive as to see peace in these empty symbols of agreement.

Moreover, those who fear this kind of "peace propaganda" fail to take into account that the offer of a pact to outlaw war, for instance, might have a greater psychological impact in the Soviet Union than in the United States. After all, the peoples of the Soviet bloc have been conditioned to believe that such a pact would really prevent war. The Soviets might experience great difficulty in justifying the need for the "dictatorship of the party" when the chief reason for its existence, the hostile capitalist threat of the United States, has been nullified by such a pact of peace, widely-touted throughout the world.

How would this clear-cut division between diplomacy and propaganda on our part affect Soviet diplomacy-propaganda? It would, by the very nature of our procedure, require that the Soviets adopt the same pattern. Once we treat Soviet "open-diplomacy" as propaganda, countering with pure propaganda of our own, conventional diplomacy would remain the only avenue left open to both sides for serious negotiations.

There are risks in waging propaganda for peace. But there are equally grave hazards in continuing the present policy. It is only by recognizing the dual purpose of Soviet diplomacy-propaganda as it is used today that we can combat its effectiveness and its tendency to accentuate conflict. If we insist on a return to diplomacy as non-public discussion and negotiation, and only that, we will preserve the sole remaining tool of serious agreement and at the same time leave ourselves free to wage propaganda in a more effective and much less dangerous fashion than is now the case.

FIGHT FALSE PROPAGANDA
WITH TRUTH*

HARRY S. TRUMAN
President of the United States

HARRY S. TRUMAN *was the thirty-third President of the United States (1945–1953). He served as Chief Executive during the early period of the cold war and through the Korean War (1950–1953).*

I am happy to be here today with this group of editors. You and I have a great many important problems in common, and one of the most important of these is the responsibility we share in helping to make the foreign policy of the United States of America. That is why I am going to take this opportunity to discuss with you some aspects of that policy.

No group of men in this country is of greater importance to our foreign policy than the group your society represents.

* Speech delivered to the American Society of Newspaper Editors, Washington, D.C., April 20, 1950.

In a democracy, foreign policy is based on the decisions of the people.

One vital function of a free press is to present the facts on which the citizens of a democracy can base their decisions. You are a link between the American people and world affairs. If you inform the people well and completely, their decisions will be good. If you misinform them, their decisions will be bad; our country will suffer and the world will suffer.

You cannot make up people's minds for them. What you can do is to give them the facts they need to make up their own minds. That is a tremendous responsibility.

PARTISANSHIP OPPOSED

Most of you are meeting that responsibility well—but I am sorry to say a few are meeting it badly. Foreign policy is not a matter for partisan presentation. The facts about Europe or Asia should not be twisted to conform to one side or the other of a political dispute. Twisting the facts might change the course of an election at home, but it would certainly damage our country's program abroad.

In many other countries today the papers print about foreign affairs only what their governments tell them to print. They can't add anything or cut anything. In the democracies, the papers have a free hand.

Only in a democracy is there such mutual trust and confidence among citizens that a private group is given such an all-important role in determining what the nation as a whole shall do. There is too much nonsense about striped trousers in foreign affairs. Far more influence is exerted by the baggy pants of the managing editor.

There has never been a time in our history when there was so great a need for our citizens to be informed and to understand what is happening in the world.

The cause of freedom is being challenged throughout the world today by the forces of imperialistic communism. This is a struggle, above all else, for the minds of men. Propaganda is one of the most powerful weapons the Communists have in this struggle. Deceit, distortion and lies are systematically used by them as a matter of deliberate policy.

RED PROPAGANDA ATTACKED

This propaganda can be overcome by truth—plain, simple, un-varnished truth—presented by newspapers, radio and other sources that the people trust. If the people are not told the truth, or if they do not have confidence in the accuracy and fairness of the press, they have no defense against falsehoods. But if they are given the true facts, these falsehoods become laughable instead of dangerous.

We can have confidence that the press of the United States and most of the other free nations will keep us from being deceived by Communist propaganda. But in other parts of the world the struggle between falsehood and truth is far more intense and dangerous.

Communist propaganda is so false, so crude, so blatant, that we wonder how men can be swayed by it. We forget that most of the people to whom it is directed do not have free access to accurate information. We forget that they do not hear our broadcasts or read impartial newspapers.

We forget that they do not have a chance to learn the truth by traveling abroad or by talking freely to travelers in their own countries.

All too often the people who are subject to Communist propaganda do not know Americans, or citizens of the other free nations, as we really are. They do not know us as farmers or as workers. They do not know us as people having hopes and problems like their own. Our way of life is something strange to them. They do not even know what we mean when we say "democracy."

This presents one of the greatest tasks facing the free nations today. That task is nothing less than to meet false propaganda with truth all around the globe. Everywhere we must meet it and over-come it with honest information about freedom and democracy.

In recent years, there has been tremendous progress all over the world in education and the exchange of ideas. This progress has stirred men everywhere to new desires and new lives, they want to be masters of their own affairs. We have helped and encouraged these people. But the Communists have seized upon their desires and ambitions and are seeking to exploit them for their own selfish purposes.

In the Far East, for example, millions are restlessly seeking to break away from the conditions of poverty and misery that have surrounded them in the past. The Communists understand this situation very well. They are trying to move in and take advantage of these aspirations.

FALSITY OF PROMISES

They are making glittering promises about the benefits of communism. They reach directly to the peasant or the villager in these vast areas, and talk to him directly in his own tongue about the things he has learned to desire. They say that they can get these things for him. And too often he hears no voice from our side to dispute them.

We know how false these Communist promises are. But it is not enough for us to know this. Unless we get the real story across to people in other countries, we will lose the battle for men's minds by default.

The Communist propaganda portrays the Soviet Union as the world's foremost advocate of peace and the protector of defenseless peoples. The contradiction between what the Communist leaders have promised and what they have actually done is so startling that we are amazed that anyone can be deceived.

In Berlin, in Czechoslovakia, in the Balkans, in the Far East, they have proved, time after time, that their talk about peace is only a cloak for imperialism. But their intended victims will not learn these facts from Soviet propaganda. We are the ones who must make sure that the truth about communism is known everywhere.

At the same time, we must overcome the constant stream of slander and vilification that the Communists pour out in an effort to discredit the United States and other free nations.

Soviet propaganda constantly reviles the United States as a nation of "warmongers" and "imperialists." You and I know how absurd that is. We know that the United States is wholly dedicated to the cause of peace.

We have no purpose of going to war except in defense of freedom. Our actions demonstrate that we mean exactly what we say. But when men throughout the world are making their choice between communism and democracy, the important thing is not what we know about our purposes and our actions—the important thing is what they know.

ECONOMIC STORIES

Communist propaganda also seeks to destroy our influence in the world by saying the American economy is weak and about to collapse. We know this is preposterous.

The industrial production of the United States is equal to that of the rest of the world combined. Our agricultural production is more than adequate for our needs. Our people enjoy the highest standard of living in the world's history. Our economic strength is the bulwark of the free world.

From every standpoint, our free way of life is vastly superior to the system of oppression which the Communists seek to impose upon mankind. In many parts of the world, however, where men must choose between freedom and communism, the true story is going untold.

We cannot run the risk that nations may be lost to the cause of freedom because their people do not know the facts.

I am convinced that we should greatly extend and strengthen our efforts for making the truth known to people in all the world.

Most of us have recognized for years, of course, how important it is to spread the truth about freedom and democracy. We are already doing some very good work—through the Voice of America and the United States Information Offices and Libraries in many parts of the world, through the exchange of students, through the United Nations and its affiliated organizations, and in other ways.

But events have shown, I believe, that we need to do much more, both ourselves and in collaboration with the other free nations. We must use every means at our command, private as well as governmental, to get the truth to other peoples.

APPEAL TO PRIVATE GROUPS

Private groups and organizations have an important part to play. Our labor unions have already done fine work in communicating with labor in Europe, in Latin America, and elsewhere. The story of free American labor, told by American trade unionists, is a better weapon against Communist propaganda among workers in other countries than any number of speeches by government officials.

The same principle applies to other groups. The best way for farmers in other countries to find out about us is to talk directly with our own farmers. Our business men can speak directly to business men abroad. We need to promote much more direct contact between our people and those of other countries.

We should encourage many more people from other countries to visit us here, to see for themselves what is true and what is not true about our country.

We should find more opportunities for foreign students to study in our schools and universities. They will learn here the skills and techniques needed in their own countries. They will also see at first hand the rights and duties of citizens in our land of democratic institutions.

Our colleges should train more Americans to go abroad as teachers, especially to teach modern methods of farming, industry, and public health—and, by example, to teach our concepts of democracy. The notable record of our many charitable and religious organizations who send teachers abroad is proof of what can be done.

Another major part of our effort must be carried out through our great public information channels—newspapers and magazines, radio, and motion pictures. We must strive constantly to break down or leap over barriers to free communication wherever they exist. We must make full use of every effective means of communicating information, in simple, understanding form, to people whose backgrounds and cultures are different from ours.

"AN ENORMOUS CHALLENGE"

This poses an enormous challenge to groups such as yours, a challenge which can be met only by extraordinary inventiveness and enterprise. I am confident that the American press can and will make a tremendously useful contribution toward finding new solutions.

The Government's programs for telling the truth about the United States to the peoples of the world also need constant improvement. Our present overseas information and educational exchange program is getting results. For example, the Voice of America has been carrying to people behind the Iron Curtain the true story of world events.

It has been so successful that the Soviet Government is using a vast amount of costly equipment in an attempt to drown out our broadcasts by jamming. We must devise ways to break through that jamming and get our messages across. And we must improve and strengthen our whole range of information and educational services.

This is not a conclusion reached by government officials alone. We have had the valuable aid of the United States Advisory Commission on Information created by the Congress. Your own society is ably represented on that commission by Mr. Mark Ethridge and Mr. Erwin D. Canham.

The members of the commission have given intensive study to the overseas information program and have made repeated recommendations that it be substantially expanded. Similar recommendations for the exchange program have been made by the Advisory Commission on Education, headed by Dr. Harvie Branscomb.

CONGRESSIONAL MOVES PRAISED

I have been glad to see that many members of the Congress have urged an improved and expanded program in these fields—as shown, for example, by the resolution introduced recently by Senator Benton for himself and a number of his colleagues.

Because of the pressing need to increase our efforts along this line, I have directed the Secretary of State to plan a strengthened and more effective national effort to use the great power of truth in working for peace. This effort will require the imagination and energies of private individuals and groups throughout the country. We shall need to use fully all the private and governmental means that have proved successful so far—and to discover and employ new ones.

Our task is to present the truth to the millions of people who are uninformed or misinformed or unconvinced. Our task is to reach them in their daily lives, as they work and learn. We must be alert, ingenious, and diligent in reaching peoples of other countries, whatever their education and cultural backgrounds may be.

Our task is to show them that freedom is the way to economic and social advancement, the way to political independence, the way to strength, happiness, and peace.

This task is not separate and distinct from other elements of our foreign policy. It is a necessary part of all we are doing to build a peaceful world. It is as important as armed strength or economic aid. The Marshall Plan, military aid, Point Four—these and other programs depend for their success on the understanding and support of our own citizens and those of other countries.

We must make ourselves known as we really are—not as Communist propaganda pictures us. We must pool our efforts with those of the other free peoples in a sustained, intensified program to promote the cause of freedom against the propaganda of slavery. We must make ourselves heard round the world in a great campaign of truth.

We have tremendous advantages in the struggle for men's minds and loyalties. We have truth and freedom on our side. The appeal of free institutions and self-government springs from the deepest and noblest aspirations of mankind. It is based on every man's desire for liberty and opportunity. It is based on every man's wish to be self-reliant and to shape his own destiny.

As we go forward with our campaign of truth, we will make lasting progress toward the kind of world we seek—a world in which men and nations live not as enemies but as brothers.

A COOPERATIVE PEACE FOR ALL MANKIND: THE FREE FLOW OF INFORMATION AND ITS BALANCED PRESENTATION*

DWIGHT D. EISENHOWER
President of the United States

DWIGHT D. EISENHOWER *was a United States Army General and Commander of the NATO forces in Europe before he was elected the thirty-fourth President of the United States (1953–1961).*

. . . Eight years ago—almost to the day—I addressed the bureau of advertising. At that moment, the horror of war was a bitter memory of the recent past. A revulsion against war or any re-

*A speech delivered before the American Newspaper Publishers Association, New York, April 22, 1954.

minder of war possessed our people. The atmosphere was charged with emotionalism that could have destroyed our military strength. Fortunately, our newspapers did not then permit us, nor are they now permitting us, to forget the ever-present reality of aggressive threat.

Aggression is still a terrible reality, though on all of the continents and the islands of the earth, mankind hungers for peace. This universal hunger must be satisfied.

Either the nations will build a cooperative peace or, one by one, they will be forced to accept an imposed peace, now sought by the Communist powers as it was by Hitler.

But free men still possess the greater portion of the globe's resources and of the potential power to be produced from those resources. They possess scientific skill, intellectual capacity and sheer numbers in excess of those available to the Communist world. Consequently, free men can have a cooperative peace if with hearts and minds cleansed of fear and doubt together they dedicate themselves to it in unity and in understanding and in strength.

It is urgent that we try to clarify our thinking about the prospect. Let us start with our own present position. This nation is a marvel of production, rich in total wealth and individual earnings; powerful in a unique combination of scientific, military, economic and moral strength. For generations our country has been free from the devastation of war in her home land and is blessed with stanch and friendly neighbors. We covet no nation's possessions. We seek only the friendship of others. We are eager to repay this priceless gift in the same coin.

Surely, the United States—by all the standards of history—should possess a genuine peace and tranquility.

But our nation today is not truly tranquil. We, her people, face a grave danger, which, in essence at least, all of us understand. This danger, this peril calls for two far-reaching policies or purposes behind which all in our country should be solidly united. They are:

First: All our efforts must be bent to the strengthening of America in dedication to liberty; in knowledge and comprehension; in a dependable prosperity widely shared; and in an adequate military posture.

Second: This strength must be devoted to the building of a cooperative peace among men.

These are the fixed purposes of the vast majority of our people. But in a world of ideological division, competitive rivalry, turbulent crisis in one place and political upheaval in another, their achievement demands far more than good intentions or glowing words.

If we are to build and maintain the strength required to cope with the problems of this age, we must cooperate one with the other, every section with all others, each group with its neighbors. This means domestic unity, about which I talk incessantly. Unity does not imply rigid conformity to every doctrine or position of a particular political figure. But it does require a common devotion to the cardinal principles of our free system, shared knowledge and understanding of our own capacities and opportunities and a common determination to cooperate unreservedly in striving toward our truly important goals. This type of unity is the true source of our great energy—our spiritual, intellectual, material and creative energy.

Furthermore, our people, strong and united, must cooperate with other nations in helping to build a cooperative peace. Such cooperation requires the American people to increase their understanding of their fellowmen around the globe. Likewise, the nations beyond our shores must come to understand better the American people—particularly our hopes and our purposes. And, because of the relatively greater stake we have in world stability, because history has decreed that responsibility of leadership shall be placed upon the nation, we must take the initiative in the development of that genuine international understanding on which a cooperative peace must be built.

MUST END MISUNDERSTANDING

In these truths I find my justification for this appearance before you. The increase of understanding and knowledge is a task that cannot be accomplished solely by our schools or our churches or from political platforms. The malignant germs of misunderstanding and misinformation are at work in the minds of men twenty-four hours every day. To combat them challenges the study and the effort of every individual who occupies any position of influence on public opinion.

Every newspaper, every magazine, every radio and television

station has the mission of bringing home to all our people and to as many other people of the world as we can reach, the facts of existence today. But this is not enough.

Every agency of human communication also must help people achieve perspective with respect to facts. Suppose the American press should faithfully report the details of every crime committed in our country, but should be invariably silent on the apprehension and punishment of criminals. Would there not soon be created a universal impression of national lawlessness, disorder and anarchy? Facts must be related one to the other in truthful perspective. Only within such framework shall we reach clear decisions in the waging of the continuous struggle for a stronger America, a peaceful world.

Domestic unity and strength as well as international understanding depend, therefore, in great part on the free flow of information and its balanced presentation.

I am not suggesting that the cause of domestic unity would be served by any attempt of yours to slant the news, or to turn your news columns into editorials. The consequent loss of public respect and confidence would soon destroy the influence of the press. But I do believe most earnestly that the press should give emphasis to the things that unite the American people equal to that it gives to the things that divide them.

News of events which divide may be more spectacular than news of developments which unify. But a free press can discharge its responsibility to free people only by giving all the facts in balance. Facts in perspective are vital to valid citizen judgments. Sound judgment is crucial to the preservation of freedom. Hence a free press can sustain itself only by responsibly reporting all the facts and ideas—the spectacular and unspectacular, the unifying facts and the divisive.

NEWS NEEDS STRESSED

Could not reader-understanding be as powerful a criterion in newspaper offices as reader-interest?

Need these two qualities be incompatible? I think not. Certainly, the great journalists of our day, in critically examining and reporting on a legislative proposal, must inevitably deal with such constructive questions as:

Does it or does it not tend to sustain our economy; to provide needed military strength; to increase our understanding of others or others' understanding of us? Does it give us a more secure position internationally? Does it promise to preserve and nurture love of liberty and self-dependence among our people? Does it improve our health and our living standards? Does it insure to our children the kind of nation and government we have known?

If proposed laws and policies are described only as mere battle grounds on which individuals or parties seeking political power suffer defeat or achieve victory, then indeed is the American system distorted for us and for the world. If the fortunes of the individual supporting or opposing a measure become, in our public accounts, as important as the principle or purpose of the project and its effect upon the nation—then indeed are we failing to develop the strength that understanding brings. If the day comes when personal conflicts are more significant than honest debate on great policy, then the flame of freedom will flicker low indeed.

I trust you do not view my remarks as an attempt to tell you how to run your own business. I am, however, willing to take the risk of your misinterpretation. James Madison wrote: "A popular government without popular information or the means of acquiring it is but a prologue to a farce or to tragedy or perhaps both." So we are talking of a problem that the responsible governmental official cannot ignore, just as none of you can close your eyes to it.

We are not moving toward farce or tragedy. But knowledge of the facts and of their interrelationships is more than ever essential to the solution of human problems.

I know that to present the facts in perspective is a difficult task. The haste of living creates reader impatience. It discourages complete explanation and places a premium upon clichés and slogans. We incline to persuade with an attractive label, or to damn with a contemptuous tag.

CATCHWORDS NOT HELPFUL

But catchwords are not information. And, most certainly, sound popular judgments cannot be based upon them.

On the steady, day-by-day dissemination of complete information depends our people's intelligent participation in their own Government. For them that is no light thing. The decisions they must make are crucial in character and world-wide in scope. On them depends all the necessaries and comforts of life—from the amount of money in their pocketbooks, the pavement on their highways, the housing in their towns, to the sort of country they will leave behind as a heritage to their children. They need full and accurate information. Your newspapers can give it to them. On every question where they have it, their decisions will be sound.

Now if increased knowledge and understanding are necessary to promote the unity of our people, they are equally necessary to the development of international cooperation. At this juncture in world affairs, ignorance of each other's capacities, hopes, prejudices, beliefs and intentions can destroy cooperation and breed war.

Nowhere on this planet today is there an impregnable fortress, a continent or island so distant that it can ignore all the outer world. If this is not to be the age of atomic hysteria and horror, we must make it the age of international understanding and cooperative peace. Even the most rabid Marxist, the most ruthless worshipper of force, will in moments of sanity admit that. International understanding, however, like domestic unity, depends, in large part, on the free, full flow of information and its balanced presentation.

But recent reports state that 75 per cent of all the people who inhabit the earth live under censorship. Illiteracy affects vast numbers in many areas of the globe. And, of course, there are language and cultural barriers. Understanding cannot, under these circumstances, be easily or quickly achieved. Into the vacuum caused by censorship and illiteracy pours the positive and poisonous propaganda of the Soviets. For twenty-four hours each day it pours in.

The Communist propaganda machine, for instance, tirelessly tells the world that our free enterprise system inevitably must collapse in mass unemployment, industrial strife, financial bankruptcy. Time and again, communistic propaganda has shifted and reversed its tactics. But this one charge is firmly fixed in the party line from Marx to Malenkov.

Our United States Information Service, cooperating with similar efforts by friendly nations, seeks to combat propaganda with truth. Every dollar we put into it, when wisely used, will repay us dividends in the triumph of truth and the building of understanding. But our official information service is properly limited in purpose, as it is in size. The mass of information of us and to us must flow through the established publicity media of the several nations. Of all these we think ours the best and the most efficient.

Yet, a study in which, I am told, many of you cooperated shows that the average daily newspaper in the United States prints about four columns a day of news stories from abroad. I do not know whether this is too little, too much, or about right. But I do know that in this amount of daily space it is hard to inform the American people about relative happenings in all other countries.

Two-thirds of this foreign news was found to be about important official ceremonies and events in other countries—about their internal political crises, their foreign relations involvements, their official statements and pronouncements. Very little of the news had to do with the man in the street, or with his social, educational, cultural, civic and religious life and history. Yet an understanding of these is indispensable to an understanding of a nation.

The same specialists who studied this question also examined many European newspapers. There, too, news about the average American was scant. Those among you who have spent years abroad have undoubtedly been amazed by the frequency with which misleading or distorted opinions of our individual and national life are expressed by citizens of other countries.

It is always disconcerting to hear foreign friends speak disparagingly of the American civilization as a collection of shiny gadgets. It is alarming to know that we are considered so immature in world politics as to be ready to provoke a war needlessly and recklessly. It is even worse to learn that we are often judged as power-hungry as the men in the Kremlin.

Because of a tragic failure to understand us and our purposes, the citizen of Western Europe frequently looks upon America and the U.S.S.R. as two great power complexes, each seeking only the most propitious moment in which to crush the other by force. He believes also that, in the meantime, each seeks alliances with nations throughout Europe with the sole purpose of using them as pawns when the moment of crisis arrives.

PEACE BY COOPERATION

We know that we seek only peace by cooperation among equals. Success in this great purpose requires that all others know this also.

As individuals we are frequently pictured abroad as rich, indifferent to all values other than money, careless of the rights of others and ignorant of the contributions others have made to the progress of western civilization.

Undoubtedly these misconceptions are partially the result of Communist propaganda. But they flourish in the lack of comprehensive, truthful two-way information.

Here at home we need fuller and better information of others if we are wisely to direct our policies toward real security. Many of us incorrectly assume that all other countries would like to live under a system identical or similar to ours. Some believe that all foreigners are lazy or decadent, that few pay taxes, that they hate us for the sole reason that we are prosperous. We hear often that the people of a particular nation are cowardly, or have no love of country or pride in their citizenship. Too often we think of them as physically weak, intellectually shallow and spiritually defeated.

Of course there are individuals everywhere who fit these descriptions, but it is dangerous to us and to peace when we carelessly speak in generalities of this kind, characterizing an entire nation.

We live in a small world, and only by a cooperative effort of the free peoples occupying important areas can we build security and peace. It is not a question of turning the press, radio, television and newsreels into media of sugar-coated propaganda, "selling" America to the Frenchman, France to the German and Britain to the American.

It is quite different from that. I repeat: for understanding we need the facts and the perspective within which they fit. I am sure that the free press in all free countries has made real progress in this direction. But I think a lot more can, and by all means should, be done. The future of all of us depends upon it.

No group can be more effective in such accomplishment than you of the American Newspaper Publishers Association. Here, indeed, is an endeavor worthy of your talents and skills.

MILLIONS ON OUR SIDE

Within the framework of friendly alliances, we are joined with hundreds of millions among the free nations in working agreements, primarily concerned with military security, but inescapably dealing with every hope and every concern of daily life. Together we live in a mighty arena bounded by the Polar regions, particularly encircling the globe, peopled by men and women of independent nations. These peoples, with scanty information and understanding of one another, are now allies of convenience under Communist threat; but tomorrow they could be full partners permanently joined in mutual understanding, impelled by common aspirations. Among the nations of that vast arena, at least, war can become unthinkable— quickly. A cooperative peace among them is no mirage of the dreamer.

Within the United Nations we possess a global forum where we can plead the cause of peace so that even the men of the Kremlin must listen. Their ears may be stopped to the spirit of our words. Their minds, however, cannot forever be shut to the facts of the age within which we—and they—must live, physically separated one from the other by a few hours of flight.

We cannot hope with a few speeches, a few conferences, a few agreements to achieve the most difficult of all human goals—a co-operative peace for all mankind.

Here may I say, my friends, that your representatives in the diplomatic world have no other thought or no other purpose than that which I have just stated—the achievement of a co-operative peace among the free nations. And eventually to enlarge that by appealing to the common sense, representing the facts of the world as they are today to all others, so that even the Iron Wall must crumble and all men be enjoined together. . . .

V

─────────

Cessation of Nuclear Testing: A Case Study in Propaganda of the *Word*

The stream of propaganda in the cold war runs full all the time. It covers many subjects and in many ways. There are some issues, however, which seem to get more play than others and which continue in the forefront of psychological exchange for years. The "nuclear testing" issue is one of these. It is important as a domestic issue in every nation which possesses nuclear capabilities and in some which could have such programs if they decided to initiate them. It is an international issue not only between the United States and the Soviet Union but one also involving almost every nation in which fallout is a real or an imagined problem.

Official Announcements

Five official documents are quoted below. They are arranged in chronological order beginning with the announcement of unilateral suspension of nuclear testing by the Soviet Union on

March 31, 1958. Two official American reactions are included: A State Department reply of the same day and Secretary Dulles' news conference the following day. The last two documents are letters exchanged by Communist Party First Secretary Khrushchev and President Eisenhower.

TEXT OF SOVIET ANNOUNCEMENT*

The question of the cessation of atomic and hydrogen weapon tests gains a greater significance for the cause of peace and the welfare of the people with every year and with every month. At the present moment the cessation of tests is demanded by the overwhelming majority of the world's population.

Despite the fact that for many years now people have persisted in their demands for the termination of these tests, the tests continue to be held, a circumstance which leads to the creation of new types of lethal nuclear weapons, increases the concentration of radioactive elements in air and soil, poisons human organisms, and threatens the normal development of further generations.

The Soviet Union has made persistent and consistent efforts aimed at reaching agreement with the powers in possession of atomic and hydrogen weapons, on the subject of immediate and unconditional termination of nuclear tests. For this purpose the U.S.S.R. Supreme Soviet and the Soviet Government reiterated over the past few years concrete proposals for terminating the tests, on the basis of which an accord on this matter could have been achieved a long time ago.

In the appeal to the U.S. Congress and the British Parliament of May 10, 1957, the U.S.S.R. Supreme Soviet called upon the U.S. Congress and the British Parliament to cooperate in concluding an agreement between the governments of the U.S.S.R., the United

---

* Text of a decree passed by the Supreme Soviet of the U.S.S.R. on March 31, 1958, following an address by the Soviet Foreign Minister, Andrei A. Gromyko. Reprinted from the *Department of State Bulletin*, Vol. 38 (April 21, 1958).

States, and Great Britain on an immediate termination of the experimental explosion of atomic and hydrogen bombs. At its last session, in December 1957, the U.S.S.R. Supreme Soviet, expressing the striving of the Soviet people toward peace, proposed that the U.S.S.R., Great Britain, and the United States take upon themselves the obligation to terminate, from Jan. 1, 1958, all tests of atomic and hydrogen weapons.

However, the United States and Great Britain did not respond to these proposals of the U.S.S.R. Consequently, experimental explosions of atomic and hydrogen bombs are continuing in various parts of the globe as before, a fact which bears witness to the further intensification in the field of production of ever more dangerous types of mass destruction weapons.

Guided by the endeavor to make a practical beginning to a universal termination of atomic and hydrogen weapon tests, and thus to make the first step in the direction of the final salvation of mankind from the threat of destructive atomic war, the U.S.S.R. Supreme Soviet decides:

1. To terminate tests in the Soviet Union of all types of atomic and nuclear weapons. The U.S.S.R. Supreme Soviet expects that the parliaments of other states in possession of atomic and hydrogen weapons will, on their part, do everything in their power in order that experimental explosions of these types of weapons will be terminated also in those countries.

2. To charge the U.S.S.R. Council of Ministers with undertaking the necessary measures aimed at the implementation of the first point of this decision and with making an approach to the governments of other states possessing atomic and hydrogen weapons with an appeal for the adoption of analogous measures so as to secure the termination of atomic and hydrogen tests everywhere and forever.

Should the other powers that possess atomic and hydrogen weapons continue to test these weapons, then the Government of the Soviet Union will, understandably, act freely in the question of the testing of atomic and hydrogen weapons in the Soviet Union, in conformity with the above mentioned circumstances, and bearing the interests of the security of the Soviet Union in mind.

The U.S.S.R. Supreme Soviet sincerely hopes that the initiative of the Soviet Union for the cessation of nuclear weapons tests will receive due support from the parliaments of other states and is profoundly convinced that if, in response to the decision of the Soviet Union, other states possessing nuclear weapons should in their turn cease testing these weapons, then by this very act an important practical stride will have been taken on the road to the consolidation of peace and the strengthening of the security of all peoples.

Such a step would undoubtedly have great significance as regards the restoring of the whole of the international situation to health and would be conducive to the liberation of mankind from oppressive alarm for the fate of the world, for the fate of future generations.

THE SUPREME SOVIET OF THE U.S.S.R.
Moscow, the Kremlin, March 31, 1958.

UNITED STATES VIEWS ON SOVIET ANNOUNCEMENT OF CESSATION OF BOMB TESTS*

The Soviet statement about nuclear testing will, of course, be studied in detail. But some general observations can be made at once.

The Soviet statement comes on the heels of an intensive series of secret Soviet tests. They should arouse world opinion to the need to deal in an orderly and dependable way with the testing and related aspects of the disarmament problem.

Soviet official propaganda incessantly seeks to create abroad the image of a peace-loving Soviet Government. But that same Government openly defies the United Nations with respect to both the substance and the procedure of disarmament.

The charter of the United Nations gives that organization

* Department of State statement on March 31, 1958, regarding an announcement by the Union of Soviet Socialist Republics that it would terminate tests in the Soviet Union of all types of atomic and nuclear weapons. Reprinted from the *Department of State Bulletin*, Vol. 38 (April 21, 1958).

broad authority with reference to principles of disarmament and the regulation of armaments. In the exercise of that authority the United Nations General Assembly has, by an overwhelming vote, approved a comprehensive first-stage disarmament proposal and called on the nations concerned to begin at once technical studies as to how these proposals might be carried out. These studies included the studies needed for a supervised suspension of nuclear testing. The United States stands ready instantly to respond to that resolution. But the Soviet Union refuses to comply.

The same General Assembly reconstituted and enlarged its Disarmament Commission. The United States wants that Commission to carry out its mandate. But the Soviet Union boycotts the Commission.

The charter makes the Security Council responsible for formulating plans for the establishment of a system for the regulation of armaments. The United States has recently proposed to the Soviet Union that this responsibility be discharged. But the Soviet Union refuses to cooperate.

The Soviet Government declines to deal with the subject of armament in any of the several ways prescribed by the United Nations Charter. It prefers elusive formulations of its own.

It is elemental that free nations which want to remain free will not, and should not, forgo their indispensable collective capacity to deter and defend against aggression merely in reliance on a Soviet statement of intentions for which there is no system of verification, which can be evaded in secrecy and altered at will.

The United States again calls on the Soviet Union to deal with the vital problem of disarmament in an orderly way, in accordance with the United Nations Charter, to which the signature of the Soviet Union is affixed. That charter constitutes a solemn agreement. If it is nullified by the Soviet Union, why should the world place confidence in new Soviet engagements?

SECRETARY DULLES' NEWS
CONFERENCE OF APRIL 1, 1958*

SECRETARY DULLES: I am ready for questions.

QUESTION: Mr. Secretary, yesterday was the Soviet announcement about suspending nuclear tests. A lot of the practical aspects of this seem to be missing. For example, do you have any information through diplomatic channels as to when the suspension would become effective and how long it would last, under what circumstances it might be terminated? If you don't have such information, which would bear up details of it, are we correct in reading into yesterday's statement the implication that in your view this whole announcement is just phony?

ANSWER: The last part is easier to answer than the first. We do not think that there is anything new of substance in the statement made yesterday by Mr. [Andrei A.] Gromyko [Soviet Foreign Minister].

To go to the earlier part of your question, we have no information through diplomatic channels or any other channels as to the details of the proposed suspension. The Soviets have just concluded their most intensive series of tests, and it would be normal, almost inevitable, that there would be a considerable lapse between that series of tests and the inauguration of a new series of tests. We have always found that that was inevitable in our own practice. We have not had any tests for some little time. We are resuming some the latter part of this month, I believe. So that some periodic suspensions of testing are, from a technical standpoint, a necessity.

Now the Soviets say that they will suspend testing but that, if we resume testing, they reserve the right to resume it. Now, of course, they know that we have this series of tests which has been planned and announced for many months and which will start in the very near future. Therefore, as far as the language of the pronouncement is concerned, they would be free to resume tests at any time in the light of the fact that we expect to begin testing within the next few weeks.

QUESTION: Mr. Secretary, what is the United States policy on the

* Reprinted from *The Department of State Bulletin*, Vol. 38 (April 21, 1958).

nuclear testing? For example, have any of the studies been concluded within the administration on the possibility of our halting such tests?

ANSWER: We have always been willing to halt tests as part of a program which would lead to the effective elimination of nuclear weapons from the arsenals of the nations. Now, the problem has been whether or not to suspend testing without any such elimination. That raises some very serious problems which have been known and discussed for some time.

The actual situation today is that the Soviet Union has, as we have, enough large thermonuclear weapons to destroy the other and perhaps a large part of humanity. The Soviet Union is willing apparently to let it go at that. We are not willing to let it go at that. We want to do either of two things: either to cut down on this and to eliminate nuclear weapons effectively from the international arsenals, or, if that is not going to be done, to develop the weapons so that they can be effectively used as a defensive weapon without a mass destruction of humanity. Either course seems to us to be one which we could choose. We prefer the first choice—have always preferred the first choice.

The Baruch plan, offered some ten years ago, would have prevented any thermonuclear atomic weapons. The Eisenhower proposals for atoms-for-peace, followed by the more detailed proposals made in the Disarmament Subcommittee, would have led to the gradual elimination under effective controls of nuclear weapons through the transfer from war stocks to peace stocks of the existing stockpiles. That is what we want; that is what we are going to try to get; but that, so far, the Soviet Union has rejected.

Now if that rejection is final and we have to go along with this situation, then, as a country which is governed by humane considerations, which do not always apply to some other countries and governments, we want to get away, if we can, from having these weapons inevitably involve a vast destruction of humanity and turn them into smaller, tactical, cleaner weapons which can be used effectively for defensive purposes without this great possible danger to humanity. Also, I may say, develop their uses for peaceful purposes.

Our first preference, of course, is the original preference indicated by the Baruch plan and by our more recent plans to have an effective way of getting rid of them. If you can't do that, then the question is, do you keep them only in such shape that they then threaten the existence of humanity or do you refine them, develop them into distinctive, discriminating weapons which can be used defensively for military purposes?

QUESTION: Mr. Secretary, it was reported on the Moscow proposal in an Italian newspaper that Mr. Khrushchev stated, "United States atomic bases undermine Italy's security because they might become a means for attacking other countries without Italian knowledge." I wonder, Mr. Secretary, whether you care to say anything about such statements?

ANSWER: The reference, I suppose, is to the possible establishment of intermediate-missiles bases in Italy?

QUESTION: Yes.

ANSWER: I may say, if that is the case, first, there is no such agreement at the present time. And the pattern for any such agreements has been set by our arrangement with the United Kingdom, where it is expressly stipulated that there cannot be any use of those bases except with the consent and participation of the Government of the United Kingdom, and the same would presumably apply to Italy.

DEVELOPMENT OF SMALLER, CLEANER WEAPONS

QUESTION: Mr. Secretary, what is your understanding from the scientific advice you have as to how long it would take, in terms of testing, for the United States to develop a weapon, a smaller, cleaner, tactical weapon, if that is the choice that has to be made?

ANSWER: I don't recall that any date has been put on this by our advisers. I think we will know a great deal more about it after the conclusion of the now projected series of tests. It is never possible in advance of testing to know just what the tests will show. But we would hope, at least, that much of the information that we want will be obtained from the present series of tests.

Now there is another aspect of the matter, which probably will not be resolved by the present series of tests, and that is the possible use of nuclear power to create a defense against intercontinental or intermediate missiles. That is a phase of the matter which has not yet developed to a point where we would, I think, expect to get any definitive results out of the present series. But, as far as it relates to the making of smaller, cleaner weapons, it could very well be that

that area would be pretty well exhausted by the present series of tests or perhaps supplementary tests that might be conducted entirely in a sealed compartment underground so that there would be no danger at all of any fallout or effect on human life.

QUESTION: Mr. Secretary, do we have any evidence of the nature of this recent series of Soviet tests, specifically whether or not they may have tested the smaller, cleaner, defensive type of weapons you are talking about?

ANSWER: Well, our knowledge, of course, depends upon what we pick up. And, for instance, we know what we know, but we don't know what we don't know. Now we cannot know whether or not there have been tests of which we have not gained any knowledge by the instruments that we have outside for detection purposes. The information that we have indicates that the tests have covered a considerable range from the smaller type measured in kilotons to the larger type measured in megatons. But it is entirely possible that there have been tests of still smaller weapons—that we haven't, perhaps, picked up yet. That we don't know.

QUESTION: Have any of these tests been announced within the Soviet Union—I mean, since February 22?

ANSWER: I think, in fact I am quite certain, that there has been no announcement made within the Soviet Union. There was one announcement made some months ago in the Soviet Union of a single test. But in the main these tests have been conducted in an atmosphere of complete secrecy, insofar as the Soviet Union could impose complete secrecy, and that has been total insofar as its own people have been concerned, with the one exception which, I think, occurred last fall.

QUESTION: Mr. Secretary, when you say there was no substance-- I think that was the phrase you used—in this announcement of yesterday, what do you mean by that?

ANSWER: What I mean by that is that it has added nothing to what has been known for quite a long time—that is, that the Soviet Union would like to bring about a cessation of testing on the part of the United States and itself and the United Kingdom and any third countries. They want to do that, however, quite apart from and unrelated to any program for doing away with the weapons themselves. Now they talk about banning the bomb and so forth, but they have neither proposed nor have they been willing to accept any program which would effectively bring about any diminution in the accumulation of weapons stockpiles.

QUESTION: Mr. Secretary, didn't they make such a proposal last August 29?

ANSWER: No, not that I am aware of. We proposed a cutoff in the use of fissionable material. We also proposed that weapons stocks be diminished in some proportion to be agreed upon. We didn't say on a basis of equality. We pointed out that probably we have larger stocks of fissionable material than the Soviets had and therefore that we would assume that their contribution from war stocks to peace stocks should be proportionately less than our own. But they have never accepted either of those proposals.

QUESTION: Mr. Secretary, in one of your previous comments I believe you said—you referred to the now projected series of tests. Is any thought being given to calling off these tests?

ANSWER: No, no thought has been given to calling them off. . . .

PROPAGANDA ADVANTAGES WEIGHED

QUESTION: Mr. Secretary, regardless of the validity, or lack of it, of Mr. Gromyko's announcement yesterday, do you not agree that it is a fact that it has put us sharply—"us" meaning the West—sharply on the defensive, from a propaganda point of view? And is it not necessary for us to respond in a way beyond the initial apparent impact of calling it little more than an April Fool's joke?

ANSWER: I think that it has given them a certain propaganda victory, or at least a success, and I may say that in that respect we are not surprised.

We had a meeting recently of the principal top officials involved in this situation with President Eisenhower. And we discussed very seriously this prospect and the question of whether it would be wise and prudent and in the best interests of the United States to try to steal a march on the Soviets by ourselves announcing a suspension of testing, at least for a time. We weighed very carefully all the pros and cons, and particularly some of these things that I have alluded to—the fact that unless there can be a program which goes to the heart of this problem, namely, the existence of nuclear weapons, we really ought to try to make these weapons into something that could be usable without vast human destruction and which could make progress toward their utility as more of a tactical weapon.

Now I don't say that they ever will be a very nice thing to be hit by. But it wasn't very nice to be hit by all the bombing that hit Berlin or by the fire bombs that were dropped on Tokyo. But there is a difference between a weapon which will destroy on impact a very considerable area and a weapon which through fallout will destroy or impair human life through areas of a thousand miles or more of diameter. We considered this problem, and we decided that we could not, in fairness to our responsibilities and our duties to the American people, perhaps to humanity, desist in a program which we believe to be sound, merely for propaganda advantages. We deliberately accepted this propaganda thrust, knowing we were going to have to take it, rather than do something which we felt was basically unsound.

Now we operate, I think, under some disadvantages from a propaganda standpoint. We operate under conditions that are totally different from those which surround the Soviet Union.

We operate, as is visible right here, in terms of a free and independent and highly intelligent press. If I came before you with something that was a phony, you would recognize it in a minute and tear it apart publicly.

We operate in terms of an opposition political party, which is alert and prepared to expose, here at home and for reporting abroad, anything which does not seem to be thoroughly sound.

We operate in terms of an American public opinion which is highly intelligent and properly critical of its Government—when I say "critical," I don't mean necessarily antagonistic but which holds government up to high standards.

And we operate with allies who have to be consulted; they are not just dummies that we can lay down the law to, like the Soviet satellites are.

Now all of those conditions make it very difficult for us to carry on a type of propaganda such as the Soviets carry on. I don't say that we are doing the best job that we can do—I know we are not; we ought to do it better. But I do say that we face conditions which are totally different from those of the Soviet Union, and I thank God that we do. I wouldn't for a minute give up, in order to get a propaganda advantage in the world, any of these things I have talked about. I wouldn't give up our free press; I wouldn't give up our intelligent political opposition; I wouldn't give up the dedication of the American people to high principles; and I wouldn't give up our allies' being free people that we have to work with, persuade, consult with, and we just can't shoot from the hip without regard to their views.

Now I think these things which we cherish so much, which are an inherent part of our free world, have to be retained and not sacrificed in an effort to get propaganda advantage. And, indeed, I don't think we could get a pure propaganda advantage in the face of those conditions of our free society, which we honor and cherish and which we would never forgo merely to get conditions for a more effective propaganda.

I recall back in the United Nations in '49, I think it was, when Mr. Vyshinsky made a great speech. He said, "We are not using atomic energy for war purposes; we are only using atomic energy to move mountains, to shift rivers, for irrigation purposes," and so forth and so on. Why, it was just a wonderful speech. There wasn't a single word of truth in it, and it was never printed, of course, in the Soviet Union.

Well, do we want to have conditions where we can pull off propaganda stunts of that sort? Surely we do not.

Here you had yesterday the Head of the Government of the Soviet Union quietly removed—not a word of praise, not a word of blame, not a word of explanation. He just goes back to being a teller in a bank. (*Laughter*) Well, we don't want conditions like that in this country.

QUESTION: Mr. Secretary, could you tell us whether this meeting of which you spoke was last week?

ANSWER: Well now, when you fix me on the date, I can't say. It was within ten days or two weeks.

QUESTION: Mr. Secretary, returning to those alternatives that you outlined at the beginning, are we to understand you to mean that, when we have achieved a smaller, cleaner, tactical bomb, we will then be prepared to eliminate from our atomic arsenal the megaton bombs and the kiloton bombs?

ANSWER: Well, this operation that I refer to involves a considerable making over of existing weapons into smaller or cleaner weapons. In other words, it is a process of transformation. You don't throw them away; the material is too valuable.

QUESTION: But will we not retain any of the megaton bombs and kiloton bombs in the arsenal?

ANSWER: I just don't know what the program is in that respect, and it is quite a long ways off before we could get to that, and I think that is a rather academic question at the moment. I assume we might retain some, but that will be a military decision, probably to be made maybe five or ten years from now.

QUESTION OF SHARING NUCLEAR INFORMATION

QUESTION: Mr. Secretary, there is considerable doubt on the Hill about the administration's proposal to share nuclear military information with allied governments. The chief point of opposition appears to be a fear that this will encourage the development of fourth-country nuclear powers. Can you give any assurance that it is not this Government's intention to do anything that would help fourth nuclear powers, beginning with France?

ANSWER: The program which we have, which permits of sharing some of our nuclear knowledge with our allies, is not designed to, nor would it be used primarily to, expand the number of countries which have nuclear weapons. However, the idea that we can stop that expansion by trying to keep our information secret is illusory. Today, with atomic material increasingly being used for power purposes around the world, with increasing knowledge about the art, it is no great trick. It takes some money, but almost anybody who has enough money and some reasonably educated scientists can make at least a crude atomic or nuclear weapon, and the crude ones are the worst from the standpoint of their damaging effect on vast masses of people.

I believe myself that a program which enables the United States with discrimination to share its knowledge is more apt to keep the development of nuclear weapons under control than a very futile effort, thinking that we can stop this movement by not sharing our knowledge. And, of course, not sharing our knowledge with some countries—like the United Kingdom, which has already got a program of this sort—strikes me as a complete folly. All that it does is it calls for a vast duplication of expense. It is very silly for the United Kingdom, which is cooperating with us in this type of program, to have to spend hundreds of millions of pounds to learn something which we can give it for nothing, and then we may have to help them out economically in order to make up for the unnecessary financial burden that we imposed upon them for nuclear weapons. . . .

LETTER FROM KHRUSHCHEV
TO EISENHOWER*

DEAR MR. PRESIDENT:

One of the most urgent problems in present international relations which very deeply agitates millions of people in all countries of the world is that of the necessity of the immediate discontinuance of tests of atomic and hydrogen weapons of various kinds. It is easy to understand the deep alarm which the continuing experimental explosions of nuclear weapons arouse among all strata of society, from political personages, scientists, and specialists to ordinary people, the rank-and-file workers of city and village, to mothers of families. These tests stimulate the armaments race and promote the development of new and ever more destructive and deadly kinds of nuclear weapons, and thereby still further intensify the threat of atomic war which hangs over mankind.

Moreover, systematic explosions of atomic and hydrogen weapons for experimental purposes even now, in peacetime, are causing damage to the health of peaceful, unsuspecting, and entirely innocent inhabitants of various countries. In the petition signed by 9235 scientists of 44 countries, including many prominent scientists of the United States of America and of the Soviet Union, and delivered in January of this year to the Secretary General of the United Nations, it is stated that each test of a nuclear bomb increases the quantity of radioactive fallout, thereby causing harm to the health of people throughout the entire world and threatening the normal development of coming generations.

* Reprinted from the *Department of State Bulletin*, Vol. 38 (April 21, 1958).

Taking all this into account the Soviet government has come to the conclusion that it is impossible to postpone any longer the solution of the question concerning the discontinuance of nuclear weapon tests because it is impossible to allow the health of the people to be irreparably harmed.

Today only three powers so far—the U.S.S.R., the U.S.A., and Great Britain—possess nuclear weapons, and therefore an agreement on the discontinuance of nuclear weapon tests is comparatively easy to reach. However, if the tests are not now discontinued, then after some time other countries may become possessors of nuclear weapons and under such conditions it will of course be a more complicated matter to reach an agreement on the discontinuance of the tests.

During the last three years the Soviet government has repeatedly approached the governments of the United States of America and of Great Britain with proposals to discontinue tests of atomic and hydrogen weapons. In as much as both the Government of the United States and the Government of Great Britain have not wished to agree to discontinue nuclear tests without specifying a time limit, the Soviet Union advanced a proposal of its own, that is, to discontinue these tests, at first even for a limited time, for two or three years, for example. The proposals of the U.S.S.R. on this question provide for the establishment of the necessary international control for the discontinuance of tests.

Despite all this, it has unfortunately been impossible up to now to come to an agreement for settling the question concerning an unconditional and immediate discontinuance of nuclear tests, or even concerning a temporary suspension.

Guided by the desire to make a practical beginning to the discontinuance of tests of atomic and hydrogen weapons everywhere and thereby take the first step in the direction of a final liberation of mankind from the threat of a destructive atomic war, the Supreme Soviet of the Union of Soviet Socialist Republics has decreed the discontinuance in the Soviet Union of tests of all kinds of atomic and hydrogen weapons.

The Soviet Government, implementing this decree of the Supreme Soviet of the U.S.S.R., *decided to discontinue unilaterally, as of March 31, 1958, tests of any kind of atomic and hydrogen weapons.*

The Soviet Government addresses to the Government of the United States of America, and also to the Government of Great Britain, a proposal to join in these measures.

If the governments of the countries which now have nuclear weapons at their disposal support this proposal of the U.S.S.R. and in their turn adopt a decision to renounce further tests, then the question which so deeply agitates the peoples of the whole world will finally be resolved and a great step will thereby be taken toward the establishment of genuine trust among states and toward the strengthening of peace.

However, if the governments of the countries with the nuclear weapons at their disposal do not wish to respond to this decision of the Soviet Government and prefer to leave things as they were before and continue experiments with atomic and hydrogen weapons, then in such case the Soviet Union, in the interests of ensuring its own safety, will of course have no alternative other than that of considering itself freed from any obligation undertaken by it in regard to the discontinuance of nuclear tests. The Soviet Government would not like to see matters take such a course.

The Government of the U.S.S.R. expresses the sincere hope that the Government of the United States of America will join in the initiative of the Soviet Union and will thereby make possible the discontinuance forever of nuclear weapon tests everywhere.

In the opinion of the Soviet Government it would be appropriate if our two countries—the U.S.S.R. and the U.S.A., which were the first to create atomic and hydrogen weapons and to possess considerable stocks of these weapons—would come forth as leaders in the noble cause of the immediate cessation of nuclear tests.

This first practical step on the path toward the protection of mankind against the calamities with which it is threatened by modern nuclear weapons would enormously facilitate the advance toward a solution of the problem, that is, the complete liberation of peoples from the threat of an atomic war. Hardly anyone will deny that the discontinuance of experiments with atomic and hydrogen weapons would greatly improve the international political atmosphere as a whole and would create more favorable conditions for the settlement of other unsolved international problems.

Permit me, Mr. President, to express the hope that the proposals of the Soviet Government stated above will meet with a favorable attitude on the part of the Government of the United States of America.

With sincere esteem,

N. KHRUSHCHEV

April 4, 1958

EISENHOWER'S REPLY TO
KHRUSHCHEV*

DEAR MR. CHAIRMAN:

I have your communication of April 4 repeating, in substance, the already widely publicized statement of the Soviet Government with reference to the suspension of nuclear testing.

It seems peculiar that the Soviet Union, having just concluded a series of tests of unprecedented intensity, should now, in bold headlines, say that it will not test again, but add, in small type, that it may test again if the United States carries out its already long announced and now imminent series of tests.

The timing, wording, and manner of the Soviet declaration cannot but raise questions as to its real significance.

The position of the United States on this matter of testing is well-known. For several years we have been seeking a dependable ending to the accumulation of nuclear weapons and a dependable beginning of the steady reduction of existing weapons stockpiles. This was my "Atoms for Peace" proposal, made in 1953 before the United Nations. Surely, the heart of the nuclear problem is not the mere testing of weapons, but the weapons themselves. If weapons are dependably dealt with, then it is natural to suspend their testing. However, the Soviet Union continues to reject the concept of an internationally supervised program to end weapons production and to reduce weapons stocks. Under those circumstances of the Soviets' making, the United States seeks to develop the defensive rather than the offensive capabilities of nuclear power and to learn how to minimize the fissionable fallout.

It goes without saying that these experiments, so far as the United States is concerned, are so conducted that they cannot appreciably affect human health.

Perhaps, Mr. Chairman, you recall the Joint Declaration made by the Governments of the United Kingdom and the United States at Bermuda on March 24, 1957. We then declared that we would conduct nuclear tests only in such a manner as would keep world radiation from rising to more than a small fraction of the levels that

* Reprinted from the *Department of State Bulletin*, Vol. 38 (April 21, 1958).

might be hazardous. We went on to say that we would continue publicly announcing our test series well in advance of their occurrence with information as to their location and general timing.

We further said that we would be willing to register with the United Nations advance notice of our intention to conduct future nuclear tests and to permit limited international observation of such tests if the Soviet Union would do the same.

The Soviet Union has never responded to that invitation. Its latest series of tests was conducted behind a cloak of secrecy, so far as the Soviet Union could make it so. Nevertheless, as I recently stated, it is the intention of the United States to invite observation by the United Nations of certain of our forthcoming tests.

Not only did the Soviet Union ignore our Bermuda proposal on testing, but it has persistently rejected the substance of my "Atoms for Peace" proposal. It refuses to agree to an internationally supervised cut-off of the use of new fissionable material for weapons purposes and the reduction of existing weapons stocks by transfers to peaceful purposes. During the five years since I first proposed "Atoms for Peace," the destructive power in our nuclear arsenals has steadily mounted, and a dependably controlled reduction of that power becomes ever more difficult.

Mr. Chairman, now that you have become head of the Soviet Government, will you not reconsider your Government's position and accept my proposal that fissionable materials henceforth be manufactured only for peaceful purposes?

If the Soviet Union is as peace-loving as it professes, surely it would want to bring about an internationally supervised diversion of fissionable material from weapons purposes to peace purposes.

If the Soviet Union is unwilling to accept "Atoms for Peace," there are other outstanding proposals by which the Soviet Union can advance the cause of peace. You will recall, Mr. Chairman, my "Open Skies" proposal made to you and Chairman Bulganin in Geneva in 1955. You will also recall my proposals for the international use of outer space for peaceful purposes emphasized in my recent correspondence with Chairman Bulganin. These proposals await Soviet acceptance.

The United States is also prepared, in advance of agreement upon any one or more of the outstanding "disarmament" propositions, to work with the Soviet Union, and others as appropriate, on the technical problems involved in international controls. We both recognize that international control would be necessary. Indeed, your present letter to me speaks of "the establishment of the necessary 'international control for the discontinuance of tests."

What is "necessary"? The question raises problems of considerable complexity, given the present possibility of conducting some types of tests under conditions of secrecy.

If there is ever to be an agreed limitation or suspension of testing, and the United States hopes and believes that this will in due course come about as part of a broad disarmament agreement, plans for international control should be in instant readiness. Why should we not at once put our technicians to work to study together and advise as to what specific control measures are necessary if there is to be a dependable and agreed disarmament program?

The United Nations General Assembly has called for technical disarmament studies, in relation both to nuclear and conventional armaments. The United States says "yes." I urge, Mr. Chairman, that the Soviet Union should also say "yes." Then we can at once begin the preliminaries necessary to larger things.

Sincerely,
DWIGHT D. EISENHOWER

Press Reactions in the United States and Japan

If it were the purpose of this book to study the nuclear testing question per se, many other aspects of the problem would have to be covered. Most of them are pertinent also to the single subject of the Soviet announcement as propaganda.

To get a complete picture of its propaganda effect one would have to study the announcement's reception in many different parts of the world. The following readings give a brief idea of reactions in the United States and Japan.

IT'S OUR MOVE NOW*

We hardly thought it could happen again, but it has. It was only yesterday, it seems, that we ran an editorial entitled "Thank You, Sputnik!" Now, much as we resent it, we have to thank the men in the Kremlin again—this time for their announcement that they are suspending their tests of atomic weapons.

Our gratitude, unlike the effusions pouring into Moscow from other parts of the world, is not for Soviet motives, which will continue to be grounded on their own self-interest, whether economic, political, or strategic. Nor is it for their recently concluded series of atomic tests, which have contributed heavily to the world's perambulant cloud of radioactive fallout and, according to the AEC, to the fact that the northeastern part of the United States, where we happen to live, is now "one of the hottest places in the world." Our gratitude is rather for the fact that the Soviets have administered a further shock—not to our national complacency, which vanished along with Sputnik I and full employment—but to the caution in Washington which replaced that complacency, and which has produced much the same kind of policymaking inertia.

For whether Mr. Dulles likes it or not, this latest Soviet move makes our acceptance of a summit conference inevitable. The nettle has been presented to us with all the world looking on, and prickles and all, we must grasp it. Had we grasped it sooner, rather than haggling over preliminary details, we could be arriving at the summit with greater bargaining power. At least we could have more to say about the agenda. As it is, the principal item on the agenda has already been established by the Kremlin: it will certainly be the suspension of atomic tests and the related problems of inspection and cutoff of production. By the time we arrive at the summit, having presumably completed our own scheduled tests in the Pacific, the Soviets may well have stolen a further march by announcing a unilateral ban on production.

When the President called the Soviet test suspension "a gimmick," he was not affronting the Kremlin, as some have asserted; he was simply handing Mr. Khrushchev another means of per-

* Reprinted from *The Reporter,* Vol. 18 (April 17, 1958), p. 2.

suading the world that Washington, listening only to men of narrow vision and special commitments, has become indifferent to the growing clamor for nuclear disarmament and considers it, in the words of Edward Teller, "a lost cause." The truth is, as the President and his advisers know very well, that it is not Soviet power but the power of public opinion—and only incidentally Mr. Khrushchev's exploitation of it—that is forcing us to the conference table.

Yet so far our leaders have not managed to turn this knowledge to America's advantage. It is unnerving to contemplate, but it would seem to be the Soviet leaders rather than our own who are moving us toward a fuller exercise of our national resources and skills. The first satellite that they flung into orbit drove us to new exertions in technology, science, and education. Their suspension of tests demands of us a more aggressive and imaginative use of diplomacy, another of our national resources that has been suffering somewhat from disuse.

JAPANESE REACTION TO SOVIET A-TEST HALT STATEMENT*

The Soviet declaration of March 31 on the suspension of nuclear tests was welcomed in Japan. While expressing some doubt as to the motives of the Soviet Union in making the declaration, both Japanese Government and press circles emphasized their hope that the United States and Great Britain would also suspend their nuclear tests.

PRIME MINISTER'S STATEMENT

At a press conference on April 2, Prime Minister Kishi stated the views of the Japanese Government on the Soviet declaration. Following is a translation of his statement:

* Reprinted from the *Japan Report,* issued by the Consulate General of Japan, San Francisco (April 20, 1958), pp. 4-7.

"The Supreme Soviet of the USSR recently adopted a resolution for unilateral suspension of nuclear tests.

"While the true motives of the Soviet Union regarding this decision are not necessarily clear and even though the Soviet Union has reserved the freedom to resume nuclear tests, the statement to the effect that nuclear tests will be unilaterally suspended is welcomed.

"As the only nation in history to suffer from atomic bombs, the Japanese people firmly believe that the prohibition of nuclear bombs is a humanitarian requirement for the survival and welfare of humanity, which precedes political, military and all other requirements and that Japan has a moral responsibility to appeal to the world on this matter.

"Taking this position, the Japanese Government hopes that the Soviet Union will continue its action of unilateral suspension of nuclear tests, irrespective of whether or not the other countries possessing nuclear bombs conduct tests. At the same time, it requests that the other countries possessing nuclear bombs also promptly suspend their tests.

"The Japanese Government hopes furthermore that with suspension of nuclear tests as the first step the countries concerned will concentrate serious efforts on attaining agreement on unconditional prohibition attended by international controls of nuclear weapons, the discontinuation of nuclear weapons production, and the complete scrapping of existing stockpiles; and that the countries will from the broad standpoint of ensuring the survival and welfare of humanity, promptly arrive at an unanimity of views at the forthcoming East-West summit conference or at the United Nations."

EDITORIAL REACTION

The Soviet declaration also evoked wide editorial reaction in the Japanese press. Following are excerpts from editorials appearing in the newspapers *Asahi, Mainichi* and *Yomiuri*—the "Big 3" of Japanese journalism:

Asahi (April 1)—"Soviet Announcement on Nuclear Test Suspension":

"The Soviet announcement . . . while it had been rumored, is still a welcome thing.

"Ever since the Bulganin letter at the end of last year, the Soviet Union carried out a total of seven, both large and small, nuclear tests. Judging from this, it was surmised that the Soviet Union intended to carry out as many tests as possible before announcing their suspension. Now that the Soviet Union has officially made such an announcement, however, the international repercussions could be very great.

"The Soviet announcement said, however, if the Western nations do not follow suit, that it reserves the right to resume the tests, while making no reference to how long the test suspension will last. We are not fully satisfied on this point.

"There is no gainsaying that the United States and Great Britain have been placed in an extremely disadvantageous position by the latest Soviet statement. Under the present circumstances it can be surmised that both the United States and the Soviet Union possess enough nuclear weapons to destroy each other. Consequently, continuation of nuclear tests and increased production and stockpiling of nuclear weapons will . . . not have an absolute military significance.

"If such is the situation, should not the Western nations indicate their decision to suspend nuclear tests permanently? We feel that the political effects of such a statement would adequately cover any military loss resulting from test suspension. Further, if the Western nations use the test suspension as a stepping stone to take the initiative and call on the Soviet Union for suspension of nuclear weapons production and for general disarmament, their wisdom and efforts will be highly praised."

Mainichi (April 2)—"Irrespective of Soviet Intentions":

"The Soviet declaration of a unilateral suspension of its nuclear tests should in itself be welcomed. If, however, the declaration has been made simply as a diplomatic device aimed at propaganda effect, we must become critical. The reason for such concern is that the Soviet declaration contains the condition of 'reserving the freedom to resume tests if the United States and Great Britain do not follow suit.'

"The Soviet Union has just carried out a series of nuclear tests from the latter part of February for one month. Thus, even without making the present declaration, the Soviet Union may be at a stage where it may not be necessary to carry out tests for some time to come. However, the United States is pushing a program to test in the Pacific the results of two years of laboratory research. . . . Thus, for the United States to suspend the tests could be to suffer a two year handicap in comparison with the Soviet Union. . . .

"If the United States goes through with the Eniwetok tests, the Soviet Union not only will be freed from its declaration of unilateral suspension but also can seize an opportunity to give the world the impression that it is a peace-loving nation which is taking the initiative in suspending nuclear tests while the United States is playing foul by preparing for a nuclear war. However, if the . . . United States calls off the tests, the Soviet Union will be able not only to enter the truce in the nuclear test competition on advantageous ground but also to say it is taking the initiative in peace diplomacy. Therefore, in making such a declaration, the Soviet Union has essentially much to gain and nothing to lose.

"The thinking of the United States is understandable from the standpoint of logic. The United States fears that suspension of its tests would create, at least, an East-West imbalance in military strength in the field of extremely vital weapons. . . . Nevertheless, if the United States is not careful, it may not be impossible that the United States will . . . come to shoulder a big political 'minus' by going ahead with the tests in order to gain a military 'plus.' That is why we feel it would be wise, at this juncture, for the United States to take the Soviet Union by surprise, by calling off the Eniwetok tests."

Yomiuri (April 1)—"Soviet Suspension of Nuclear Tests Welcomed":

"We hope that the United States and Great Britain will willingly take the same action that the Soviet Union has taken, without being swayed by face-saving considerations or by what has happened in the past. To date the Western powers, particularly the United States, have primarily given three reasons for not being able to suspend nuclear tests. These are:

"*Firstly* . . . that the present level of technological achievement is not sufficient to ensure that secret nuclear tests can be detected. However, the test explosion of a small nuclear device at the end of a deep tunnel in Nevada last September was detected as far away as Alaska. . . .

"*Secondly* . . . that 'clean hydrogen bombs' are being manufactured in the United States and that there need be no worry about 'death ashes.' Nevertheless, in a report summarizing the testimony given by fifty representative scientists at the United States Congressional hearings last summer, it was stated that every nuclear explosion causes a deadly fallout and that there can be no such thing as a clean bomb.

"*Thirdly* . . . that the West could not, for national defense reasons suspend nuclear tests unless the other side did likewise. The Soviet Union, however, has now announced a suspension of nuclear tests. . . .

"The United States, Great Britain and the Soviet Union now possess nuclear weapons, both large and small and of various types, with which they could not only annihilate one another but the whole of mankind as well. What reason on earth can be advanced in favor of continuing these dangerous tests?

"The Soviet declaration of unilateral suspension of nuclear tests is indeed a good pumpprimer. If the United States and Great Britain follow suit, the mistrust between East and West would be markedly alleviated and the door would be opened wide for a ban on nuclear weapons, which is the earnest prayer of mankind."

Epilogue

As Paul Nitze pointed out in an article reprinted above, there are some international negotiations pursued more for their propaganda value than for their likely contributions to the resolution of international conflicts. The nuclear test ban talks would seem to fall in this category. The talks which were pursued at Geneva during the three-year de facto *moratorium came to a halt in the spring of 1961. Perhaps too much progress was being made to let them continue unless the parties all were serious about a permanent cessation. In any event the resumption of testing by both sides followed too soon on the collapse of the talks not to have been planned well before the negotiators left Geneva. The dramatic Soviet resumption in the late summer of 1961 on the eve of the Belgrade "neutralist" conference may have been at the price of any propaganda gains which accrued from the 1958 cessation. The American resumption—at first underground and not involving fallout—may not have been so costly in terms of propaganda losses.*

The readings below are selected from numerous notes, statements and speeches by leaders of both cold war camps, and the Epilogue concludes with an exchange of letters between President Kennedy and Prime Minister Ikeda of Japan and a letter from Prime Minister Ikeda to Nikita Khrushchev. These letters were written in February and March of 1962, on the eve of a new round of nuclear testing in the atmosphere by the United States. All of the selections are included primarily to illustrate the importance which each side places on countering the propaganda of the other. Taken as a whole, the psychological impact of the testing question is unique because it involves almost exclusively the attempt by both camps to counter the negative impact of their deeds *with any positive impact they might make in* words.

U.S. AND U.K. PROPOSE

BANNING NUCLEAR TESTS

IN ATMOSPHERE*

WHITE HOUSE STATEMENT, AUGUST 30

The Soviet Government's decision to resume nuclear weapons testing[1] will be met with deepest concern and resentment throughout the world. The Soviet Government's decision to resume nuclear weapons testing presents a hazard to every human being throughout the world by increasing the dangers of nuclear fallout. The Soviet Government's decision to resume nuclear weapons test-

---

* The three statements reprinted here were 1961 White House press releases dated August 30, August 31 and September 1, respectively. The joint U.S.–U.K. proposal was contained in a White House press release (Hyannis, Mass.) dated September 3, 1961. Reprinted from *The Department of State Bulletin* (September 18, 1961), pp. 475-477.

[1] The Soviet Union announced its decision to resume testing on Aug. 31 (Moscow time) and began a series of tests in the atmosphere on Sept. 1.

ing is in utter disregard of the desire of mankind for a decrease in the arms race. The Soviet Government's decision to resume nuclear weapons testing presents a threat to the entire world by increasing the dangers of a thermonuclear holocaust. The Soviet Government's decision to resume nuclear weapons testing indicates the complete hypocrisy of its professions about general and complete disarmament.

For 3 years world attention has centered on the negotiations in Geneva for a treaty to secure an end to nuclear testing. Until last March it appeared that slow but encouraging progress had been made. At that time the Soviet Union reversed its own earlier positions on key issues, refused to discuss seriously the genuine efforts made by the United States and the United Kingdom to meet known Soviet views, and blocked the path toward a nuclear test ban treaty. In order to avoid missing any possible opportunity to arrive at an agreement, the United States and the United Kingdom remained at the negotiating table. Only this week Ambassador Dean has made additional proposals in the hope of moving toward a test ban under effective international control. Urgent discussion of this issue had been scheduled at United States initiative at the forthcoming session of the General Assembly in the hopes that constructive debate could show the way to surmount the impasse at Geneva.

The pretext offered by the announcement for Soviet resumption of weapons testing is the very crisis which they themselves have created by threatening to disturb the peace which has existed in Germany and Berlin. It is not the first time they have made such charges against those who have dared to stand in the way of Soviet aggresssion. In addition, the announcement links the Soviet resumption of testing with threats of massive weapons which it must know cannot intimidate the rest of the world.

The purpose and motivation of this Soviet behavior now seems apparent: The Soviet Government wished to abandon serious negotiations in order to free its hand to resume nuclear weapons testing.

The United States continues to share the view of the people of the world as to the importance of an agreement to end nuclear weapons tests under effective safeguards. Such an agreement would represent a major breakthrough in the search for an end to the arms race. It would stop the accumulation of stockpiles of ever more powerful weapons. It would inhibit the spread of nuclear weapons to other countries with its increased risks of nuclear war.

These results, with their prospects for reducing the possibility of a nuclear war, have been blocked by the Soviet unilateral decision to resume nuclear testing. The Soviet Union bears a heavy responsibility before all humanity for this decision, a decision which was made in complete disregard of the United Nations. The termination of the moratorium on nuclear testing by the Soviet unilateral decision leaves the United States under the necessity of deciding what its own national interests require.

Under these circumstances, Ambassador Arthur Dean is being recalled immediately from Geneva.

WHITE HOUSE STATEMENT, AUGUST 31

The President met this morning [August 31] with members of the National Security Council and with congressional leaders to discuss the resumption of nuclear testing by the Soviet Union. It was recognized that the Soviet announcement was primarily a form of atomic blackmail, designed to substitute terror for reason in the present international scene.

What the Soviet Union is obviously testing is not only nuclear devices but the will and determination of the free world to resist such tactics and to defend freedom.

The President is entirely confident that the size of the U.S. nuclear weapons stockpile and the capabilities of individual weapons and delivery systems are wholly adequate for the defense needs of the United States and of the free world.

The President shares the disappointment registered throughout the world that serious and sustained attempts to ban nuclear testing have come to this abrupt end.

STATEMENT BY ARTHUR H. DEAN, SEPTEMBER 1[2]

In recent weeks, Chairman Khrushchev has been boasting about a hundred megaton bomb, a weapon far too large for military ob-

[2] Made at the White House following a meeting with President Kennedy. Ambassador Dean is U. S. Representative to the Geneva Conference on the Discontinuance of Nuclear Weapon Tests.

jectives. Two days ago the Soviet Government announced its intention to resume nuclear tests.

These events, at a time when the world could have had a workable treaty banning nuclear explosions, show a determined Soviet purpose to rest its future policy on the terrorization of humanity.

The Soviet policy is the policy of overkill. But the Soviet Government underestimates the people of the world if it thinks they will capitulate to a strategy of blackmail and terror.

JOINT U.S.-U.K. PROPOSAL, SEPTEMBER 3

The President of the United States and the Prime Minister of the United Kingdom propose to Chairman Khrushchev that their three governments agree, effective immediately, not to conduct nuclear tests which take place in the atmosphere and produce radioactive fallout.

Their aim in this proposal is to protect mankind from the increasing hazards from atmospheric pollution and to contribute to the reduction of international tensions.

They urge Chairman Khrushchev to cable his immediate acceptance of this offer and his cessation of further atmospheric tests.

They further urge that their representatives at Geneva meet not later than September 9 to record this agreement and report it to the United Nations. They sincerely hope that the Soviet Union will accept this offer, which remains open for the period indicated.

They point out that with regard to atmospheric testing the United States and the United Kingdom are prepared to rely upon existing means of detection, which they believe to be adequate, and are not suggesting additional controls. But they reaffirm their serious desire to conclude a nuclear test ban treaty, applicable to other forms of testing as well, and regret that the Soviet Government has blocked such an agreement.

U.S. RESUMES NUCLEAR
TESTING IN LABORATORY
AND UNDERGROUND*

In view of the continued testing by the Soviet Government, I have today [September 5] ordered the resumption of nuclear tests, in the laboratory and underground, with no fallout. In our efforts to achieve an end to nuclear testing, we have taken every step that reasonable men could justify. In view of the acts of the Soviet Government, we must now take those steps which prudent men find essential. We have no other choice in fulfillment of the responsibilities of the United States Government to its own citizens and to the security of other free nations. Our offer to make an agreement to end all fallout tests remains open until September 9.

DECLARATION OF PREMIER
KHRUSHCHEV**

The Soviet Government has studied the joint statement of the U.S. President and the Prime Minister of Great Britain of 3 September of this year on the question of nuclear weapon tests. How can one evaluate such a statement?

Primary attention is drawn to the fact that the leaders of the United States and Britain have not uttered a single word about the acuteness of the present times or about the tense international atmosphere, although it should be clear to them that the question of nuclear tests cannot be examined without any reference to this atmosphere.

* This statement was made by President Kennedy and published in a White House press release dated September 5, 1961. Reprinted from *The Department of State Bulletin* (September 18, 1961), p. 475.

** The declaration was handed to the U.S. and U.K. Ambassadors at Moscow on September 9, 1961, by the Soviet Ministry of Foreign Affairs. This is an unofficial translation. Reprinted from *The Department of State Bulletin* (September 25, 1961), 515-517. (This is an unofficial translation.)

It is precisely from the Governments of the United States and Britain who carry out activities in the Western military blocs that the peoples believe they can expect a clear and direct answer as to when they will stop rattling weapons and stop pushing the world toward the catastrophe of a nuclear war. Leaving all this aside, Mr. Kennedy and Mr. Macmillan not only separate the question of nuclear tests from the disarmament problem—of which it is a part—but they also try to examine it alone, as in a test tube without any relationship to events in international life.

Each line of the statement of the U.S. President and the Prime Minister of Great Britain reveals the tendency of the Western Powers and their allies in the aggressive blocs to insure at any cost unilateral military advantages at the expense of the interests of the security of the Soviet Union and other socialist states. And at that the leaders of the United States and Britain have even tried to represent the case as if their statements in the joint declaration had been dictated by their solicitude for easing international tension and were in the interest of all humanity.

Whatever grandiloquent words the leaders of the Governments of the United States and Britain may choose in their attempts to defend their course of action in connection with nuclear weapons, they will not help to present their aggressive policy as a policy of peace or barbarity as humanity. To clarify the aims of this statement let us see what the concrete contents are.

The announcement put forward the proposal that the Soviet Union, the United States, and Britain should immediately agree not to hold nuclear weapon tests in the atmosphere but that the question of tests underground and in the cosmos should not be touched upon in such an agreement.

It is not so very difficult to get to the bottom of this proposal. It has been proposed to us that the United States and Britain—not to mention France, which in general is not affected by this proposal —should reserve the right to perfect nuclear weapons in the future. The question is to see whether it is possible to tie the hands of the Soviet Union even more in the improvement of its defense measures. In other words, with one propaganda shot they want to kill two birds: to have the blessing of approval of the Soviet Union for their military preparations in the sphere of nuclear weapons and at the same time to trip up their partner in negotiations, the Soviet Union.

In reality it is known that the program for the creation of new types of nuclear weapons in the United States is at present dependent on underground tests—that is, the type of tests for which the green light for American-British proposals is to be given. For several years at the three nuclear powers' conferences in Geneva the United States tried to achieve legalization of underground nuclear tests, which was one of the main obstacles to the conclusion of a treaty of total cessation of nuclear tests.

It is no secret that underground tests have long been planned in the United States and that the necessary shafts and gigantic underground caverns are ready in Nevada.

If more proofs were needed to show that the aims pursued in the common declaration of the President of the United States and the Prime Minister of Great Britain are covered by white threads, such proof was given by Mr. Kennedy himself, in ordering the resumption of underground testing of nuclear weapons on 5 September, i.e., one day after appealing to the Soviet Union. . . .

Confronted with the feverish war preparations of the NATO countries directed against the Soviet Union and socialist countries, we had no other choice but to take such measures as are dictated by the necessity to withstand threats and to be ready to meet aggression well armed. Such a necessity has arisen against our will; it was created not by us but by this policy of saber-rattling and inciting war which is now being carried out by the main NATO countries, especially in connection with the question of concluding the German peace treaty.

The Soviet Union has decided to resume nuclear tests because in the present circumstances to overlook the possibility of an aggression unleashed against it would be tantamount to frivolity.

In reaching the decision to resume tests the Soviet Government has obviously taken into account that at first there may be people who would be unable to evaluate the entire complex international situation and would show their well-known lack of understanding of this Soviet step. We knew beforehand that some people in the West would not pass up the opportunity to make propaganda capital from it. However, the Soviet Union could not have acted differently. Having weighed all the pros and cons, the Soviet Government, with sorrow and heartache, has to decide to resume experimental explosions.

We have no doubt that a great majority of mankind rightly interprets the measures undertaken by the Soviet Government. Strengthening the defenses of the Soviet Union means at the same time strengthening the forces of peace in the entire world. An aggressor should know that there is a reliable force able to safeguard peaceful labor, freedom, and independence of peoples.

The joint American-British statement touches on the question of the growing danger of polluting the atmosphere with radioactive matter. One cannot find words to express how undesirable this is. The Soviet Union is taking all measures to reduce to the minimum all harmful consequences of the tests for living organisms.

It is right, however, to ask the question: Why did the Government of the United States, or the Government of Britain, not lament the pollution of the atmosphere when for several years the rumble of explosions of atomic and hydrogen bombs taking place far from the vital centers of these states—on the islands of Bikini, Eniwetok, Christmas—did not cease? Enormous quantities of radioactive precipitation poisoned not only the earth's atmosphere but also infected the waters of the Pacific Ocean and, through the products of the sea, passed into the bones and blood of completely innocent people.

Why have the Governments of the United States and Britain not found a word of condemnation for the actions of the French Government which, during the course of nearly two years, has poisoned the earth's atmosphere by carrying out nuclear tests in the Sahara?

The solicitude over the poisoning of the earth's atmosphere expressed in the American-British statement proves artificial and ostentatious when brought to the test. Would it not be more honest to tell the peoples what really awaits them if events develop further in the same direction in which they have gone in recent months as a result of the growing aggressiveness of the policy of the NATO powers. Events are taking such a turn that if the policy of the Western Powers is not changed in time mankind may be caught by a whirlwind of nuclear-rocket war. In the fire of such a war dozens and hundreds of millions of people would be burned.

The present policy of the NATO powers leads to the knowledge that it is not the radioactive fallout that has to be feared but the falling of the actual nuclear weapon—of all its death-bearing and destructive force—on the heads of the peoples. If you balance the harm of nuclear tests to the health of the people against the consequences of the military application of nuclear weapons, it will be obvious to everyone what choice has been put before mankind today and how much hypocrisy is concealed in the statements of the Governments of the Western Powers on the subject of experimental nuclear tests.

No, the Soviet Union cannot agree to risk the lives of millions and millions of people. The Government of the U.S.S.R. would not have fulfilled its duty if it did not fittingly look after the security of the Soviet people. If it is now faced with the dire necessity to resume experimental nuclear tests, this is only so that our people, and also all mankind, may not experience themselves—as happened in the Japanese towns of Hiroshima and Nagasaki—the explosion of these weapons under war conditions.

The Soviet Union is striving to prevent people from becoming victims of atomic, hydrogen, and neutron bombs which are talked about in the West by those who oppose the real humanity of socialist society and our external policy more than their own man-hating policy in which peoples are fuel in the crucible of a nuclear war and the material and cultural riches created by the peoples are but potential loot—military trophies for the imperialist aggressors.

Who does not know that the Soviet Union has carried out many times fewer nuclear tests than the United States, Britain, and France? We have every reason, from both the moral standpoint and also from the standpoint of the security of our state interests, to claim the right to hold the same number of experimental tests as the Western Powers. . . .

JAPAN PROTESTS RESUMPTION
OF NUCLEAR TESTS*

This is an exchange of letters between President Kennedy and Prime Minister Ikeda of Japan and a letter from Prime Minister Ikeda to Nikita Khrushchev concerning the intention of the United States to conduct a series of nuclear tests in the atmosphere in the spring of 1962.

President John F. Kennedy on February 28 informed Prime Minister Ikeda by letter (two days prior to his nation-wide broadcast to the American public) that the United States would resume the testing of nuclear weapons in the atmosphere in the middle of April in the light of the Soviet Union's unilateral breaking of the moratorium of such testing. The following are the texts of letters from President Kennedy to Prime Minister Ikeda, Prime Minister Ikeda's reply to President Kennedy and Prime Minister Ikeda's letter to Premier Khrushchev:

PRESIDENT KENNEDY'S LETTER TO PRIME MINISTER IKEDA

28 February 1962

DEAR MR. PRIME MINISTER:

Recognizing the deep concern with which your Government and your nation view the testing of nuclear weapons, and in the light of our agreement last June to consult together on issues of great international significance, I have asked Ambassador Reischauer to convey to you this personal message.

After deep consideration, I have with great reluctance reached a decision that I must order the resumption of nuclear weapons testing in the atmosphere. I am issuing this order, in the knowledge that it will bring disappointment to many, both in my own country and abroad, upon the single and decisive ground that such tests

* Reprinted from the *Japan Report,* Vol. 8, No. 5 (March 25, 1962), pp. 2-4. *Japan Report* is edited and distributed by the Japan Information Service, Consulate General of Japan, New York City, for Japanese diplomatic and consular establishments in the United States.

are now necessary for the military security of the entire Free World. The nuclear test moratorium which was so brutally broken by the Soviet Union in 1961 cannot now be kept by our side alone, if we are to avoid the hazard of advances by the Soviet Union which might imperil us all.

I cannot stress too strongly that this decision is governed by strictly military considerations. Study and analysis of the recent series of atmospheric tests by the Soviet Union reveal strides in technique and design which could, over time, shift the balance of military power in favor of that nation. While some have maintained that an American resumption of atmospheric testing would be morally wrong, I believe that it would be the ultimate in immorality to allow the deterrent force of the United States to decline, relative to that of the Soviet Union, to the point where the United States and its allies might become vulnerable to diplomatic extortion or even direct military action.

I wish to assure you, Mr. Prime Minister, that this nation will continue to press vigorously for nuclear and other disarmament under a reasonable system of international controls and safeguards. The Soviet Union, with its test series of 1961 has dramatically intensified the nuclear arms race—my Government will not rest until this race, with all its dangers, is brought to a close. To this end we have proposed that a supreme effort be made at the forthcoming 18-nation conference on disarmament.

While I am ordering that nuclear tests be resumed, the series which is in preparation will not begin until the middle of April, and between now and then we shall be urging the Soviet Government once again to join with Great Britain and with us in an effective nuclear test ban treaty. If such a treaty can be signed in this period, there will be no American atmospheric tests.

The position of this Government will be more fully explained in a major address which I shall make on Friday, March 2nd, to the American people. I trust that this letter and my coming address will make it plain to you with what regret I have come to this necessary decision and how deeply I hope that the Soviet Government may be brought to accept the necessity of effectively controlled disarmament, especially in this dangerous area of nuclear testing.

I ask your understanding, and that of the Japanese people, for this action which my Government is forced to take in the vital security interest of all Free World nations.

Sincerely,

JOHN F. KENNEDY

PRIME MINISTER IKEDA'S LETTER TO PRESIDENT KENNEDY

2 March 1962

DEAR MR. PRESIDENT,

I wish to express to you my appreciation for your personal message conveyed to me by Ambassador Reischauer, explaining to me, prior to official announcement of your decision to resume nuclear weapons testing in the atmosphere, the circumstances which led you to this decision. This is in line with our understanding of last June to consult with each other on major issues of international significance, and is also indicative of your understanding of the deep concern and anxiety with which the Government and people of Japan view the testing of nuclear weapons.

The circumstances which compelled you with great reluctance to make this decision, as explained in your letter, came about, I believe, because the Soviet Union, in complete defiance of the hopes of mankind, unilaterally broke the moratorium on nuclear weapons testing and vigorously conducted a series of some fifty such tests.

However, as I made clear at our talks last June, it has been and continues to be the constant and earnest hope of Japan that the testing of nuclear weapons is never conducted whatever its reasons be. The Japanese people who have experienced the tragic consequences of nuclear explosion deeply deplore nuclear weapons testing in the atmosphere.

At present when nuclear weapons have been developed to an extraordinary degree and when we are cognizant of the urgency of securing the welfare and security of mankind and the peace of the world, it is obvious that the nuclear race should not be continued endlessly between East and West. I must express my earnest hope, Mr. President, that you will reconsider your present decision to resume testing.

From these considerations, may I hope that before you actually resume your tests you will make a supreme effort, as you have indicated in your letter, to bring about together with the countries concerned an agreement for the suspension of nuclear weapons testing under effective international control and inspection.

From what I have expressed in this letter, I trust, Mr. President, that you and the people of your country will show a most serious regard to the feelings of the Government and people of Japan.

Yours sincerely,

HAYATO IKEDA

Prime Minister of Japan

PRIME MINISTER IKEDA'S LETTER TO CHAIRMAN KHRUSHCHEV

10 March 1962

His Excellency N. S. Khrushchev
Chairman of the Council of Ministers
Union of Soviet Socialist Republics

EXCELLENCY:

The Government of the United States announced on March 2nd its decision to resume nuclear weapons tests in the atmosphere.

To Japanese, the only people who have experienced the horrors of atomic explosions, the utilization of nuclear energy for military purpose is absolutely intolerable. The Japanese Government has forthwith protested to the United States Government against the above-mentioned announcement and asked [it] to cancel the proposed experiments.

A total and permanent prohibition of nuclear weapons tests is the fervent wish of all Japanese as Your Excellency is well aware.

The moratorium on nuclear weapons testing which was maintained for about three years among the United States, the United Kingdom and the Soviet Union following their conference of October, 1958 on the discontinuance of such testing raised our hopes and expectations for the banning of the tests for all time.

Unfortunately this moratorium was broken by the sudden Soviet resumption of tests on an extensive scale in September last year. On that occasion the Japanese Government communicated in writing to the Soviet Government our apprehensions that the Soviet action might prompt other powers to do likewise, creating a vicious circle of such tests. Sure enough, the United States Government has now decided on resumption of its atmospheric testing, and the world is exposed once more to the menace of nuclear arms race.

We earnestly hope to see all the countries currently engaged in the development of nuclear weapons lose no time in agreeing to a test ban. We believe the most urgent task for the coming 18-nation disarmament conference is the speedy conclusion of an international agreement on stopping all nuclear weapons tests under an effective system of inspection and control.

I am convinced it is the paramount responsibility we Japanese owe to history and mankind to appeal unremittingly in order to see that the tragedy we have experienced is never again repeated on earth. This appeal, transcending race and political ideology, is directed equally to all countries which possess nuclear weapons and all countries which conduct the testing of such weapons. I have already appealed to the President of the United States in the same manner as I am doing to Your Excellency now.

On the other hand, the United States Government has declared its intention of abandoning its test program in the event of an early conclusion of an effective nuclear test ban treaty. Whether or not such an agreement materialize[s] depends now, Your Excellency, upon your decision.

I cannot but urge most strongly upon Your Excellency that in answer to the fervent wish of mankind that you make the utmost effort to the end of outlawing forever all nuclear weapons tests.

Yours sincerely,
HAYATO IKEDA
Prime Minister of Japan

VI

The Peace Corps: A Case Study in Propaganda of the *Deed*

In one of the selections reprinted below President Kennedy says that the Peace Corps was not designed as propaganda but to help the peoples of the world to find a better way of life. Yet in another selection one of the Peace Corps officials says that it was "conceived as a key component in the weapons system" in the struggle against tyranny, poverty, disease and war. And in the Peace Corps Act itself Congress specifies as one of the program's major purposes, "to help promote a better understanding of the American people . . ."

Students of international relations will be more than casually interested in this apparent paradox. It reflects basic changes which are taking place in the nature of the international system under the stresses of intertwined technological and political revolutions. Perhaps historians of this period will one day record that national statesmen finally found that they could achieve the selfish objectives of national states only through the development of inter-national and finally supranational institutions. Or, as it has been so well put by some contemporary writers, perhaps it will become

218

clear to modern man that there is "realism in idealism" and that no nation-state can be truly secure or prosperous as long as any nation-state is weak and underdeveloped.

In any case it has already become clear that successful propaganda must be more than just words and that the propaganda of the deed *must be more than a selfish act. The Peace Corps may meet this critical modern test of successful propaganda only by not being designed or used as propaganda at all.*

The readings that follow provide a good outline of the ultimate propaganda problem faced by the United States: to convince the world that Americans really care about their fellow inhabitants of the planet Earth.

In the first selection Roger Tubby summarizes the propaganda problem which the United States faces for the decade of the sixties and the role which the Peace Corps may play in resolving that problem. President Kennedy's statement and his message to Congress requesting Peace Corps legislation describe the official hopes of the United States that the Corps will be a "new dimension in our overseas program." The Act itself which established a permanent Peace Corps is more specific about the benefits to the United States but also emphasizes the service aspect of the program. Sargent Shriver's description of the Peace Corps reflects the deep idealism of the officials and volunteers. The report of the first overseas activity of the Corps (in Ghana) is indicative of the emphasis on education which the President stressed in his request for permanent legislation. Finally the article by Lawrence Dennis analyzes the first year of the Peace Corps in operation. Mr. Dennis proposes the further development of the Peace Corps idea into a program of "universal public service" in which Americans can once again find the "path of their purpose."

THE CRISIS AND
AMERICA'S IMAGE*

ROGER W. TUBBY

ROGER W. TUBBY, *government official and newspaperman, is Assistant Secretary of State for Public Affairs.*

Years ago, before I left Washington to edit a country daily in northern New York, someone put a sign on my office door at the Department of State. The sign said, "Crisis Every Half Hour." Some days then that seemed no exaggeration, nor does it now.

It is perhaps worth bearing in mind how difficult and full of crises the situation was in the late 1940's. Italy and France were close to going Communist; the Communist armed forces were at the very gates of Athens; Russian troops were holding Azerbaijan in northwest Iran; Russia was threatening seizure of the Turkish Districts of Kars and Ardahan; Tito was moving on Trieste; free Europe's economy was shattered by war; Russia seized Czechoslovakia and implacably refused to honor her pledges made at Yalta for free elections in Poland and the Balkan States; Japan was broken, many of her industries in ruins; the Philippines was starting a difficult recovery after the ravages of war; the Indian subcontinent was in the heartrending convulsions of partition; Latin America was caught in the sudden cutback of U.S. war industry orders for her minerals and metals, fibers, rubber, and many other products—and in America we had our own severe readjustment problems as millions of servicemen returned to civilian life. Then there was the blockade of Berlin, the sudden savage onslaught on south Korea. There were crises aplenty. They were met by the Greek-Turkish aid program, the Marshall plan, point 4, the creation of NATO and other defense alliances, by the Berlin airlift, by the hard and successful struggle to save south Korea.

* This is an address made before the Eastern Labor Press Conference at Washington, D.C., on June 3, 1961 (press release 365). Reprinted from *The Department of State Bulletin*, Vol. 44, No. 1147 (June 19, 1961), pp. 972-975.

220

With respect to Europe, President Kennedy in Paris on Thursday said, "In many ways the experience of Europe in the last 10 years has confounded all of those who believed the tide of history was running against us."

Today we again have crises in many parts of the world. While this is no cause for despair, it is cause for concern. Millions and millions of people want and insist on having better living conditions, and if the Communists can help them faster than we, or even if it only appears that the Communists can do so, many will turn to the Communists.

President Kennedy in his *Alianza para Progreso* speech March 13th* said,

> . . . our unfulfilled task is to demonstrate to the entire world that man's unsatisfied aspiration for economic progress and social justice can best be achieved by free men working within a framework of democratic institutions.

COMMUNIST-BLOC ACTIVITIES

The Communist powers claim, on the contrary, that their system will more efficiently satisfy mankind's unfulfilled aspirations. They claim that the balance of power has shifted in their favor. They boast of rapid economic, scientific, and military progress, conveniently ignoring the even greater strides taken by many of the nations of the free world. And, not satisfied with economic competition conducted on the basis of quality, price, and service, the Communists are engaged in skillful and ruthless efforts to undermine free governments, to create chaos wherever possible, to subvert or overrun free countries. Sabotage, forgeries, outrageous distortions of the truth are among the weapons used. In Laos and south Viet-Nam guerrilla warfare is also employed, together with terroristic murders of freely elected officials. Secret arms shipments are made to more and more areas.

Communist-bloc international broadcasting continues to increase steadily in hours on the air and in range and effectiveness. There's been a massive expansion in radio propaganda by Communist China during the last year. Broadcasts to Africa by the Communist bloc as a whole almost doubled in 1960.

* BULLETIN of Apr. 3, 1961, p. 471.

Bloc educational exchanges with underdeveloped countries show that Soviet exchanges were up 50 percent in 1960, with emphasis especially on impressing and influencing students of underdeveloped or newly independent countries. There has been a steady flow of visits of high government officials between these countries and the U.S.S.R. and Red China.

The most notable feature of Communist China's "people's diplomacy" has been the dramatic increase of so-called people-to-people contacts with African countries. At least 157 delegations from African and Near Eastern countries visited Red China last year compared to 42 in 1959, an increase of over 370 percent.

Latin American delegations to Communist China increased from 37 in 1958 and 107 in 1959 to 178 in 1960 (25 from Cuba alone).

Almost one-half of the Asian delegations to visit Communist China during 1960 came from Japan; there were 65 Japanese groups representing various political hues, economic interests, and "friendship" organizations. In 1959 there were only 29 such groups.

In the labor field Communists prefer, wherever practicable, to use propaganda media and techniques which insure the active participation of the largest possible number of people, regardless of efficiency or cost. Thus hundreds of "factory newspapers" and other local publications are published, often poorly edited and crudely mimeographed, but nevertheless they are effective in appearing to be close to the interests of the workers.

Communist successes in Cuba and Laos, the Gagarin circuit of the earth, growing Soviet military and economic power, psychological warfare gains in some areas—all this no doubt is heady stuff for Communist leaders.

But neither they, nor we, should forget that the free world possesses great resources, the greatest of all being our freedom.

Yet if we do not marshal these resources effectively, if we do not move rapidly enough to meet the aspirations of the peoples of the underdeveloped lands, if we do not strengthen our own economy and defenses, and if our major allies do not do likewise, then there will most likely be further attrition, further losses to the so-called "Democratic People's Republics"—countries that are not democratic, do not belong to the peoples, and which are not republics. Parenthetically, if we resist them, their leaders call us warmongers; if we defend the right of neutrals to independence, we are charged with being provocative and imperialistic.

SUCCESS OF COMMUNIST PROPAGANDA

Indeed, as we know, Communists do not recognize any "objective" or "eternal" truth; they consider words and thoughts as weapons, not as reflections of reality; and they use lies, deception, suppression or distortion of facts as "normal" means in their struggle for power. Their propaganda is differentiated (1) on different levels and (2) according to different audiences. The substantive contents of these differentiated propaganda messages may differ from, or directly contradict, each other, but their underlying purposes serve the same Communist cause. They have been fairly successful in this complicated and seemingly "self-refuting" orchestration of their propaganda because

a. any specific audience receives only one type of propaganda message (e.g. the Indonesian peasant does not read what the Communists tell Russian or Chinese peasants);

b. most people have short memories and rarely notice that the Communists tell them today a story conflicting with their story of 6 months ago or that the Communists predicted a development last year which failed to materialize. For instance, the Communists predicted a depression in the U.S. at the end of World War II;

c. only a fraction of the audiences reached by Communist propaganda is also reached by anti-Communist propaganda (which could expose these contradictions, false predictions, and other vulnerabilities);

d. a large part of anti-Communist propaganda—and of free-world mass media in general—simply condemns communism as "bad" and does not turn Communist words against their authors.

Of course within every Communist country Communist propaganda enjoys an absolute and complete monopoly; no newspaper can be printed, no broadcast can be made, no book can be published, no motion picture can be produced without the explicit permission of the Communist Party, given either directly or through the party-controlled Government apparatus. This insures that any item—whether news, feature, poem, motion picture, or anything else—admitted into media channels reaches only the audiences chosen by party authority, at the time and especially in exactly the shape prescribed by that authority.

I mention these things not because they are new to any of us but only as a reminder of the scope and effectiveness of the opposition we are up against. The czars of Russia and the emperors of the great Chinese dynasties were successful in their conquest of neighboring territories, but their operations were crude compared to those of their modern successors.

THE FUTURE OF FREEDOM

The seeking for a true understanding between the Communist and the free world, a searching for a lessening of tension, the hope for an end of atom bomb testing, for disarmament, for joint efforts in eliminating the terrible scourges of sickness and hunger and illiteracy, for exploring space, for sharing of a myriad of scientific discoveries, including conversion of salt water to fresh water—all these things depend largely on recognition by Russia and Red China that, while no free-world nation today has territorial ambitions, the United States and its free-world allies will stand firm against Russian or Red Chinese efforts to dominate others. If they desist, we can then work together on programs of value to all.

"This Nation is engaged in a long and exacting test of the future of freedom," President Kennedy said in his address on urgent national needs,* "a test which may well continue for decades to come. Our strength as well as our convictions have imposed upon this Nation the role of leader in freedom's cause. . . . We are not against any man, or any nation, or any system, except as it is hostile to freedom."

We believe that men should have a free choice—of government, of jobs, of religion. We believe in working to create, hard and disheartening though the task will be, a world of law and order by strengthening the U.N. and by working in co-operation with many nations in economic, health, and other agencies.

But what we can do, how effectively we can carry out the revolutionary beliefs of our forefathers, whether we can help "those people in the huts and villages of half the globe struggling to

---

* For text, see H. Doc. 174, 87th Cong., 1st sess.

break the bonds of mass misery,"* depends in great measure on our own understanding of the needs, our own willingness to sacrifice, the image *we* present to the world.

So, as we face many crises, crises which together challenge our survival, we do need in the United States to demonstrate what is meant by freedom—freedom for Negroes as well as Yankees, for Mexican-Americans as well as the Amish of Pennsylvania, for the workers in textile mills, for members of college faculties, or for clerks in stores on Main Street.

UNDERSTANDING THE ISSUES

And to do these things we should, all of us, understand clearly what the issues are. We must recognize especially how terribly damaging our remaining racial intolerance is to the image of America.

You in the labor press do a tremendous job of informing your readers of problems between labor and management and of legislation of major concern to labor. I wonder, however, if you could not most usefully carry more general news, more news or comment especially on foreign affairs, possibly a column regularly of foreign affairs highlights. Would it be helpful to you—would you be interested in briefings on foreign affairs problems, or in State Department releases or pamphlets, if you're not already getting them? Our business is very much yours—how we carry it on, whether we represent your interests effectively, how foreign aid will boost our economy, our job opportunities, while helping others, even as our exports to Germany, France, and Great Britain soared during and following the Marshall plan.

But most essential, it seems to me, is for us all in Government, in the press, to arouse our people from complacency about our situation. We cannot afford ignorance and apathy; we cannot, or certainly should not, if we aim to survive, turn our backs on poverty and injustice either at home or abroad. When Adlai Stevenson returned from Latin America last year he said, "If the free way of life does not help the many poor, it will never save

* For text of President Kennedy's inaugural address, see BULLETIN of Feb. 6, 1961, p. 175.

the few rich." We cannot or should not ignore what the Communists are doing in greatly expanded broadcasting, in distribution of magazines and books, in bringing African and Near Eastern and other students from underdeveloped countries to their schools and colleges. We ignore at our peril subversive activities around the world as in our unions or anywhere else in our own society.

The seizure of Cuba by the Communists has shocked us in the United States, as the Red seizure of Czechoslovakia shocked Western Europe in 1948. Whether Cuba's loss, the plight of Laos and south Viet-Nam, the danger to Berlin—whether these things concern us deeply enough to get us moving as far and as fast as we should, depends really on our understanding of what is happening, our interest in the contest between dictatorship and freedom, our willingness to pool our resources and energies.

We are already moving forward vigorously with the President's programs, both those strengthening our domestic economy and our foreign policy. Indeed a strong U.S. economy is an essential prerequisite for a successful foreign policy. An expanded and longer range foreign aid legislation is before Congress; $500 million has already been approved for the *Alianza para Progreso* program for Latin America. The Food-for-Peace and Peace Corps programs, both new and imaginative and needed in helping others abroad, have received strong support already among our people. So have Presidential proposals to strengthen our military and space programs. We are moving forward once again, as we did in the forties. And we are working in far closer harmony and understanding with our allies around the world.

The President in Vienna is seeking to find an acceptable and workable basis for improving relations with Russia. He will, however, make clear to Khrushchev our capacity and resolve to resist Communist aggression and subversion.

This capacity and resolve, of course, depends on us all. We surely have what it takes if we'll but use it. However, we hope that Mr. Khrushchev will make possible peaceful solutions of world problems; that, instead of seeking to weaken or wreck the U.N. he will help strengthen it; that he will agree to disarmament with reliable inspection and control machinery.

If Russia and Red China will renounce imperialism, which has happily gone out of fashion in the rest of the world, what marvelous opportunities will then exist for them and all of us to work far more effectively against all forms of human misery and to move on to an age of achievement in science, industry, the arts —an age far more productive than any we have known.

Unfortunately, however, Russia and Red China are not likely to be as sensible as we would wish—at least not for some time, not until they are convinced by the propaganda of our acts, by the continued demonstration of our strength, that their imperialism is costly and extremely hazardous. So we probably will have numerous other crises in the months and years immediately ahead. Some will be hard to handle, with no easy solutions, and innumerable suggestions as to what should be done. But we have surmounted problems before, as in the 1940's, problems tough as any we face today. And we will do so again.

STATEMENT BY
PRESIDENT KENNEDY *

JOHN F. KENNEDY

JOHN F. KENNEDY *served in the House of Representatives and as United States Senator from Massachusetts before he was elected President of the United States in 1960.*

I have today [March 1] signed an Executive order providing for the establishment of a Peace Corps on a temporary pilot basis. I am also sending to Congress a message proposing authorization of a parmanent Peace Corps. This Corps will be a pool of trained American men and women sent overseas by the U.S. Government or through private institutions and organizations to help foreign countries meet their urgent needs for skilled manpower.

* This statement was read by President Kennedy at his news conference on March 1, 1961 (White House press release). Reprinted from *The Department of State Bulletin* (March 20, 1961), p. 400.

It is our hope to have 500 or more people in the field by the end of the year.

The initial reactions to the Peace Corps proposal are convincing proof that we have, in this country, an immense reservoir of such men and women—anxious to sacrifice their energies and time and toil to the cause of world peace and human progress.

In establishing our Peace Corps we intend to make full use of the resources and talents of private institutions and groups. Universities, voluntary agencies, labor unions, and industry will be asked to share in this effort—contributing diverse sources of energy and imagination—making it clear that the responsibility for peace is the responsibility of our entire society.

We will only send abroad Americans who are wanted by the host country—who have a real job to do—and who are qualified to do that job. Programs will be developed with care, and after full negotiation, in order to make sure that the Peace Corps is wanted and will contribute to the welfare of other people. Our Peace Corps is not designed as an instrument of diplomacy or propaganda or ideological conflict. It is designed to permit our people to exercise more fully their responsibilities in the great common cause of world development.

Life in the Peace Corps will not be easy. There will be no salary, and allowances will be at a level sufficient only to maintain health and meet basic needs. Men and women will be expected to work and live alongside the nationals of the country in which they are stationed—doing the same work, eating the same food, talking the same language.

But if the life will not be easy, it will be rich and satisfying. For every young American who participates in the Peace Corps—who works in a foreign land—will know that he or she is sharing in the great common task of bringing to man that decent way of life which is the foundation of freedom and a condition of peace.

MESSAGE TO CONGRESS*

TO THE CONGRESS OF THE UNITED STATES:

I recommend to the Congress the establishment of a permanent Peace Corps—a pool of trained American men and women sent overseas by the U.S. Government or through private organizations and institutions to help foreign countries meet their urgent needs for skilled manpower.

I have today signed an Executive order establishing a Peace Corps on a temporary pilot basis.

The temporary Peace Corps will be a source of information and experience to aid us in formulating more effective plans for a permanent organization. In addition, by starting the Peace Corps now we will be able to begin training young men and women for oversea duty this summer with the objective of placing them in overseas positions by late fall. This temporary Peace Corps is being established under existing authority in the Mutual Security Act and will be located in the Department of State. Its initial expenses will be paid from appropriations currently available for our foreign aid program.

Throughout the world the people of the newly developing nations are struggling for economic and social progress which reflects their deepest desires. Our own freedom, and the future of freedom around the world, depend, in a very real sense, on their ability to build growing and independent nations where men can live in dignity, liberated from the bonds of hunger, ignorance, and poverty.

One of the greatest obstacles to the achievement of this goal is the lack of trained men and women with the skill to teach the young and assist in the operation of development projects—men and women with the capacity to cope with the demands of swiftly evolving economies, and with the dedication to put that capacity to work in the villages, the mountains, the towns, and the factories of dozens of struggling nations.

* This message is House Document 98, 87th Congress, 1st session. Reprinted from *The Department of State Bulletin* (March 20, 1961), pp. 401-403.

The vast task of economic development urgently requires skilled people to do the work of the society—to help teach in the schools, construct development projects, demonstrate modern methods of sanitation in the villages, and perform a hundred other tasks calling for training and advanced knowledge.

To meet this urgent need for skilled manpower we are proposing the establishment of a Peace Corps—an organization which will recruit and train American volunteers, sending them abroad to work with the people of other nations.

This organization will differ from existing assistance programs in that its members will supplement technical advisers by offering the specific skills needed by developing nations if they are to put technical advice to work. They will help provide the skilled manpower necessary to carry out the development projects planned by the host governments, acting at a working level and serving at great personal sacrifice. There is little doubt that the number of those who wish to serve will be far greater than our capacity to absorb them.

The Peace Corps or some similar approach has been strongly advocated by Senator Humphrey, Representative Reuss and others in the Congress. It has received strong support from universities, voluntary agencies, student groups, labor unions, and business and professional organizations.

Last session, the Congress authorized a study of these possibilities. Preliminary reports of this study show that the Peace Corps is feasible, needed, and wanted by many foreign countries.

Most heartening of all, the initial reaction to this proposal has been an enthusiastic response by student groups, professional organizations, and private citizens everywhere—a convincing demonstration that we have in this country an immense reservoir of dedicated men and women willing to devote their energies and time and toil to the cause of world peace and human progress.

Among the specific programs to which Peace Corps members can contribute are teaching in primary and secondary schools, especially as part of national English language teaching programs; participation in the worldwide program of malaria eradication; instruction and operation of public health and sanitation projects; aiding in village development through school construction and other programs; increasing rural agricultural productivity by assisting local farmers to use modern implements and techniques. The initial emphasis of these programs will be on teaching. Thus the Peace Corps members will be an effective means of implementing the development programs of the host countries—programs which our technical assistance operations have helped to formulate.

The Peace Corps will not be limited to the young, or to college graduates. All Americans who are qualified will be welcome to join this effort. But undoubtedly the corps will be made up primarily of young people as they complete their formal education.

Because one of the greatest resources of a free society is the strength and diversity of its private organizations and institutions much of the Peace Corps program will be carried out by these groups, financially assisted by the Federal Government.

Peace Corps personnel will be made available to developing nations in the following ways:

1. Through private voluntary agencies carrying on international assistance programs.
2. Through overseas programs of colleges and universities.
3. Through assistance programs of international agencies.
4. Through assistance programs of the U.S. Government.
5. Through new programs which the Peace Corps itself directly administers.

In the majority of cases the Peace Corps will assume the entire responsibility for recruitment, training, and the development of oversea projects. In other cases it will make available a pool of trained applicants to private groups who are carrying out projects approved by the Peace Corps.

In the case of Peace Corps programs conducted through voluntary agencies and universities, these private institutions will have the option of using the national recruitment system—the central pool of trained manpower—or developing recruitment systems of their own.

In all cases men and women recruited as a result of Federal assistance will be members of the Peace Corps and enrolled in the central organization. All private recruitment and training programs will adhere to Peace Corps standards as a condition of Federal assistance.

In all instances the men and women of the Peace Corps will go only to those countries where their services and skills are genuinely needed and desired. U.S. operations missions, supplemented where necessary by special Peace Corps teams, will consult with leaders in foreign countries in order to determine where Peace Corpsmen are needed, the types of job they can best fill, and the number of people who can be usefully employed. The Peace Corps will not supply personnel for marginal undertakings without a sound economic or social justification. In furnishing assistance through the Peace Corps careful regard will be given to the particular country's developmental priorities.

Membership in the Peace Corps will be open to all Americans, and applications will be available shortly. Where application is made directly to the Peace Corps—the vast majority of cases—they will be carefully screened to make sure that those who are selected can contribute to Peace Corps programs, and have the personal qualities which will enable them to represent the United States abroad with honor and dignity. In those cases where application is made directly to a private group, the same basic standards will be maintained. Each new recruit will receive a training and orientation period varying from 6 weeks to 6 months. This training will include courses in the culture and language of the country to which they are being sent and specialized training designed to increase the work skills of recruits. In some cases training will be conducted by participant agencies and universities in approved training programs. Other training programs will be conducted by the Peace Corps staff.

Length of service in the Corps will vary depending on the kind of project and the country, generally ranging from 2 to 3 years. Peace Corps members will often serve under conditions of physical hardship, living under primitive conditions among the people of developing nations. For every Peace Corps member service will mean a great financial sacrifice. They will receive no salary. Instead they will be given an allowance which will only be sufficient to meet their basic needs and maintain health. It is essential that Peace Corps men and women live simply and unostentatiously among the people they have come to assist. At the conclusion of their tours, members of the Peace Corps will receive a small sum in the form of severance pay based on length of service abroad to assist them during their first weeks back in the United States. Service with the

Peace Corps will not exempt volunteers from selective service.

The United States will assume responsibility for supplying medical services to Peace Corps members and insuring supplies and drugs necessary to good health.

I have asked the temporary Peace Corps to begin plans and make arrangements for pilot programs. A minimum of several hundred volunteers could be selected, trained, and at work abroad by the end of this calendar year. It is hoped that within a few years several thousand Peace Corps members will be working in foreign lands.

It is important to remember that this program must, in its early stages, be experimental in nature. This is a new dimension in our oversea program and only the most careful planning and negotiation can insure its success.

The benefits of the Peace Corps will not be limited to the countries in which it serves. Our own young men and woman will be enriched by the experience of living and working in foreign lands. They will have acquired new skills and experience which will aid them in their future careers and add to our own country's supply of trained personnel and teachers. They will return better able to assume the responsibilities of American citizenship and with greater understanding of our global responsibilities.

Although this is an American Peace Corps, the problem of world development is not just an American problem. Let us hope that other nations will mobilize the spirit and energies and skill of their people in some form of peace corps—making our own effort only one step in a major international effort to increase the welfare of all men and improve understanding among nations.

JOHN F. KENNEDY

The White House
March 1, 1961

THE PEACE CORPS ACT,
SECTION 2*

DECLARATION OF PURPOSE

SEC. 2. The Congress of the United States declares that it is the policy of the United States and the purpose of this Act to promote world peace and friendship through a Peace Corps, which shall make available to interested countries and areas men and women of the United States qualified for service abroad and willing to serve, under conditions of hardship if necessary, to help the peoples of such countries and areas in meeting their needs for trained manpower, and to help promote a better understanding of the American people on the part of the peoples served and a better understanding of other peoples on the part of the American people.

THE PEACE CORPS**

R. SARGENT SHRIVER

R. SARGENT SHRIVER *is Director of the Peace Corps. Before his appointment he was President of the Board of Education in Chicago, Illinois.*

When someone asks me, "What is the Peace Corps[?]" I begin not with the concept or the organization or the program but with the men and women—they are the Peace Corps.

Some of them are teachers. Others are surveyors and farmers and engineers. Some are skilled craftsmen. There are nurses and home economists. And doctors.

* Reprinted from Public Law 87-293, 87th Congress, H. R. 7500, September 22, 1961.

** Reprinted from *The Peace Corps* (p. 1), an information pamphlet published by The Peace Corps Office of Public Affairs, Washington, D.C., 1961. This reading is taken from the Introduction to the pamphlet.

They come from every state in the Union. Their backgrounds are diverse and reflect the wide spectrum of American life.

But they all have one thing in common: they have chosen to serve their country. They have all asked themselves one question: "What can I do?"

The Peace Corps is their answer.

They have been called the silent generation, these men and women who are volunteering to serve in the Peace Corps—as surveyors in Tanganyika, farm extension workers in Colombia, teachers in rural schools in the Philippines, as community development workers in Chile. They have come quietly to enlist for two-year terms of hard work in Africa, Asia, and Latin America. They have come with a spirit of determination, and idealism.

I am convinced that faith in democracy, the belief in a civilization based on the dignity of the individual human being, the readiness to sacrifice to enable such a civilization to live and grow, the willingness to serve another person—these are waiting to be tapped, and have been tapped, by the Peace Corps.

"Yours was the first revolution," Ashadevi, a spirited woman associate of Ghandi, said to me in India. "Do you think young Americans possess the spiritual values they must have to bring the spirit of that revolution to our country? There is a great valuelessness spreading in the world, and in India, too. Your volunteers must not add to this. They must bring more than science and technology. They must be carriers of your best values and ideals. Can your Peace Corps touch the idealism of America and bring that to us?"

My answer was, Yes. And the Volunteers . . . are the reason I believe it is so.

It is not easy to serve in the Peace Corps, for the tests are thorough, the interviews are probing, the training is rigorous. But once accepted, their contribution—and yours—will have come at a critical hour in the life of the world. And if anyone asks why this should be done, why this should have been your choice and theirs, you need only recall the words of Edward Everett Hale more than half a century ago: "I am only one, but still I am one. I cannot do everything, but still I can do something."

THE FIRST PEACE CORPSMEN
REPORT FOR WORK: GHANA*

Early on the morning of September 15, 1961, a young American stood before a desk in a Ghanaian classroom and introduced himself to the eager students seated there.

This quiet moment—though few were aware of it—marked the beginning of the Peace Corps on the job.

And today the 50 men and women in this first group of Volunteers are busily and devotedly continuing the work they had begun as pioneers among pioneers.

Fittingly, they are teaching in the secondary schools of Ghana, which in 1957 became the first African country south of the Sahara to achieve independence.

The Volunteers, who received their preparatory training at the University of California in Berkeley, are teaching in 27 different schools throughout Ghana. At 17 of these schools, there is only one Volunteer at work. At the others, they are in groups of two to five.

Each Volunteer is teaching at least one of the following subjects: physics, biology, chemistry, history, mathematics, geography, general science, Latin, French, or English. In nine cases, Volunteers are teaching two of the subjects listed above.

Throughout Ghana, the school day begins early. A typical schedule starts with the first class at 7:30 a.m. and runs until 2 p.m., with a half-hour break for brunch. At about 4:30 p.m., when it is less hot, the students participate in sports or manual work.

President Kwame Nkrumah has often expressed Ghana's intense interest in expanding and improving the country's educational resources.

"We must concentrate all our efforts on education," he told the opening of Parliament on July 4, 1961. "It is only through universal education that we can give our people the full opportunity to develop their latent abilities and intelligence."

And it is toward this goal that the Peace Corps Volunteers are bending their efforts.

* Reprinted from *The Peace Corps* (pp. 3-4), an information pamphlet published by The Peace Corps Office of Public Affairs, Washington, D.C., 1961.

THE PEACE CORPS:
A NEW DIMENSION
OF PUBLIC SERVICE*

LAWRENCE E. DENNIS

LAWRENCE E. DENNIS *is Director of Training for the Peace Corps. He is on leave of absence as vice president in charge of academic affairs, Pennsylvania State University.*

Several commentators have suggested that the class of '61 will be remembered as the "Peace Corps class," because of the high degree of excitement generated on college campuses by what Secretary Rusk has called "a sparkling new idea." The enthusiasm for the Peace Corps among young adults carries with it, I believe, a profound meaning for our time: In face of charges of materialism, cynicism, and conformity that have been hurled against them for the better part of their lives, and despite the despair and despondency and pessimism of their elders, the young men and women of today's America are seeking to find something above and beyond themselves with which to identify and give meaning to their personal lives. They are asking themselves what they can do for their country, as the President has enjoined us all to do.

President Kennedy, underscoring the basic U.S. foreign policy lines that thread their way back to the Truman Doctrine and the Marshall Plan, has called on the American people "to bear the burden of a long twilight struggle . . . against the common enemies of man: tyranny, poverty, disease, and war itself." The Peace Corps has been conceived as a key component of the weapons system in that struggle. It envisions "a pool of trained American men and women sent overseas by the U.S. Government or through private organizations and institutions to help foreign countries meet their urgent needs for skilled manpower . . . men and women with the skill to

* This article is adapted from a commencement address given by Mr. Dennis at Cornell College, Mount Vernon, Iowa, June 5, 1961. It is reprinted from *Higher Education*, Vol. 17, No. 8 (May-June 1961), pp. 3-5.

teach the young and assist in the operation of development projects —men and women with the capacity to cope with the demands of swiftly evolving economies, and with the dedication to put that capacity to work in the villages, the mountains, the towns, and the factories of dozens of struggling nations."

As outlined in the President's message to Congress, Peace Corps volunteers are to be made available to developing nations in the following ways:

1. Through private voluntary agencies carrying on international assistance programs.
2. Through overseas programs of colleges and universities.
3. Through assistance programs of international agencies.
4. Through assistance programs of the United States Government.
5. Through new programs which the Peace Corps itself directly administers.

Several months have now passed since the President established the Peace Corps on a pilot basis by executive order. What have we learned in that time?

We know, first of all, a great deal more about the need for Peace Corps volunteers which manifests itself in the economies of the less developed countries of the Far East, South Asia, Africa, and Latin America. This need for trained manpower spans a wide variety of fields, including surveying, geology, civil engineering, agronomy, animal husbandry, community development, nursing, home economics, sanitation, health technology, law, social work, forestry, public administration, business management, and—most important of all, perhaps—teaching. In every country visited by the director of the Peace Corps, Mr. Shriver, on his trip abroad last spring, the need for elementary and secondary teachers and teaching aides was given top priority by the leaders of the host governments.

As a matter of fact, education in the new nations of the world is more than just a "need." It is a passion, an all-consuming desire that means to be satisfied, the same burning thirst for knowledge that has given freedom its thrust in all the epochs of history. Americans have never been strangers to this passion. We have the same responsibility to nourish it and inflame it elsewhere as we have here at home, where all too often we seem to take our schools and colleges for granted.

We know, secondly, that Peace Corps volunteers are not only needed but wanted overseas. Peace Corps projects have already been negotiated with governments or private agencies in Tanganyika, Colombia, the Philippines, Chile, and Ghana; others are presently being formulated. There is no question now but that we shall have at least 500 Peace Corps volunteers trained and on assignment overseas by the end of 1961, which was the goal first set by President Kennedy. By commencement time next year, we hope to have three times that number abroad, assuming that Congress enacts the legislation establishing the Peace Corps on a permanent basis.

We have also learned some things about the kind of training Peace Corps volunteers must have if they are to work successfully in their overseas assignments. For work, of course, is what the Peace Corps is all about: A developing nation wants a job done; they want it done well; they are in a hurry; they want to learn how to do it themselves; we have volunteered to help them. To accomplish this task, the Peace Corps volunteer must know how to do it, how to teach it, and the timetable for getting the job done.

But there are crucial elements other than technical skill that will contribute to the volunteer's maximum effectiveness. He must be in top physical condition. He must know his own capacities, the demands of the job, and the nature of the setting. He must learn how to live at the level of his counterparts in the society in which he is working. He must know how to raise the level of their aspirations, rather than threaten them. He must have a mastery of the language of the host country sufficient for social understanding. He must understand his own country's history and the role America plays in the world scene. He must be familiar with the culture to which he has been assigned. He must be equipped to cope with political, emotional, and physical stress.

In other words, the Peace Corps training program—for whatever project—will be comprehensive, balanced, and rigorous. The volunteer will serve abroad as a representative of his country. The way he conducts himself while in service overseas will reflect the values in which he believes, the way of life he holds most precious.

We also know now, from the tremendous public response to

the Peace Corps, that there is a deep reservoir of motivation toward public service among people from every walk of life, regardless of age or status. But we know, too, that it is up to our institutions of higher education to tap that reservoir with imaginative Peace Corps programs that can capture and sustain the public interest.

In the last analysis, in fact, the success of the Peace Corps and other international service projects is going to depend on whether our colleges and universities are willing to assign top priority to the establishment in the curriculum of programs of education for public service and responsibility.

The men and women who may be selected for service in the Peace Corps this year and in subsequent years will one day return to their homes and communities in this country. Similarly, countless numbers of their college classmates who might not have served overseas will also be appointed or elected to positions of public responsibility in a highly specialized yet wholly interdependent society that is now undergoing a fantastic rate of profound social, economic, cultural, and technological change. How well these young men and women will be equipped to shoulder public responsibilities—how they will fare as tomorrow's leaders—is largely up to our institutions of higher education.

I believe we have arrived at a point in our history when we should think seriously about an imaginative proposal advanced in a commencement address over a decade ago by David Lilienthal—the proposal that the United States adopt a program of *universal public service*. Under this concept, every educated person who is qualified to do so would be expected to set aside a number of years for the rendering of service in the legislative or executive branches of his local, State, or national government, either at home or abroad. Out of the best and most productive years of each man's life, he would carve a segment in which he would put his private career aside to serve his community and his country—and thereby the cause of freedom itself.

What Mr. Lilienthal envisioned was "a fluid kind of citizen-service, in which men and women move from private life into public service for a period of years, and then back to private life." Then, on their return to private life, "these citizens will be experienced in first-hand knowledge of public affairs and of the special difficulties that beset the public servant; we will have public servants whose judgment will be enriched by recent experience in the day-to-day problems of private affairs."

Certainly the Peace Corps idea has within it the seed corn for a universal public service program. And when we speak of concepts of "public service" and "public responsibility" we are in the realm of education—for these are value concepts that denote an attitude toward one's fellow man—a "public philosophy," if you will. Dealing with such concepts should be the primary mission of higher education in our time. It is, in fact, part of the public responsibility of every college and university to nourish and stimulate a sense of commitment to public service in the minds of all students and alumni.

In the long run, as I have indicated, it will require just such a sense of public commitment to build and sustain and strengthen the Peace Corps. To judge by the exciting and enthusiastic response to President Kennedy's plan from all over the country these past few months, there is already a deep reservoir of interest among people from every walk of life, regardless of age. The Gallup Poll reported last winter that 71 percent of a representative population sample interviewed said they favored the Peace Corps program, and 66 percent of the same sample said they would favor participation by their sons and daughters.

We should not be surprised at this phenomenon. For there has been frustration in the American heart, and it has mounted slowly, through wars both cold and hot, in a revolutionary age where anxiety substitutes for peace and machines supplant men. For almost a generation now, we have been groping to find again the path of American purpose.

It has been there all along, of course, and we needed only to part the underbrush to discover it. As a nation, we were always happiest when we had a sense of physical mission, when we had something to *do,* above and beyond self. As long as the frontier could be pushed farther back at home, we had it—"happiness in the doing," as one commentator phrased it, "and not in the deed." The fullest meaning of the Peace Corps to modern America is that we can busy ourselves in the *doing* once again—not only in this country, nor in this continent alone, but in half the world itself.

We know that we cannot transplant a culture to the millions of people in the world's underdeveloped nations who are only now beginning to realize and to ask what can be theirs in terms of health and learning and opportunity. Their way of life, of course, must be their own; it must be indigenous to their native soil. But we can help them get started and work with them to achieve a better way of life.

The mission of the Peace Corps, then, can be, I believe, a moral and blessed mission that could occupy us an entire lifetime. Though it is fraught with many pitfalls, and could result in dismal failure if higher education should shirk its own responsibilities, the Peace Corps can give us the impetus, the thrust we need to find ourselves.

In the words of Judge Learned Hand:

> By some happy fortuity man is a projector, a designer, a builder, a craftsman; it is among his most dependable joys to impose upon the flux that passes before him some mark of himself, aware though he always must be of the odds against him. His reward is not so much in the work as in its making; not so much in the prize as in the race. We may win when we lose, if we have done what we can; for by so doing we have made real at least some part of that finished product in whose fabrication we are most concerned—ourselves. And if at the end some friendly critic shall pass by and say, "My friend, how good a job do you really think you have made of it all?" we can answer: "I know as well as you that it is not of high quality; but I did put into it whatever I had, and that was the game I started out to play."

Conclusion

There are differences of opinion about the nature of propaganda and about its role in international affairs. For some, the word has distinctly negative connotations of distortion and untruth. For others, it is a neutral word describing a variety of ways in which a nation might make its position known to others. But whether "propaganda" is synonymous with "lies" or with "information" it describes some phase of an important attempt at conflict resolution in international affairs.

Psychological elements in the resolution of international conflicts have grown increasingly important in the nuclear age. Whether they have become as important as the physical ingredients of those conflicts is a matter of dispute among scholars and other commentators. However, it is clear that no nation can now afford to ignore the power of propaganda, at least as it is used by opposing nations to create false and unflattering images in the minds of others. A nation might decide not to be "guilty" of propagandizing others, but even this restraint is potentially dangerous in a world where the competition for minds and for markets is so intense.

Both of the major powers in contemporary world affairs, the United States and the U.S.S.R., have established agencies of information or propaganda. The American effort, because of the democratic nature of the society from which it comes, is less inclusive on the official level than the Soviet program. On the other hand the Russian effort, because of the totalitarian nature of communist control, is less extensive on the unofficial level than the United States program.

Americans are faced with the problem of weighing the relative advantages of official and unofficial activity in the information field. Some authorities believe that the reporting of the American story is done adequately by private agencies and individuals. Some of these same authorities also believe that the amount of information which is reported is less important that what is reported—in other words the deed is more important than the word. Others suggest that both the deed and the word are essential elements in a successful presentation of the American position in world affairs.

Every American citizen is exposed to propaganda every day in what he reads, sees, experiences, or hears from outside his own country. Conversely, by what he himself does and says, every American citizen is a source of information about the United States and thus a contributor to the images which others have of "America."

Whatever may be his conclusions on the nature and role of propaganda, on the success of our information activities in the past or on the proper divisions of functions between the government and private persons, no American can avoid propaganda. What average Americans do about it may well determine the outcome of the cold war.